THE GIFT OF THE STRANGER

The Gift of the Stranger

Faith, Hospitality, and
Foreign Language Learning

DAVID I. SMITH *and* BARBARA CARVILL

WILLIAM B. EERDMANS PUBLISHING COMPANY
GRAND RAPIDS, MICHIGAN / CAMBRIDGE, U.K.

© 2000 Wm. B. Eerdmans Publishing Co.
255 Jefferson Ave. S.E., Grand Rapids, Michigan 49503 /
P.O. Box 163, Cambridge CB3 9PU U.K.
All rights reserved

Printed in the United States of America

04 03 02 01 00 99   7 6 5 4 3 2 1

ISBN 0-8028-4708-0

For Nathaniel, Miriam, and Amy

Wally, Jim, and Mia

Contents

CONTENTS

III. Practice: Implications for the Classroom

Foreword

This book is a product of the Calvin Center for Christian Scholarship (CCCS), which was established at Calvin College in 1977. The purpose of the CCCS is to promote creative, articulate, and rigorous Christian scholarship that addresses important theoretical and practical issues.

The present volume is the result of the collaboration of Barbara Carvill and David Smith, who have worked together for three years under a grant from the CCCS. Right from the beginning of this project, we at the CCCS knew this would be a unique contribution to Christian academic thought and practice. As the authors will suggest, there is a stunning silence about a Christian approach to teaching foreign languages — and this despite a considerable amount of theorizing about epistemological and pedagogical issues. In order to fill in these gaps in the literature, Carvill and Smith will take the reader through the promises, as well as some of the problems, that this rearranged discourse can offer. Then, there is plenty of attention to practical and applied concerns, all done — we believe — in a winsome way, so as not to allow this merely to be a methodology book.

The point of this book, in the end, is not so much to make an ultimate statement about Christian thinking and foreign language teaching as to open up a considered discourse in which language teachers in many countries and in many languages can join with their colleagues and these authors in rethinking their craft. The CCCS is delighted to have provided the support that made this excellent project into a reality.

RONALD A. WELLS
Director, CCCS
December 1999

Acknowledgments

We would like to thank the many friends who have encouraged and supported us in this project. Our gratitude goes above all to the Calvin Center for Christian Scholarship, under the helpful leadership of Ron Wells, for its generous institutional and financial support. We also thank all the people who gave us helpful comments during the different stages of the manuscript: Phyllis Mitchell, James Wilkins, Edna Greenway, Herman de Vries, Thea van Til Rusthoven, Clarence Joldersma, Mary Vander Goot, Neil Plantinga, Janice Walhout, Calvin Seerveld, Christine Pohl, Shirley Dobson, Lori Meed, John Shortt, Trevor Cooling, Robert Sweetman, Brian Walsh, and Pennylyn Dykstra-Pruim. Barbara Carvill would like to express her deep gratitude to her faithful and encouraging friends at the Department of Germanic Languages at Calvin College. It is from James Lamse and Wallace Bratt that she has learned how to practice hospitality in the setting of a foreign language department. In many respects, the ethos of this book reflects the educational practice of these two wonderful colleagues. David I. Smith would like to thank the Stapleford Centre for giving him time to work on the manuscript and the Institute for Christian Studies in Toronto, where some of the ideas in this book took shape. He is also very grateful to numerous people for ideas, support, or timely encouragement, including Richard Parrish, Dave Baker, Keith Heywood, Catherine Worth, Helen Gillingham, David Smith, Ward Evans, Paul and Sarah Williams, Elmer Thiessen, James Olthuis, Doug Blomberg, the members of Eastwood Community Church, and, above all, Julia, who has accompanied this project with much patience and loving support.

Our very special thanks goes to Wallace Bratt for editing our manuscript with such care, dedication, and fierce love for detail.

Introduction

Les Cadeaux de Dieu qui me font sourire

La lumière du soleil un jour de pluie, le bruit d'un enfant qui rit, l'odeur des fleurs parfumées au printemps, le baiser de la rosée sur l'herbe fraîche du matin —

Les arcs-en-ciel   Les couleurs du soleil

Les flocons
de neige

Les chatons, la mer bleu-foncé

The poem reproduced above expresses gratitude. Comprised of a small collection of familiar words — rainbows, snowflakes, children's laughter, the scent of flowers, the blue of the sea — it was written by two second-year French students[1] but could just as well have been penned by a beginner flipping through a dictionary to find the words for some of her favorite things. Obviously, as part of a French lesson, the words of the poem could have been arranged as a vocabulary list, perhaps to be memorized for a test the next day. Or they could have been chanted in unison, built into a computer-based exercise, or worked into dialogues. But arranged as a smiling face under the title "Les Cadeaux de Dieu qui me font sourire" (The gifts of God which make me smile), they take on a different spirit: they become an expression of gratitude for the gifts of creation.

This book, which is written for teachers of foreign languages, is interested in "rearrangements." It looks at the ordinary and necessary elements involved in teaching and learning a foreign or second language and asks whether they can be designed to express a different spirit. In particular, it asks whether reflection on foreign language education from the standpoint of Christian faith can lead to a meaningful rearrangement of the words, phrases, aims, resources, and techniques with which all foreign language educators are concerned.

This notion will likely seem strange to many readers. There seems at first glance little possible connection between Christian faith and language teaching. Is the unwary reader about to be treated to some bizarre new method that claims religious authority? Or to pious attempts to squeeze the Bible into every corner of the foreign language curriculum?

No, our aim in this book is to investigate some of the ways foreign language education can be arranged and patterned and to ask whether a Christian approach would warrant some patterns rather than others. We do this not only to explore how foreign language learning can become a more consistently integrated part of Christian education, but also to ask whether a rearrangement informed by Christian belief might contribute something worthwhile to foreign language education beyond and outside of Christian circles.

One reason a Christian approach to foreign language education strikes many as odd is the virtual absence of discussion on this matter today. Among Christian theorists there presently is a growing and lively body

---

1. Betsy McLaughlin and Jackie McConnell; see Barrick, 1993, 38.

of literature on Christian education,[2] including works on specific areas of the curriculum, but until now that discussion has not included systematic attention to foreign language education. Furthermore, it hardly need be said that the vast literature on foreign language learning outside of Christian circles devotes virtually no space at all to the possible relevance of Christian educational ideas. And let's be honest: the idea that the Bible has something to do with learning, say, Spanish sounds forced. To many, at least, the present volume may appear to be a voice trying to make noise in a vacuum.

Part I of this book aims to counter such a notion by sketching a biblical and historical background to our inquiry. The first chapter, in which we ask whether there are biblical themes that are significant for foreign language education, gives one kind of context to our discussion: if our exploration claims to be Christian, it must be guided by relevant Christian beliefs. The key Christian themes set out in this chapter will guide the rest of our inquiry. The next two chapters show that the absence of Christian discussion about foreign language learning is only a recent phenomenon. The common current perception that such discussion seems odd says more about our lack of historical awareness than about the viability of the discussion itself. Christian faith has, in fact, played a significant role in the history of foreign language education. Chapters 2 and 3 describe that role by outlining some relevant episodes, thus providing a second, historical context for our exploration, one that shows this study to be merely a small and late contribution to a long-standing tradition of Christian reflection on this topic.

Part II, the heart of the book, talks about the goals of foreign language instruction in the light of the Christian themes described in Part I. What should the basic aims of foreign language education be? What does foreign language study contribute to general educational goals? Are the aims that currently dominate foreign language education adequate? These are the questions chapters 4, 5, and 6 address. Central in these chapters is an exploration of how the biblical theme of hospitality to the stranger provides an ethical imperative for rethinking the basic objectives and emphases of foreign language education.

Part III gets down to everyday practice. Even if there is a tradition of

---

2. See, for instance, among recent publications, Cooling, 1994; Fowler, Van Brummelen, and Van Dyk, 1990; Shortt, 1997; Stronks and Blomberg, 1993; Van Brummelen, 1994b.

INTRODUCTION

Christian reflection on foreign language education and a way of thinking ethically about basic goals, how does this affect what goes on from day to day in the classroom? Will the end of our theorizing be something really odd — or, conversely, merely a reissue of current practice with some Bible verses tacked on? In this part we confront these questions and suggest how our approach might look in daily practice.

Chapter 7 reviews some teaching materials used in foreign language classrooms, examining in particular how the materials and their arrangement convey an implicit vision of the world. Here we are interested not only in whether such materials have religious content, but also in the assumptions they make about human existence in the foreign culture. How do the people who walk the pages of textbooks or multimedia packages handle ethical decisions? What do they believe? Do they suffer as well as shop? Do the images these teaching materials offer provide an adequate basis for a meaningful encounter with strangers made in God's image?

The next two chapters deal with the question of teaching methods, a question at the heart of so much current discussion in the field of foreign language education. Chapter 8 reviews the changing understanding of the nature of teaching methods over the last few decades, focusing in particular on the growing awareness that beliefs play a role in the construction of methods. The view that methods are value-free is no longer viable. We will show that although particular beliefs do not give rise to unique individual techniques, they do shape the overall pattern of teaching. Chapter 9 offers a case study of two pedagogical approaches and explores their compatibility or incompatibility with particular Christian beliefs.

Finally, chapter 10 looks at examples of activities and units of work developed as part of the Charis Project. This project, based at the Stapleford Centre in Nottingham, England, has published foreign language learning materials that respond to the requirement in England and Wales that spiritual, moral, social, and cultural development be promoted across the whole curriculum. The examples we discuss in this final chapter suggest some of the ways foreign language learning can contribute to spiritual development.

This book is for teachers of foreign languages on all levels, for practitioners in the field, methodology teachers, student trainees, textbook writers, curriculum planners, and will also be of interest to teachers of English as a second or foreign language. This study does not aim to replace a methodology textbook. It is an exploration, a provisional scouting of an area neglected in recent times, and it intends to open a discussion. As such, the book is part of a broader return to this neglected area. It complements and is, to an extent, an outgrowth of the work of such organizations as the North American Christian Foreign Language Association (NACFLA), which has been holding annual conferences and publishing their proceedings since 1991. This particular organization has recently established a website that includes the beginnings of a bibliographic project;[3] it has also launched a refereed journal.[4] We have been involved in these developments and are indebted to the work of many colleagues in this association. Similar developments have taken place in the United Kingdom, which has seen several gatherings of Christian foreign language educators and a number of publications, including a Christian response to the National Curriculum and the development of the Charis teaching materials referred to above. In Australia, too, there has been a fresh interest in the place of foreign language learning in Christian education. We hope our explorations will contribute to and further these recent developments. Because there is still plenty of work to be done, it is our wish that this book will stimulate foreign language educators everywhere to reflect and explore further, to refine and correct our work, and to develop new insights of their own.

DAVID I. SMITH *and* BARBARA CARVILL

3. http://www.spu.edu/orgs/nacfla/.
4. *Journal of Christianity and Foreign Languages.*

PART I

BACKGROUND:
SETTING THE STAGE

CHAPTER ONE

From Babel to Pentecost

Punishing errors in pronunciation by executing offenders on the spot does not seem the most promising of instructional strategies. Yet the Bible, in the course of describing a dark chapter of Israel's history, mentions just such an incident. When the ancient Gileadites captured the fords of the Jordan, they asked all who passed that way to say the word "Shibboleth" as a test of their ethnic identity. Those whose faulty pronunciation revealed them to be Ephraimites were promptly slain (Judg. 12:4-6). Admittedly, this action is not put forward for us to emulate, and it was not carried out with educational intent — we may safely assume that helping the Ephraimites improve their pronunciation was far from the minds of their executioners. This narrative does, however, seem to be as close as the Bible gets to mentioning any of the typical practices of the foreign language classroom. Not much to go on, it would seem, when it comes to relating biblical faith to foreign language education.

It gets worse. Some years ago, toward the end of my (David Smith) undergraduate studies, I spent considerable time thinking and praying about which career to pursue. One sunny morning I was strolling through the college with a close friend, explaining to him my growing conviction that my calling lay in education and that I should train as a foreign language teacher. His reply was both immediate and disconcerting: "Well, foreign language teachers are a product of the fall, aren't they? I mean, just look at Babel!"

While he intended his reply as little more than humor at my expense, it was close enough to some established patterns of Christian thinking to be disturbing. There is a substantial tradition that cites the Babel story as clear evidence that "linguistic and cultural diversity is presented in Scripture as a whole, and in Genesis especially, as a result of the fall, an act of judgment on humanity."[1] This view sees the diversity of languages and cultures that surrounds as, at best, a restraint imposing formidable barriers to cross-cultural communication. These barriers are intended to limit the human tendency toward evil — the very tendency that led to scenes such as those at the fords of the Jordan — by keeping us divided into local groups. It seems to follow that diversity of languages is not to be celebrated, but should rather be mourned or tolerated while we wait in hope for a promised future restoration of unity.

Christians understand the Bible to be authoritative for human living. If this authoritative text does not mention foreign language teaching, and even appears to have a gloomy view of differences in language and culture, it is little wonder that many Christian language teachers have difficulty meaningfully relating the Scriptures in which they trust to their professional calling. Little wonder also that the growing literature on Christian education has not seemed to know quite what to do with foreign language learning, and that Christian teachers of foreign languages can find themselves struggling to justify their contribution within Christian educational settings.[2]

To abandon hope here would, however, be premature in the extreme. This chapter will suggest that the gloomy picture sketched above is wrong — wrong in its assessment of the potential contribution of Christian language teachers and wrong in its interpretation of the Bible. There are, in fact, rich biblical resources for reenvisioning the callings of both teachers and learners of second languages. In exploring these resources our aim is not to devise a forced matching of Bible texts to teaching practices. Our intention is rather to make clear the outlines of the worldview that shapes our approach to foreign language education, and to ask how the concerns of foreign language educators might relate to the overall biblical story. We aim to be suggestive rather than exhaustive, to establish a vantage point

---

1. Hill, 1996, 15.

2. For instance, a U.K. bibliography of evangelical writings on education with over two thousand entries contains but a single entry under the heading "Modern Languages" — a three-page magazine article stating the benefits of foreign exchange visits (Schwarz, 1990).

from which to view the issues discussed in the remaining chapters.[3] And we begin at the very beginning . . .

From Formlessness to Fruitfulness

"In the beginning God created . . ." These well-known words signal, among other things, that Babel is not the beginning. In the beginning God created . . . well, a whole host of things. The Creator portrayed in the opening chapter of Genesis is a God who makes space for — no, who *enjoys* — diversity. As the biblical narrative parades the acts of separation that turn creation from a formless void into a spectacularly diverse cosmos, the repeated refrain declares that "God saw that it was good" — even "very good" (Gen. 1:4, 10, 12, 18, 21, 25, 31).

The climax of this opening episode in the Genesis narrative is the creation of human beings. At the end of a process in which various parts of creation become differentiated, we meet creatures who are not simply different, but made to image God. Very much creatures of the earth (thus the name "Adam," literally the one who comes from the *"adamah,"* the earth), they are nonetheless able to speak with the God who spoke worlds into being. They are able to make responsible, fateful choices and can enter into relationships of personal intimacy and moral depth. They can act creatively and reflectively, respond spiritually, and reflect in their lives something of the character of the God who displays compassion, grace, patience, love, faithfulness, forgiveness, and justice (Exod. 34:6-7).[4]

These remarkable creatures are commanded to be fruitful, to spread across the earth, and to take genuine, creative responsibility for the world God made. Humans are not mere puppets, or machines following a preprogrammed pattern, but are called to a responsible role in the continuing task of caring for and developing the potential of creation.

This role is evocatively sketched in the story of Adam naming the animals (Gen. 2:19-20), where God himself waits expectantly to see what will happen, and must respond to the results of Adam's creative choices. Nothing in this narrative suggests that, when it came to giving each animal a name, there was a single correct answer that God was looking for; this was

3. For a more detailed discussion see Smith, 1996b.
4. Cf. Ward-Wilson and Blomberg, 1993.

not the first vocabulary test! On the contrary, we are told that God wanted "to see what he would name them" (v. 19), that Adam "gave names" (v. 20), and that "whatever the man called each living creature, that was its name" (v. 19). In other words, from now on, if in conversation with Adam God wants to refer to one of the animals, he must use the name given by Adam! At the same time, the message of the story is not that humans enjoy unbounded freedom, that anything goes. The entire narrative takes place against the background of Adam's responsibility to image God, to reflect God's character and desires as he responds to the tasks before him.[5]

Given such a divine endorsement of human creativity in the realm of language, it is by no means self-evident that language was designed to remain uniform as people responded to God's desire for them to spread, to invent, and to name. *Spreading, creativity, diversity — all are rooted in creation prior to the fall.* One reflection of the variety of human responses is the diversity of languages and dialects.[6] If people are to spread out over the earth, and are also to freely give names and develop their language, then, as time passes, diversity seems assured. God's affirmation of linguistic creativity in the story of Adam naming the animals surely casts doubt on the idea that, were it not for sin, the languages of the world would be one.

However, the celebration of creation's riches is quickly disrupted by temptation and disobedience. The fall brings a thorny tangle of thistles that

---

5. This side-by-side portrayal of divine creation and human creativity is unusual. Other accounts that associate the origins of language with a divine reality tend to downplay human creativity. In Islamic accounts, the Arabic language is of divine origin and the Koran is an Arabic book, debased by being translated (cf. Surah 43.2). The Arabic language is itself regarded as part of Allah's revelation, and the words of the Koran are seen as containing no human elements. Similarly in Hindu lore Sanskrit is the language of the gods, and the Bhagavad Gita is debased if translated. The human creativity involved in language is suppressed in the name of religious authority.

Modern secular accounts, on the other hand, have at times tended to the opposite extreme, emphasizing an unbounded human freedom and glorying in the idea that "the vast enterprise of turning our world into a machine that spins for human comfort was made possible by man's capacity for symbolism, interwoven with every thought and object but compacted with all the power of human intellectuality in the computer-like program that we call language" (Bolinger, 1980, 10). Creativity in Bolinger's account is autonomous and self-serving. The subduing of creation reduces it to a machine, and the guiding vision is not God's glory or creation's well-being, but human comfort. The Genesis account, in contrast, sees the Creator's gift and call as enabling and setting the true context for creative human response (Olthuis, 1993).

6. For further discussion see Yallop, 1993.

thread themselves among the fruits of responsive human creativity. of sharing in the joyful creativity of the divine task, the human task be͟ͅomes painful, marked by sweat and struggle (Gen. 5:29). Relationships between people become violent and broken, and it becomes harder to associate difference straightforwardly with celebration. The development of all human cultures now knows both good and evil, and it is no longer possible to declare that all that is different is very good. In this new situation, no culture can assume that everything it has to offer, or that everything that comes to it from strangers, is a gift.[7] Diversity is not a good in itself. Nevertheless, even in the midst of growing evil there is still grace; the call to spread and the blessing on the diversity of peoples remain (Gen. 9:1; 10:5, 18, 32).

Babel and Beyond

It is in this context that the Babel story appears. Many popular readings of this story reflect a certain amount of chronological snobbery as they picture a group of somewhat simpleminded primitives trying to build a tower all the way up to the sky in order to get to God's throne room above the clouds. A rather nervous God, genuinely afraid that they might succeed, intervenes before it is too late. This kind of reading, however, does little justice to the text. A more attentive reading reveals a significantly different pattern of events. Only the general pattern will be outlined here; the appendix contains a more detailed defense of our interpretation of the text.

The Babel narrative is primarily concerned not with a tower, but with a city, a city being built with two motives: "Come, let us build ourselves a city, with a tower that reaches to the heavens, so that we may make a name for ourselves and not be scattered over the face of the whole earth" (Gen. 11:1-4).[8] The first motive is to bolster the name of the builders, asserting their power over others; making a name for oneself is elsewhere in

---

7. As González points out, the book of Revelation presents people of every tribe, language, and nation both among the redeemed worshipers of the new creation and among those aligned with evil (cf., e.g., Rev. 7:9; 11:9) (González, 1998). See also Gundry-Volf and Volf, 1997, 33-60.

8. The desire to make a name for oneself, the project of city building, and an emphasis on the people speaking with the same speech are all associated in ancient Assyrian inscriptions with empire building and military conquest (Uehlinger, 1990); see appendix for more detailed discussion.

Scripture associated with military conquest and rule over the conquered people.[9] The second motive is to avoid obedience to God's instruction that they spread out over the earth, an instruction that echoes through the first ten chapters of Genesis like a leitmotif.[10]

In response to this overt rebellion against the call to spread, God comes down — not because humans are in danger of becoming omnipotent (an idea foreign to the Bible), but because judgment will become inevitable if they are allowed to continue in their spiraling rebellion. Having promised in Genesis 9:11 not to repeat the cataclysm of Genesis 6–8, God intervenes in a way that not only judges and disrupts the empire-building project, but also pushes the builders back onto the path God had originally set before them. The close of the Babel story twice underlines the fact that people are once more spreading out over the earth, suggesting that a more final judgment is being averted, that humankind is being returned to a path where there is the possibility of blessing. Whether the confusion spoken of in the narrative is taken to refer to a miraculous multiplying of dialects or simply to the disruption of the conspiratorial consensus of the builders,[11] it is oppressive uniformity rather than diversity that seems to be associated with sin.

Out of Egypt

As the Old Testament story progresses, Israel discovers firsthand what it is like to live as slaves under a monolithic regime. This experience was to play a profound role in the development of the Israelites' sense of identity. Oppressed as a marginal group by the arrogant words of Pharaoh, they were called to become a *hearing* people.[12] From the beginning of their exodus they also were a mixed multitude (Exod. 12:38), faced with the question of whether they would break away from Pharaoh's example in their treatment

9. The phrase occurs in 2 Sam. 8:13-14, where David made a name for himself by striking down 18,000 Edomites and subjecting Edom to his rule.

10. See Gen. 1:27-28; 9:1, 7, 19; 10:5, 18, 20, 25, 31-32.

11. See appendix.

12. Pharaoh, who refused to listen and remained oblivious to the Israelites' suffering until it was extended into his own household, is contrasted with the God who not only *heard* the cry of the Hebrew slaves but *knew* their suffering (Exod. 2:24-25). Exodus 1 hints strongly that Pharaoh's regime echoes what happened at Babel. See appendix.

of the stranger in their midst. Both of these callings — to be a hearing people and to care for the stranger — are potentially relevant to foreign language educators, and both will give direction to the present study.

Hardness of Heart and Hardness of Hearing

The proud "Come let us . . ." heard at Babel and in Egypt (Gen. 11:4; Exod. 1:10) knows little of vulnerable dependence on God or of interdependence with others. It is a sovereign monologue, a kind of speech that is focused squarely on its own benefit and demands to get its own way. It does not expect to have to reconsider. It does not expect to have to respond to the hearer's rejoinder, or to show careful concern for the hearer's needs or sensibilities. This is the kind of speech the psalmist laments and condemns in Psalm 12:

> Help, LORD, for the godly are no more;
> the faithful have vanished from among men.
> Everyone lies to his neighbor;
> their flattering lips speak with deception.
> May the LORD cut off all flattering lips
> and every boastful tongue
> that says, "We will triumph with our tongues;
> we own our lips — who is our master?" (vv. 1-4)

The psalmist contrasts such talk with God's words, which are "flawless, / like silver refined in a furnace of clay, / purified seven times" (v. 6). God's words differ radically from the arrogant assertions of would-be triumphant tongues whose clamor leads to an inability to hear either the word of God or the voice of one's neighbor (Gen. 11:7).

Israel's identity is to be different. Israel is called not first of all to speak but to *hear*: "Hear, O Israel: the LORD our God, the LORD is one" (Deut. 6:4). As Walter Brueggemann notes in another context, "to 'listen' means to be addressed, to know that life comes as a gift from another. This listening is not simply an auditory response, but requires obedient action."[13] Attentive, responsive hearing is the opposite of self-assertive au-

13. Brueggemann, 1988, 105.

tonomy. The Israelites are to speak in testimony to what they have heard from God.

But hearing also involves an open attitude toward other humans. When God judged the city of Babel, each inhabitant lost the ability to hear the other;[14] in a similar way, Pharaoh's arrogant speech was accompanied by an inability to hear the cries of the Hebrews. Many years later, when Israel in turn became like Egypt, or like Babel, the prophets repeatedly charged her with failing to hear both God and the marginalized within her own community.[15] Jesus himself came with a radical message for "those who have ears to hear."

Hearing the voice of the other takes time, commitment, sensitivity, vulnerability. When the other is a stranger, it might even involve learning the other's language.

The Voice of the Stranger

The memory of being silenced and mistreated in Egypt, of being surrounded by unresponsive ears and a foreign tongue, was to have particular consequences for the life of the emerging Israelite community. The Law that provided the framework for their existence before God contains repeated reminders to pay careful attention to the alien, the stranger:

> Do not mistreat an alien or oppress him, for you were aliens in Egypt. (Exod. 22:21; cf. 23:9)

> When an alien lives with you in your land, do not mistreat him. The alien living with you must be treated as one of your native-born. Love him as yourself, for you were aliens in Egypt. I am the LORD your God. (Lev. 19:33-34; cf. Deut. 10:19)

> Do not deprive the alien or the fatherless of justice, or take the cloak of the widow as a pledge. Remember that you were slaves in Egypt and the LORD your God redeemed you from there. That is why I command you to do this. (Deut. 24:17; cf. 27:19)

14. Gen. 11:7, translated literally.
15. See, e.g., Jer. 7:1-29, esp. 6.

Clearly, the Law takes Israel's treatment of the stranger very seriously. And who are these strangers? They are the immigrants, the temporary or permanent residents who have come from abroad, possibly to find shelter from a previous situation of exclusion or conflict.[16]

Exodus 12:38 records that when the Israelites left Egypt, "many other people went up with them." Thus the ethnic Israelites were not the sole beneficiaries of God's liberating acts; from the very moment the chosen people left Egypt, the ethnically different were in their midst. And so the promise to Abram, that all of the distant nations would be blessed through him, comes very close to home, as the foreigner shares the same pilgrimage with the descendant of Abraham and eventually sets up home in the same promised land.

In short, Israel's calling has both an outward and an inward focus. Beyond her borders she is to be a light to the other nations; within her borders she is to be a blessing to strangers, to those from other nations who have taken up residence in her midst. An ear responsive to voices that speak with unfamiliar accents or in unknown tongues will need to focus not only on nations safely distant, but also on immigrant communities close by. And for Israel, as for the contemporary modern language teacher or learner, diversity of language and culture is not safely distant, but rather very close at hand.

The laws concerning the stranger appeal to the Israelites' own experience, urging them to treat others as they themselves wish others had treated them.[17] Of course, this does not mean they are to relinquish the integrity of their identity and cultural home, or to romantically accept all things foreign, as the ongoing polemic against destructive idolatry makes clear (e.g., Exod. 34:15-17). Rather, the alien is to respect the same community standards and laws as the Israelite (e.g., Exod. 12:49). Welcoming the alien does not put Israel's faith and communal ways up for sale; it is precisely that faith and God's expectations of the community that are to motivate a loving welcome for the stranger. Israel's faith is not to be sacrificed to hospitality; instead, it undergirds it. Welcoming the stranger does not involve an abandonment of identity for Israel, any more than it does for the individual language learner or the school community. Rather, it involves the formation of an identity expressed in love.

16. Spina, 1983.
17. For a more detailed study see Van Houten, 1991.

At the most basic level, then, the Israelites are called to avoid treating others the way they themselves were treated by the Egyptians: they are not to mistreat or oppress the aliens among them or deprive them of justice. Expressed positively, they are to recognize and take steps to mitigate the vulnerability typically experienced by the immigrant, as by the widow and orphan. The least the resident alien should be able to expect is justice, and space to live and thrive.

But the Law is not satisfied with this minimal response. To the warning to avoid oppression it adds the more radical demand to "love those who are aliens" (Deut. 10:19), in fact to "love [the alien] *as yourself*" (Lev. 19:34, italics ours). This last formulation is striking, for it echoes the command given earlier in the same group of laws to "love your neighbor as yourself" (Lev. 19:18).[18] This emphasis points to a further motivation for Christian concern with foreign languages and cultures: *Loving the stranger is presented as a significant aspect of loving one's neighbor as oneself.* Not only did the prophets reiterate this command whenever Israel failed to live up to her calling,[19] but Jesus himself emphasized it as one of the two most important elements in his summary of the law.

I Was a Stranger . . .

In the Old Testament we noted two interrelated themes: the focus on Israel being a blessing to the nations beyond its borders and the call for her to love the strangers on her doorstep. In the New Testament Jesus takes up both concerns. The first is probably more familiar: in the Great Commission (Matt. 28:19-20; Mark 16:15; Luke 24:47) Jesus issued a fresh challenge to bring good news to all nations, to "go out into all the world." This commission lies at the foundation of Christian missionary endeavor.

But the second concern is also prominent in Jesus' life. In many places in the Gospel narrative he can be seen both teaching and practicing welcome for those who had been excluded, not only for "sinners" and tax

18. See Spina, 1983.

19. It is reflected not only explicitly in denunciations of sin such as Jer. 9:6, but also implicitly in a passage such as Zephaniah's vision of a humanity restored by God's intervention, whereby God will "purify the lips of the peoples, / that all of them may call on the name of the LORD / and serve him shoulder to shoulder" (Zeph. 3:9).

collectors, but also for Samaritans, Gentiles — in a word, for strangers (see, e.g., John 4:1-42; Luke 7:1-10).

We have already noted the connection between "loving your neighbor as yourself" and "loving the stranger as yourself." In Luke 10:25-37 Jesus is asked by an expert in the law what it means to love one's neighbor. In response, he tells the parable of the Good Samaritan. In this parable, contrary to what we might expect, it is not the Jewish victim of robbery lying by the roadside who turns out to be the answer to the query, "Who is my neighbor?" Jesus makes this clear at the end of the parable when he asks, "Which of these three do you think was a neighbor to the man who fell into the hands of robbers?" (v. 36). His answer: the one who had mercy on him, the Samaritan — who for the Jew was a stranger in the land, ethnically different, to be mistrusted and avoided.[20] As in Leviticus, the neighbor again turns up in the guise of the stranger.

Jesus drives the point home even more sharply in the parable of the sheep and the goats (Matt. 25:31-46). Here, as in the above parable, the question of what must be done to inherit eternal life looms large (v. 46; cf. Luke 10:25). The divine King is seen separating the righteous from the unrighteous, the sheep from the goats. The righteous are addressed as follows: "I was hungry and you gave me something to eat, I was thirsty and you gave me something to drink, *I was a stranger and you invited me in,* I needed clothes and you clothed me, I was sick and you looked after me, I was in prison and you came to visit me. . . . whatever you did for one of the least of these brothers of mine, you did for me" (vv. 35-40, italics ours). The unrighteous are those who failed to do these things.

Here, as in the Old Testament, the kind of welcome given or not given to the stranger is presented as one of the marks of discipleship, one of the signs of responsiveness to God — or its absence. With Jesus' call to follow comes an invitation to participate in the new creation, the redemption that includes a clear concern for the stranger. At Pentecost firstfruits of this new creation become visible.

---

20. Compare the discussion of Jesus' encounter with the woman at the well (John 4) in Gundry-Volf and Volf, 1997.

Hearing Restored

Luke's story of Pentecost is designed to evoke particular memories, the echoes of an earlier text and the events it described. Shared vocabulary and the overall shape of the narrative link Luke's story to the story of the city of Babel.[21] In both narratives a call to spread into all the earth echoes in the background (Gen. 9:1; Acts 1:8). In both stories people gather together, and in response, God comes down. Confusion is said to ensue (the crowd is bewildered), and the sequel is dispersion, with both Babel builders and apostles in their different ways going out into all the world.

There are, of course, significant, hopeful differences between these two accounts. First, the disciples are to heed the command to go into all the world only after a period of dependent waiting. Second, as Babel's disobedient gathering is replaced by the yielded community of Pentecost, God's descent brings empowerment and life. Third, the result now is not failed communication and mutual isolation, the inability to hear one another, but a renewed hearing, the surprise of rediscovered understanding.

These parallels and differences can be summarized as follows:

Babel (Genesis 11)	Pentecost (Acts 2)
Preceded by a call to fill the earth	Preceded by a call to go into all the world
Gathering in disobedience	Gathering in obedience
God comes down	God comes down
Confusion results	Confusion results
People cannot understand (literally "hear") one another	People miraculously hear one another
Scattering	Scattering (after some delay)

Luke seems to be making a point here: Pentecost is connected with Babel. It is in some way a redemptive answer to the tendencies that emerged in Genesis 11 and that, but for God's gracious promise, might have led a second time to cataclysmic judgment. A fresh wind blows to make all things new, including Babel.[22]

21. See J. G. Davies, 1952.
22. There are echoes here of the creation story in Genesis 1: just as God's Spirit

Now notice a striking fact about the way things happen in Acts 2. If the more pessimistic readings of the Babel story were correct, we would expect to see a return to linguistic uniformity when healing comes, an undoing of the curse of difference. It is not hard to imagine a miracle whereby the hearers are enabled to understand a single language, restoring a taste of lost linguistic oneness.[23]

But that is not what happens at all. Instead of re-creating a single language, the Spirit enables each person present to hear the wonders of God proclaimed *in his or her own language.* The gift of tongues described in the Pentecost story remarkably affirms the linguistic individuality of the hearers. Hearing, an important mark of humanity before God, is restored (cf. Gen. 11:7), and in this restoration *diversity is not negated, but affirmed.*

This episode is not only authoritative for the life of the church, which experienced its birth at Pentecost and is to be a fellowship drawn from every nation, tribe, and tongue; it also gives a promissory glimpse of God's plans for the world. Zephaniah's vision of the nations not fused into one, but serving God shoulder to shoulder (Zeph. 3:9), is not yet fulfilled in its entirety at Pentecost, but we are given a tantalizing preview in the here and now of a promised future. Here is the strongest hint that recovered uniformity may not be the best way of describing that future.

How fellowship before God is ultimately to be combined with continuing diversity of language, a diversity we so often experience as barrier and struggle, remains a mystery, but perhaps this sense of mystery is not surprising. After all, sin and brokenness do not have an ordered place in God's world; they are not to be harmonized with creation, but to be agonized over, repented of, wrestled with, hoped through. Yet we can learn from Pentecost that our solutions to the fragmentation we face will not be genuinely redemptive if they underestimate or trample on human diversity, including diversity of language.

(*ruach:* spirit, breath, wind) was involved in creation, so now a wind from God and the outpouring of God's Spirit heralds a new creation (cf. Ezek. 37:9; John 3:8). In both creation and re-creation there is a process of separating in which diversity is affirmed (cf. Acts 2:2-3, 8; Gen. 1:2-4).

23. Most of the hearers would have been familiar with Aramaic (those from the east) or Greek (those from the west), so there was not in fact an insurmountable language barrier (Bruce, 1988, 54); there is no indication that Peter's subsequent sermon underwent miraculous translation for the audience (Acts 2:14-15). The miracle of tongues should therefore be seen as more than an overcoming of practical barriers.

Who Is the Foreigner?

These themes do not end with Acts 2, for it seems unlikely that Pentecost (or, for that matter, even Babel) can have been entirely absent from Paul's mind when he wrote 1 Corinthians 14:6-12. In these verses we find once more a concern for the hearer, a focus on the community and how it should be built up, an affirmation of the basic worth of all human languages, and a recognition of the inability to hear that makes us foreigners to each other: "Unless you speak intelligible words with your tongue, how will anyone know what you are saying? You will just be speaking into the air. Undoubtedly there are all sorts of languages in the world, yet none of them is without meaning. If then I do not grasp the meaning of what someone is saying, I am a foreigner to the speaker, and he is a foreigner to me" (vv. 9-11).

Paul speaks of being unable to understand someone else's words. It is more common in such circumstances to attribute dysfunction to the speaker of the alien tongue, the "barbarian" who lacks full humanity. Paul does not, however, take himself as the immovable point of reference. He declares that if he doesn't understand the other, *he himself is a foreigner,* a stranger to that other person, just as the other is a stranger to him. This embrace of all languages as meaningful counters both the common human inclination to define full humanity in terms of the ability to speak the definer's language and the tendency in much of church history to regard most vernacular languages as too uncouth to carry God's truth.[24]

Israel's dual calling to be a hearing people and to care for the stranger in her midst, a calling that continues to echo through the New Testament, points to a need to reflect on the kind of human community we want to build. As Brueggemann comments in relation to Genesis 11, to identify unity with the good and diversity with sin is too simplistic, even dangerous:

God wills a unity which permits and encourages scattering. The unity willed by God is that all of humanity shall be in covenant with him (9:8-11) and with him only, responding to his purposes, relying on his life-giving power. The scattering God wills is that life should be peopled everywhere by his regents, who are attentive to all parts of creation, work-

24. See chap. 2.

16

ing in his image to enhance the whole creation, to bring "each in its kind" to full fruition and productivity. . . . The purpose of God is neither self-securing homogeneity as though God is not Lord, nor a scattering of autonomous parts as though the elements of humanity did not belong to each other.[25]

It is to this kind of diverse community that the various strands of the biblical story we have been following seem to point. Between the celebrations of diversity that accompany both the original creation and the beginnings of the new creation lies the call to hear and welcome the stranger in a world scarred by sin. Here, in broad outline, is a guiding vision for Christian foreign language educators working in a context of simultaneously increasing globalization and deepening pluralism. The initial impression that the Bible has little to say to foreign language educators has given way in the course of this chapter to a richer tapestry of biblical themes that will inform the rest of our study.

How does this broad vision relate to the practicalities of foreign language education? Answering this question will be the task of the second and third parts of this study, in which we will explore the basic aims, content, and methods of foreign language education in light of the themes highlighted in the present chapter. Before turning to present-day practice, however, we would like to address a further question. If the notion that the biblical story really does have some relevance for foreign language education had any validity, wouldn't it have been spotted and explored long ago?

Yes. It would have been. And it was . . .

25. Brueggemann, 1982, 99.

CHAPTER TWO

Beginnings: Early Christian Contributions to Foreign Language Education

I (David Smith) mentioned in chapter 1 my sense of being called into foreign language education and the obstacles a limited interpretation of the Bible can place in the way of seeing such a vocation as a bona fide Christian calling. As I embarked on a language teaching career, I soon found that getting the theology straight did not quite seem to be enough. It was still somehow difficult to feel that my educational role was a valuable form of Christian service. I suspect that a large part of the reason had to do with the invisibility of the past.

In the few years that I had been a Christian, virtually all the heroes presented to me for imitation and adulation had been called to some form of church ministry. The popular biographies, the stirring snippets of church history, the challenging anecdotes used to illustrate sermons, the topics covered at prayer meetings — all were concerned mainly with pastors, evangelists, missionaries, relief workers, and the like. It was only natural to end up feeling that to really serve the Lord meant following one of these vocations. I had been given little reason to suspect that anyone in the past had shared my peculiar calling or that it might have any significance in God's plans.

Needless to say, the professional literature in my field did not help much. Outside the church the fruits of past Christian contributions to shaping second-language education tend to be taken for granted; scholars are, at best, only minimally aware of the Christian origins of such contributions and scarcely even acknowledge them. In a professional context, the idea of approaching foreign language education in a Christian manner seemed odd, idiosyncratic, perhaps even illegitimate.

This sense of lacking a heritage, of not really being part of a tradition, is in fact largely a product of our highly selective memory. This chapter and the next one seek to begin to redress the balance. In them we will not offer a systematic overall history of language teaching or a thorough history of Christian involvement in the field. Our approach will be more impressionistic. We simply want to illustrate, through a few telling examples, that the kind of Christian discussion of the aims, materials, and methods of second-language teaching we attempt in this book is neither strange nor new; on the contrary, to engage in it involves getting back in touch with some of the discipline's historical roots.

In the present chapter we will sketch the ways in which the missionary interests of the church became intertwined with the development of second-language teaching, giving particular attention to the contributions of Ramon Lull and Roger Bacon to a reawakening of interest in foreign language study in the Middle Ages. We will focus primarily on attitudes to linguistic diversity and motives for foreign language learning. In the next chapter we will consider how Christian thought has influenced the *educational* shape of language learning — not merely the motives for learning other languages, but also the ways in which languages are taught. We will approach these more pedagogical issues mainly through a brief review of the work of Comenius, perhaps the greatest Christian contributor to second-language education in its long history.

Expanding Horizons: The Early Church

The attitude of the ancient Greeks to linguistic diversity seems to have been one of indifference. R. H. Robins notes that while they did have interpreters and speakers of other languages, "of serious interest in the languages themselves among the Greeks there is no evidence; and the Greek designation of alien speakers as 'barbaroi' (. . . whence our word 'barbarian'), i.e. people who speak unintelligibly, is probably indicative of their attitude."[1] In other words, the world divided into Greek speakers who were bearers of full humanity and foreigners who were considered of lesser

---

1. Robins, 1979, 11.

worth. Serious study of language did not, therefore, focus on diversity. In the classical world, the discipline of "grammar" was preoccupied with a narrower range of concerns: rhetoric, correct expression, and interpreting the poets. It was the preserve of a cultural elite, and welcoming the stranger was not a conspicuous motivation for pursuing it.

In the Romans we find similar attitudes, but their situation was more complicated. It was harder for them to focus so single-mindedly on their own language, for they were the inheritors of a prestigious Greek cultural legacy. This meant they had to develop their own literary tradition in interaction with foreign language texts, the Greek classics. As a result, education in the early Roman Empire was bilingual. According to Rita Copeland, the Romans became "the first people in the European West to exploit another language in order to achieve mastery over their own."[2]

Copeland's comment suggests the complexity of the situation; it points to a more serious interest in a foreign language than the Greeks showed, yet it also gives the impression that the motivation for this interest really revolved around the Romans' own language. Their exploitation of Greek was, Copeland argues, based in rivalry, especially as bilingualism declined and Greek came to be taught as a foreign language. The underlying aim of studying Greek was to enrich and thus bolster the status of Latin culture, to develop it to a level where it could displace Greek. As Copeland herself puts it, "Roman reverence for Greek culture was simply a corollary of the desire to displace that culture, and eliminate its hegemonic hold."[3]

This early Western dalliance with foreign language education seems, then, to have been informed by a desire to establish the supremacy of the mother tongue. As time went on, Greek was gradually eclipsed in the Roman world, signaling a "growing linguistic rupture between East and West."[4] In Western educational contexts, the primary purpose of language education became the preservation of Latin's supremacy in the face of the encroachments of vernacular languages.[5] As with the Greeks, the Romans' interest in other languages remained shot through with a sense that those languages were secondary rivals to the mother tongue. As Louis G. Kelly's summary of the situation highlights, this emphasis even shaped the expe-

2. Copeland, 1991, 11.
3. Copeland, 1991, 30.
4. Copeland, 1991, 38.
5. Copeland, 1991, 42.

rience of many for whom Latin was a foreign tongue: "Since the intellectual life of Rome was entirely formed by Greek ideas, Greek was the prerequisite for the educated and cultured. But outside a restricted area in Italy, Latin was a foreign language; and as any advancement was dependent on a good knowledge of Latin, it too was a necessity for any ambitious provincial. The local languages had no status whatsoever, and did not enter into consideration."[6]

Things changed after Christ, however. According to Holger Pedersen, the initial spread of Christianity "brought with it the first great expansion of the linguistic horizon."[7] Christians had a different worldview in which Babel and Pentecost played a significant role. They also introduced a fresh set of concerns that grew out of their interest in mission and in translating and interpreting the Bible. The result in the early Christian centuries was a growing interest in a variety of linguistic issues, and also a new practical focus: a concern for communication began to challenge earlier elitist and prescriptive emphases. Thus Augustine, though thoroughly familiar with classical linguistics, could state: "Whether we say 'inter homines' or 'inter hominibus' has no influence on him who wants to know the facts. Likewise, is barbarism anything else than to pronounce a word with other letters and sounds than they used to do who spoke Latin before us? Whether 'ignoscere' 'to forgive' is pronounced with the third syllable long or short, is of no interest to the person who asks God to forgive him his sins."[8] In other words, Augustine is suggesting that the message is more important than its form. Since early church audiences did not initially consist of a cultural elite familiar with classical writers, some of the church fathers, out of consideration for their readership, even used colloquial language in their writings.

Shrinking Horizons — the Early Middle Ages

Unfortunately, the fresh vistas that began to open up with the advent of Christianity soon began to recede from view. Hovdhaugen comments about the open attitude of early Christianity toward linguistic diversity:

6. Kelly, 1969, 366.
7. Pedersen, 1962, 34.
8. Quoted in Hovdhaugen, 1982, 113.

"Such an attitude could easily have led linguistics into a new direction where linguistic variation and language development could have come into focus. But the opposite happened: pagan grammar soon became dominant within Christian linguistics too."[9]

Gradually, the intellectual leadership of the church shifted to the Latin-speaking classes. Christian scholars such as the Roman monk Flavius Magnus Aurelius Cassiodorus (ca. 477–ca. 570) advocated the fusion of classical learning and Christianity in Christian education, with the goal of facilitating the study of Scripture. Isidore of Seville (ca. 560-636), a major figure in the early church, expressed a continued interest in linguistic diversity in his writings; he discussed the differences between language groups and stated that "every human being can either through listening acquire the mastery of any language whether of Greek or Latin or of any other nation or he can learn it from a teacher through reading."[10] However, he also clearly emphasized the growing dominance of Latin, Greek, and Hebrew at the expense of other languages:

> There are, however, three sacred languages: Hebrew, Greek and Latin which are the most excellent in the whole world. For in these three languages the notice of accusation against him was written by Pilate over the Lord's cross. Because of that and because of the obscurity of the Holy Scriptures the knowledge of these three languages is necessary so one can take recourse to another if the wording of one language brings some doubt concerning a name or the interpretation.[11]

This focus on an elevated trio of sacred languages was to influence the ministry and mission of the church for centuries to come. Hovdhaugen concludes a discussion of these developments with the verdict that, by the early Middle Ages,

> Christianity did not mean a paradigmatic shift in linguistic theory. The broadening of the study of language which is found in the earliest Christian writings on linguistic matters was soon narrowed by the recapturing of the field by traditional grammar. The period 600-1000 is domi-

---

9. Hovdhaugen, 1982, 113.
10. Quoted in Hovdhaugen, 1982, 111.
11. Quoted in Hovdhaugen, 1982, 110.

nated by Cassiodorus's approach to linguistics. . . . The interest in languages other than Latin was very limited. . . . Although more or less anecdotal references to Greek and Hebrew are found in most linguistic writings, the focus of interest in linguistics is again a mainly monolingual one.[12]

The rupture between East and West previously noted left the Western church largely focused on Latin as the preeminent language. This shift toward the dominance of Latin had a negative effect on the church's approach to missions, on the communication of the Christian faith, and increasingly on the church's understanding of the Bible.

In the East more openness to linguistic diversity remained. The development of the Slavic languages, for instance, owed much to the work of Cyril (826-69) and Methodius (815-85), the "Apostles to the Slavs." In the ninth century these linguistic pioneers created the first script for the Slavonic dialect in Moravia, where they worked as missionaries. In translating portions of the Bible and liturgical works into the local language, they laid the foundations of what is now known as Old Church Slavonic. Their efforts met with alternate approval and opposition from the Western Church, and after Methodius's death, their disciples were imprisoned and dispersed. Nevertheless, the impact of their work remained significant for the development of the Slavonic churches.

In the West, where Latin had predominated for so long, change came very slowly. However, with the onset of the thirteenth century, a fresh focus on international mission and an awareness of the ill effects of limiting oneself only to Latin nurtured new interest in the vernacular languages. After such a lengthy monolingual period of Western Church history, some rethinking was long overdue. The rest of this chapter is devoted to two individuals who committed themselves to such a rethinking and its consequences: Ramon Lull and Roger Bacon.

Ramon Lull

Ramon Lull was born about 1232 on the island of Mallorca. He was educated with a view to gaining a position at the royal court, and in time was

12. Hovdhaugen, 1982, 115.

appointed tutor to James, the son of James the Conqueror. When that task expired, he retained a position at court, where his lifestyle of deceit and sexual adventure gave rise to many colorful stories.[13]

This all changed in the summer of 1263, when the course of Lull's life was dramatically altered by a profound and startling Christian conversion.[14] In the days that followed, a number of ideas crystallized that were to form the basis of all his subsequent labors. He resolved to place his life in the service of Christian mission and to write books that would demonstrate truth and confound error. He realized, however, that his existing learning was rudimentary and to complete this task he would need to master both foreign languages and the sciences. The conviction that God had given him his ideas and plans helped him overcome fits of despondency. Considering his connections at court, he also resolved to urge rulers and popes to found colleges for foreign language instruction as a prelude to sending out missionaries.

Nine years of study followed, at the end of which he published his *Book of Contemplation,* a seven-volume treatise on religion that he wrote in Arabic and translated into Catalan. Besides mastering Arabic during these years, he also acquired a detailed understanding of the Koran and of Muslim tradition, as well as a knowledge of theology, philosophy, and the sciences. His publication of theological works in languages other than Latin was itself a departure from custom.

13. One such relates how he fell in love with a beautiful married woman who did not return his affections; one day he saw her entering a church, and was so overcome with ardor that he galloped right into the church after her on horseback, causing uproar among the worshipers, who ejected him from the building.

14. The "Contemporary Life" of Lull, written around 1311, relates, "Being one night in his chamber, seated upon his bed, imagining and thinking out a vain song and writing it in the vulgar tongue for some woman of whom he was at the time enamoured with a vile and worthless love — when his whole understanding was engaged and occupied in the composition of this vain song, he looked to his right hand and saw our Lord God Jesus Christ hanging upon the cross in great agony and sorrow" (Peers, 1927, 32). Lull experienced the vision as a powerful shock, but his stubborn will reasserted itself and the next day he discounted his vision and returned to his song. A week later, in the same place and at the same time, and again while occupied with his song, the vision was suddenly repeated, to his even greater consternation. Eventually he faced the message of the visions, that "Jesus Christ desired none other thing than that he should wholly abandon the world and devote himself to His service." After a whole night of internal debate he yielded to the summons.

In 1276 James the Conqueror died. His son James, Ramon's former pupil, inherited a share of his father's kingdom. It seems that he knew of Ramon's ambitions, for one of his first acts as James II was to found a missionary college at Miramar. This college was to be maintained annually from the royal coffers, and in it thirteen friars were to devote themselves to the study of Arabic as a prelude to missionary endeavor. The project was formally approved by Pope John XXI. Lull was overjoyed at this first great success, and he spent a year working at Miramar to establish the college.

The ensuing years he spent in activities consistent with the resolutions he had made immediately after his conversion: writing books and lecturing on them, importuning popes and leaders to organize missionary ventures and to provide for language education, and undertaking missionary endeavors himself. He eventually wrote over two hundred books, and is remembered as the father of Catalan literature.[15]

The Campaign for Language Colleges

Lull's desire that colleges be set up to teach foreign languages remained at the fore throughout his life. He felt that the Crusades were misguided and had failed; he called instead for a turn to love, prayer, and preaching.[16] A key part of his understanding of such mission was the conviction that the preaching should take place not in Latin, but in the language of the hearers.

Despite the initial success at Miramar, he met with more frustration than encouragement. He lamented in his *Book of Contemplation* the lack of interest among Christians in learning foreign languages for missionary purposes: "For the churches I see divers images and paintings made, which will beautify them; but I see few men who will learn divers languages, or who will go and preach to the infidels, or bring them into

---

15. His romance *Blanquerna*, written a hundred years before Chaucer's *Canterbury Tales*, is described by Peers as "a masterpiece, not only of Catalan literature, but of European literature" (1929, 167). Terry refers to Lull as "the Creator of Catalan literary prose," adding that "his presence as a philosopher-poet of genius at the beginning of the vernacular tradition . . . is of incalculable significance for the later history of literary Catalan" (1972, 12, 14).

16. *Book of Contemplation*, chap. 112, quoted in Peers, 1929, 31.

the true way of life and lead them from the error wherein they now are."[17] This regret was to echo through his writings for most of his life. Between 1277 and 1305 he made repeated trips to Rome to petition a series of popes for support and for the means to realize his plans. For a variety of reasons, every trip ended in a frustration he eventually expressed in his *Desconort* (Disconsolateness), a sorrowful lament whose subtitle reads: "Made by master Ramon Lull in his old age, when he saw that neither the Pope nor the other lords of the world would put forth a method for the conversion of the heathen, according as he had prayed them at many and divers seasons."[18] Besides the frustration he encountered in his efforts to instigate new projects, some unknown disaster at Miramar caused the one existing college to be abandoned soon after 1292. The fruits of Lull's labors seemed few.

Nevertheless, the prodigious flow of his books continued, as did his persistent pursuit of his ideals. In 1311 he attended the Council of Vienne, where he presented a number of proposals, including, of course, "that there should be builded certain places where certain persons, devout and of lofty intelligence should study divers languages to the end that they might preach the holy Gospel to all nations."[19]

The council's response to Lull's proposal, after he had invested almost fifty years of unstinting labor and ardent faith in the pursuit of his vision, must have delighted him immensely. Not only did the council accept his proposal; it even expanded it. Where Lull had proposed three colleges, it decided to found five, in Rome, Bologna, Paris, Oxford, and Salamanca. Hebrew, Arabic, and Chaldean were to be taught, and the church was to provide for the expenses of the colleges in Rome and Salamanca.[20]

Lull was not one to entertain ideals without acting on them, and he never forgot his early resolution to lay down his own life preaching the gospel. Between his visits to Rome, he journeyed to a great number of countries, writing, lecturing, and debating with adherents of other faiths, and his missionary journeys to Muslim Africa make dramatic reading. Stephen Neill comments that "At one time or another we find him everywhere in the Christian world of that day."[21] His last missionary venture,

17. Chap. 106, quoted in Peers, 1929, 39.
18. Quoted in Peers, 1929, 257.
19. Peers, 1927, 43.
20. Peers, 1929, 360.
21. Neill, 1986, 115.

undertaken in 1315 when he was eighty-three years old, bore the fruit of several converts among the learned Moors of Tunis. Tradition has it (though this account has been questioned) that this journey ended when Lull was stoned to death by a crowd as he began to preach Christ.

Lull's central interests were clearly missiological rather than linguistic. Neill notes that "he was not interested so much in the languages for themselves as in that to which they should lead — a competent understanding of the thought and the doctrine of the Saracens, and the possibility of elevated and charitable discourse with them on matters of religion."[22] Nevertheless, Lull's deep concern for understanding the language and culture of others and for presenting truth to them in a manner informed by that knowledge recaptured an authentically Christian impulse. His heart was set on evangelism, and he did not reflect on the broader purposes of second-language teaching. One of his contemporaries, however, did.

Roger Bacon

The available biographical information concerning Lull's eminent contemporary Roger Bacon is sketchy. We do know that he was born around 1214 in Dorset, England, and died in 1292. He studied at Oxford, where he took his M.A., and achieved fame through lectures at Oxford and Paris. He joined the Franciscans, continuing his studies and making many enemies through his sharp criticism of established figures and practices. His writings included incisive attacks on the pope and his court, on the clergy, all religious orders, the academic institutions, kings, and the experts in the legal professions.[23]

Bacon's studies were wide-ranging and intense; he wrote that "men used to wonder before I became a friar that I lived, owing to my excessive labours."[24] He is remembered particularly for his work in mathematics and science, but was also keenly interested in languages. He was an accomplished scholar of English and French, read Greek, Latin, and Hebrew, and knew some Arabic. He considered knowledge of languages a necessary

22. Neill, 1986, 116.

23. Little, 1914.

24. Little, 1914, 3. Latourette describes him as "one of the most original and creative intellects of the Middle Ages" (1939, 390).

foundation for acquiring wisdom and urged his contemporaries to promote the study of languages as a priority. S. A. Hirsch comments that "he did not stop at exhortations. He threw himself into this pursuit [linguistic study] with the same energy which characterised his efforts in the other fields of learning."[25]

Recognizing the need for suitable textbooks, he wrote grammars of Greek and Hebrew and planned to write an Arabic grammar as well. He also invited various Greek scholars to England so that he and his followers might learn from them. In his leisure time he instructed boys in science and languages.

In 1266 the pope, having received a letter from Bacon, asked for a copy of his works. Since they were as yet unwritten, Bacon hurriedly produced his *Opus Majus,* which he intended as a preamble to a systematic work on all the sciences. In its pages Bacon set out his departure from certain aspects of traditional scholastic thought. He argued that four faults were hindering the progress of wisdom: dependence on authority, yielding to established custom, allowing weight to popular opinion, and concealing real ignorance with the pretense of knowledge. He was a pioneer advocate of an experimental approach to the sciences.

The section of Bacon's writings that is of greatest interest for our purposes is the third part of the *Opus Majus,* titled "On the Usefulness of Grammar," that is, the usefulness of the study of languages. In fourteen short chapters he catalogues a variety of reasons why language learning should be promoted by and within the church. Some of these reasons reflect a decidedly superstitious view of the magical properties of certain tongues: for instance, supposedly the Greek, Latin, and Hebrew alphabets have certain mystic properties that might enable those who can interpret them to predict future events. Such curious and dated parts of Bacon's reasoning will not be detailed here, but other sections of his argument are of more interest for the purposes of this study.

"Pure Zeal for Knowledge"

In the first section of his argument, Bacon presents the case for language learning in terms of its contribution to "pure zeal for knowledge." "For it is

---

25. Hirsch, 1914, 113.

impossible for the Latins to reach what is necessary in matters divine and human except through the knowledge of other languages, nor will wisdom be perfected for them absolutely, nor relatively to the Church of God."[26]

He points out that the Bible ought to be read in its original languages if it is to be fully appreciated and understood, and makes clear his disgust at the error-ridden translations of his day, declaring: "God knows that nothing can be brought before the Apostolic Seat in need of such vigorous correction as this endless corruption."[27] Even when translated, he adds, the Bible contains foreign words such as *hallelujah* that people should understand. What is more, even where the text of the translation is correct, a poor grasp of languages can lead to misinterpretation.

He makes similar points about works of philosophy, stating that all existing translations of philosophical works are uniformly bad, and that a great deal of important work remains untranslated and can only become available through learning the language in which it is written. Even Latin writers of philosophy use many foreign words that the reader needs to understand.

Finally, he argues that ignorance of etymology and derivation, which may include the derivation of certain Latin terms from other languages, leaves the Latins with an imperfect grasp of their own language, since they have little sense of where the words came from and the shades of meaning they might carry. In short, Bacon's claim in this section of his work is that ignorance of foreign languages will lead to a more general ignorance.

The specifics of the argument are, of course, dated. With accurate translations and a glut of Bible study aids at our disposal, we are in a much better position than Bacon's contemporaries. However, Bacon's academic motivation for language learning remains relevant, and his contention that foreign language education can lead to a fuller understanding of the Scriptures is still valid today. While there is no need for all readers of the Bible to master Greek and Hebrew, a grasp of how languages work and differ from each other, and an awareness of the relevance of cultural differences for communication, could help learners approach their Bible translations more intelligently. This emphasis is still worthy of Christian educators' attention.

---

26. *Opus Majus*, pt. 3, chap. 4; quotations from the *Opus Majus* are taken from Burke, 1962.

27. Burke, 1962, 88.

"The Church of God"

In the second section of his work on the usefulness of language study, Bacon contends that speakers of various vernacular languages in Europe who have become subject to the church need Christian instruction in their mother tongue. (Later he will go on to concentrate on mission to those outside Christendom.) He declares that "of this there is proof in the fact that all the nations waver in faith and morals and neglect the orders of the Church pertaining to salvation, because a genuine plea is not addressed to them in their mother tongue. Hence everywhere among such nations there are evil Christians, and the Church is not ruled as it should be."[28] While Bacon's own focus remained on the ancient languages, this is the first of several arguments that point beyond the necessity of learning classical languages to a practical need for knowledge of the various vernacular languages.

"The Commonwealth of the Faithful"

The arguments Bacon advances on this theme have a very modern ring. He first claims that a knowledge of foreign languages will benefit Christendom's interests in international trade; in particular, such knowledge will enable traders to avoid being subjected to fraud. Second, it will enable individuals who travel abroad to secure justice before foreign judges if they are wronged or accused. Third, an increase in the study of languages will help secure peace by enabling nations to communicate more freely and effectively with one another, for "very often matters which have been set on foot with great labour and expense come to naught owing to ignorance of a foreign tongue."[29]

While these reasons have familiar present-day parallels in discussions of foreign language education, they exhibit a difference in emphasis. Where today's rhetoric tends to emphasize competition and opportunities

28. Burke, 1962, 108.
29. Burke, 1962, 110. Bacon backs up this point with an anecdote: "I learned that Soldanus of Babylonia wrote to my lord, the present king of France, and there was not found in the whole learned body in Paris, nor in the whole kingdom of France a man who knew satisfactorily how to explain a letter nor to make the necessary reply to the message. And the lord king marvelled greatly at such dense ignorance, and he was much displeased with the clergy because he found them so ignorant."

for personal or national economic gain as reasons for taking foreign language education seriously, Bacon's focus is more on issues of justice and on right relationships with citizens of other nations.

"The Conversion of Unbelievers"

In his final section Bacon echoes Lull's concern that mission attempted without a grasp of the hearer's language is ineffectual.[30] Like Lull, he complains that crusades have proved singularly ineffective and even harmful, leading not to the conversion of unbelievers but to their destruction and to a lasting hatred of the church. Conversion is instead a fruit of faithful preaching in a language understood by those who hear:

> Moreover, the faith did not enter into this world by force of arms but through the simplicity of preaching, as is clear. And we have frequently heard and we are certain that many, although they were imperfectly acquainted with languages and had weak interpreters, yet made great progress by preaching and converted countless numbers to the Christian faith. Oh, how we should consider this matter and fear lest God may hold the Latins responsible because they are neglecting the languages so that in this way they neglect the preaching of the faith. For Christians are few, and the whole broad world is occupied by unbelievers; and there is no one to show them the truth.[31]

A final argument concerns nations that will not convert to Christianity, even after hearing preaching in their mother tongue. How should they be dealt with, and how should their potential threat to the security of Christendom be countered? This task, Bacon asserts, "requires rather the way of wisdom than the labour of war."[32] Here, too, words can achieve more good than force ever will:

> At the command and at the words of the saints from the beginning of the world . . . numberless miracles were performed. But the hand of the

30. Burke, 1962, 111.
31. Burke, 1962, 111.
32. Burke, 1962, 112.

Lord is not shortened; and we should believe that if on the authority of the Church and with right intention and from desire many true and wise Christians should utter holy words for the propagation of the faith and the destruction of falsehood, that many blessings might result by the grace of God. Oh, how many tyrants and evil men have been confounded at the words of power and convicted rather than through wars![33]

Bacon shares Lull's conviction that mission must be underpinned by effective foreign language learning, and he relates this emphasis to the possibility of peace across cultural and religious boundaries. Despite his overly magical view of language, his basic idea remains evocative: holy words uttered by wise Christians in foreign languages have the power to call down God's blessing.

Taking Stock

In the pleas of Lull and Bacon that the Western Church turn its attention to learning the languages of others, we glimpse afresh the broadening of the linguistic horizon that was evident in the earliest Christian centuries. As the emergence of a Christian worldview had led to wider linguistic interests in the days of the church fathers, so likewise the concern for learning foreign languages that emerged increasingly in the late Middle Ages was connected with the recovery of authentic Christian emphases: bringing blessing to the nations, recognizing the humanity of speakers of all languages, reconciliation, caring for the stranger. In refusing to acquiesce to their fellow Christians' indifference to language learning, Lull and Bacon provided a fresh impetus for taking Pentecost seriously. Although their main emphasis fell on the relation of language learning to mission, Bacon's ideas also reflect an interest in a second theme that we discussed in chapter 1: cultivating right relationships with strangers both abroad and at home.

What is still missing from the writings of both Lull and Bacon is any discussion of language learning in a pedagogical context. Their pleas remain at the level of general arguments in favor of the church taking an interest in other languages. Thus it is no surprise that educational goals,

33. Burke, 1962, 112-13.

methods, and materials for teaching second languages continue to lie beyond the horizons of their discussion. In these areas little had changed since the Greeks and Romans.

In the centuries following Lull and Bacon, the vernacular languages grew stronger and Latin began to lose its hegemony. Various protest movements in the Western Church, such as those led by Jan Hus, Peter Waldo, and Peter Chelčicky, renewed and acted on the call to take vernacular languages seriously. The stage was now being set for second-language teaching to come into greater prominence.

CHAPTER THREE

Broadening Horizons:
From Luther to Comenius

So far we have taken a selective look at the ways Christian faith led historically to certain attitudes toward differences in language and culture. Concern for interpreting and translating the Bible, an interest in communication and the well-being of the hearer, and an emphasis on mission — all
were reasons for regarding study of the languages of others as important.
These Christian emphases motivated Lull and Bacon to push for such
study even when the attitudes of their contemporaries were less than encouraging. This strand of Christian concern for foreign language learning
is still visible today in the activities of organizations such as the Wycliffe
Bible Translators, whose work has contributed significantly to the discipline of linguistics as well as to Christian mission.

But what about foreign language *education* — pedagogy, learning
materials, educational aims and objectives, and the like? Has Christianity
intersected with language learning only in terms of general motives for
pursuing such learning, or has Christian reflection also been brought to
bear on the specifically educational questions that concern the language
teacher? The present chapter will address this question and will, as in the
previous chapter, provide significant examples rather than a complete history. We begin with a brief look at the time of the Reformation.

Decay and Reformation

The dissatisfaction and demand for change that found expression in the Protestant Reformation of the sixteenth century did not revolve exclusively around the church and its theology. The Reformers also expressed deep dissatisfaction with the state of education; in addition, they had to deal with the effects their own reforms had on educational matters.

Schooling in Germany in the sixteenth century had reached a less than healthy state. The increase in wealth generated by growing trade and industry led to popular impatience with scholastic and humanist education. For many, training the mind in the best of classical culture seemed of little relevance to the immediate task of earning a living. Moreover, since most schools were church run, the attacks of the Protestant reformers gave people further reason for turning away from the schools of the day.

Martin Luther, for one, was clearly dissatisfied with the educational situation. In 1524 he expressed his feelings about existing schools in his usual delicate, understated manner:

> What have men been learning till now in the universities and monasteries except to become asses, blockheads, and numbskulls? For twenty, even forty, years they pored over their books, and still failed to master either Latin or German. . . . Instead of worthwhile books, the stupid, useless, and harmful books of the monks, such as *Catholicon, Florista, Grecista, Labyrinthus, Dormi Secure,* and the like asses' dung were introduced by the devil. Because of such books the Latin language was ruined, and there remained nowhere a decent school, course of instruction, or method of study. . . . What else could come out of them but pupils and teachers as stupid as the books they used?[1]

He comments further:

> It is perfectly true that if universities and monasteries were to continue as they have been in the past, and there were no other place available

1. Luther, 1962, 351-52, 374, 375. The *Catholicon* was a thirteenth-century lexicon that included orthography, grammar, etymology, prosody, and rhetoric; the *Florista* (1317) was a rhymed Latin syntax; the *Grecista* (1212) was a grammatical treatise in hexameters; the *Labyrinthus* was a thirteenth-century poem; the *Dormi Secure* was a collection of sermons from 1450.

where youth could study and live, then I could wish that no boy would ever study at all, but just remain dumb. For it is my earnest purpose, prayer, and desire that these asses' stalls and devils' training centers should either sink into the abyss or be converted into Christian schools.[2]

Luther specifically complained of deficiencies in language education:

Languages and the arts, which can do us no harm, but are actually a greater ornament, profit, glory, and benefit, both for the understanding of Holy Scripture and the conduct of temporal government — these we despise. But foreign wares, which are neither necessary nor useful, and in addition strip us down to a mere skeleton — these we cannot do without. Are not we Germans justly dubbed fools and beasts?[3]

Faced with the need to counter the educational decline of the day with a more positive agenda, Luther urged not only that greater value be placed on schooling, but also that the schools themselves undergo far-reaching reform. The Reformers set themselves a goal that exceeded the vision of traditional humanist education: they proposed that elitist intellectual training be replaced by universal public education. Luther was also interested in improving the way language was taught, declaring that: "By the Grace of God it is now possible for children to study with pleasure and in play languages, or other arts, or history. Today, schools are not what they once were, a hell and a purgatory in which we were tormented with *casualibus* and *temporalibus* [cases and tenses] and yet learned less than nothing despite all the flogging, trembling, anguish, and misery."[4]

It was left to Luther's fellow reformer, Philipp Melanchthon, to actually map out such reforms. Melanchthon worked hard to that end, earning in the process fame as the reformer of German education, the *Praeceptor Germaniae*.[5] As a result of his work, the universities in Germany were reorganized and public schools were founded. His pedagogy and textbooks

---

2. Luther, 1962, 352.
3. Luther, 1962, 358. Luther comments: "In short, the Holy Spirit is no fool. He does not busy himself with inconsequential or useless matters. He regarded the languages as so useful and necessary to Christianity that he ofttimes brought them down with him from heaven" (361).
4. Luther, 1962, 369.
5. Manschreck, 1958.

also were widely adopted, including a new Latin grammar that was significantly superior to its predecessors. Widely used in Protestant schools, it went through more than fifty editions and was still in use in the eighteenth century.[6]

Nevertheless, despite the efforts of the Reformers, the sixteenth century saw little fundamental change in how languages were taught. Melanchthon's grammar, for example, was an improved version of existing medieval models rather than a radical departure. One area of improvement was his effort to provide meaningful, edifying content in textbooks whose major focus was grammatical training.[7] Language learning in the medieval era had focused on linguistic form rather than content, on mastery of grammatical minutiae rather than language in use. Latin was the medium of instruction, and was taught before or even to the exclusion of the learner's vernacular tongue. Some of the textbooks used in medieval classrooms had been written over a thousand years before. These grammars often seemed to aim for the greatest possible complexity; Latin nouns, for example, were commonly assigned to one of seven genders: masculine, feminine, neuter, common of two, common of three, promiscuous, and doubtful. The focus of language study in general was not on the outside world, but rather on the authoritative texts that formed the scholastic heritage. While the Reformers, particularly Melanchthon, did improve things significantly, a more fundamental rethinking of language learning had not yet been achieved.

Through the Labyrinth of the World

On March 28, 1592, Jan Ámos Komenský, whose life was to prove both remarkably eventful and highly significant for the subsequent history of Western education, was born to a mill owner and his wife in Nivnice, southern Moravia.[8]

Comenius, as he is now usually known, lost his parents to a plague when he was only ten and had to endure an early education that he re-

6. Manschreck, 1958, 150.

7. Manschreck, 1958, 148.

8. For more detailed (and highly readable) biographical information, see Murphy, 1995.

membered chiefly for its harshness and brutality. Nevertheless, he progressed to university and became a minister and later a bishop in the Moravian Church of the United Brethren. The times were difficult for this group of believers, and Comenius was to share fully in their tragedies during the Thirty Years' War. Twice he found himself with only the clothes on his back after his home and its contents had been destroyed in the fighting. The first time he suffered the loss of his wife and their children, all of whom fell victim to a plague that spread in the wake of the conflict. Among the material he lost during the second attack was the manuscript of a Czech-Latin dictionary that he had been working on for over forty years. With other Moravian pastors and their congregations he wandered to and fro across eastern Europe, sometimes finding safe places to settle briefly, at other times fleeing from persecution or hiding out in caves in the mountains.

In spite of these dramatic and forbidding circumstances and the burdens associated with his responsibilities first as a pastor, then as leader of the United Brethren, Comenius was remarkably productive in a variety of areas. He wrote voluminously. His spiritual allegory *The Labyrinth of the World and the Paradise of the Heart* is regarded as one of the greatest works of Czech literature. He also met Descartes and debated faith and philosophy with him.

The turbulence of his life and the breadth of his interests did not prevent Comenius from investing enormous amounts of labor in educational reform, however, and he earned a reputation as one of the greatest figures in the history of education. His writings in this field attracted a good deal of interest. He was invited to London by the British government, and carried out far-reaching programs of school reform in Sweden and Hungary. There is even evidence suggesting that he was offered the presidency of Harvard College.

One of his particular areas of eminence was his work as a language teacher. Two of his language textbooks, the *Janua Linguarum Reserata* (Gate of languages unlocked [1632]) and the *Orbis Sensualium Pictus* (World of sensory things in pictures [1658]) achieved phenomenal success. Both were widely translated and remained in print for centuries after their publication. The *Orbis Pictus* went through twenty-one editions in the seventeenth century, forty-three in the eighteenth, thirty-three in the nineteenth, and nine in the twentieth. It was translated into sixteen languages, including Arabic, Turkish, Persian, and Mongolian. In addition,

Comenius's ideas on how to teach languages laid the foundations for modern language education. J.-A. Caravolas describes his language teaching theory as "the first general and coherent one in the history of this old discipline."[9]

A considerable body of literature discusses Comenius's life and work, and his importance is generally recognized. What has not always received due emphasis in studies of his writings, though, is his insistence that all teaching should be informed by the conviction that "all that does not relate to God and to the future life is nothing but vanity."[10] Comenius's project was basically a rethinking of education from the standpoint of a consciously Christian philosophy:

> A new philosophy must be set up in a new light, so that there may be no reason for the continuance of that old philosophy of the Greeks which has been convicted in so many ways of being inferior and insufficient, confused and ill-ordered and yet noisy and impetuous, and has inflicted so many injuries on the Christian spirit. A new philosophy must be set up so that the children of Israel need no more be forced to turn to the Philistines to get their ploughs and hoes and axes and trowels sharpened, but may possess at home their own swords and all other necessary equipment, and not be found wanting in the day of battle.[11]

Inspired by this motivation, Comenius worked out a distinctive set of educational beliefs that placed him on a different trajectory from the philosophical schools of thought that had influenced him. His articulation of such a forthright overall stance invites questions about the relationship of his Christian faith to his ideas about language teaching in particular. Were they accidental to each other, coexisting side by side, or was the mod-

9. Caravolas, 1993, 145.

10. *Great Didactic* (henceforth *GD*) XXIV:24. Quotations are from the translation by M. W. Keatinge (Keatinge, 1967).

11. *Via Lucis* (The way of light) 124-25, cited in Murphy, 1995, 81. Cf. *GD* XXV, passim, e.g., 14: "to a Christian soul all is strange, and should be strange, that has any other source than the Holy Spirit; and of such a kind are the ravings of the heathen philosophers and poets," or 17: "The true light comes from heaven, from the Father of Light! Any light that is visible in human efforts arises from a few sparks that seem to shine because of the darkness that surrounds them; but what are a few sparks to us, in whose hands a blazing torch has been placed (the effulgent word of God)?"

ern project of second-language education informed at the very outset by Christian convictions?

Education for Humans

Central to Comenius's educational thinking is his understanding of what it means to be authentically human.[12] The first ten chapters of his most famous work on education, *The Great Didactic*, are devoted to what it means to be made in God's image. His summary answer to that question is as follows:

It is plain that man is situated among visible creatures so as to be

(i.) A rational creature
(ii.) The Lord of all creatures
(iii.) A creature which is the image and joy of its Creator.

These three aspects are so joined together that they cannot be separated, for in them is laid the basis of the future and of the present life.[13]

It is crucial, in Comenius's view, that these three characteristics be taken together. When combined, they convey his understanding of the significance of humankind's being made in the image of God. They also correspond to what he considered the three basic goals of education: *erudition, virtue,* and *piety.*[14]

First, Comenius considered it an essential part of our nature as rational beings to be fascinated by all aspects of creation. He had a high view of humankind's rational powers, yet rejected the rationalism of Descartes. Reason stands empty, he argued, without data from the senses. Furthermore, it is unfruitful unless guided by a will that chooses the good. Most importantly, it is vain without wisdom from the Scriptures. Thus the proper task of human rationality is to explore the world through the senses and to bring to light the harmony between the creation and divine revelation. Only when pursued in this way can mere knowledge grow into true wisdom.

12. See Čapková et al., 1989, 8.
13. *GD* IV:2.
14. *GD* IV:6 and passim.

Lordship over creation, humanity's second characteristic, should flow from such a pursuit of wisdom. Such lordship differs radically from the self-centered exploitation commonly associated with the idea of mastery over creation in our own times. In the *Pampaedia* Comenius complains: "What cruelty is inflicted everywhere on all things that are put to improper uses through the wickedness or the ignorance of men. . . . [I]t is desirable . . . that all creatures should have cause to join us in praising God."[15] An attitude of humility toward creation befits those who are aware that God is "invisibly present in all visible things."[16] Care for all creatures, concern for the neighbor's interests, self-control — these are the ingredients of true lordship, which is expressed not in domineering superiority but in servanthood.[17]

The third characteristic explored by Comenius has to do with reflecting God's perfection, with experiencing joy in God and bringing joy to God. Piety, he explains, means

> that (after we have thoroughly grasped the conceptions of faith and of religion) our hearts should learn to seek God everywhere . . . and that

---

15. *Pampaedia* II:13. Quotations are from the translation by A. M. O. Dobbie (Dobbie, 1986). Here Comenius presents universal education as equipping men for the true dominion that will lead to the liberation of creation described in Rom. 8:20. *GD* IV:4 offers this definition of lordship: "To be the lord of all creatures consists in subjecting everything to his own use by contriving that its legitimate end be suitably fulfilled; in conducting himself royally, that is gravely and righteously, among creatures . . . [not being] ignorant where, when, how and to what extent each may prudently be used, how far the body should be gratified, and how far our neighbour's interests should be consulted. In a word, he should be able to control with prudence his own movements and actions, external and internal, as well as those of others."

16. *GD* XXIV:2.

17. We are "sent into the world . . . that we may serve God, his creatures, and ourselves, and that we may enjoy the pleasure to be derived from God, from his creatures, and from ourselves" (*GD* X:8). Lordship is bound up with servanthood, and it is only on the basis of this close connection between rule and servanthood that Comenius's repeated insistence that the teacher is the servant, not the lord of nature, working along the grain of what is given, can be understood in relation to his strong affirmations of human agency and of the teacher's authority. It follows from this threefold responsibility for service that growth in humanity is not a matter of inwardness or individual perfection, but takes place in interrelation with the whole of creation, such that "whether humans are human or not becomes evident not in the individual subject but in the humanity of the world" (Schaller, 1992, 24). The goal of formative agency in the world is not appropriation of a convenient resource, but the creation of a garden of delight.

when we have found Him we should follow Him, and when we have attained Him we should enjoy Him. The first we do through our understanding, the second through our will, and the third through the joy arising from the consciousness of our union with God. We seek God by noticing the signs of His divinity in all things created. We follow God by giving ourselves up completely to His will. . . . We enjoy God by so acquiescing in His love and favour that nothing in heaven or on earth appears to us more to be desired than God Himself.[18]

God, he continues, is to be glorified in our bodies as well as our minds; in fact, inner and outer piety are inseparable. Piety embraces and enfolds the acquisition of knowledge through reason's interaction with the senses. It is also to guide the exercise of the will in virtuous action in the world. Wisdom, our "true work," is composed of knowledge, virtue, and piety; such wisdom raises us above all other creatures. The truly human person is the creature who images God and brings him delight by consciously referring everything back to its divine source.[19] When knowledge and virtue are completed and embraced by piety, then we have, in broad outline, Comenius's Christian vision of the nature and calling of the human person.

From the premise that all persons are created in God's image and are called to reflect that image, Comenius drew conclusions that were radical for his day. First, he insisted that the traditional neglect of the education of girls should be overturned; young people of both sexes should be educated equally. Second, he advocated that members of all social classes and economic strata should be educated in common. And third, he stressed that education should be available to all, regardless of their level of intellectual ability. Since God gives intellectual gifts to all in some measure and apportions them as he sees fit, differences in ability offer grounds neither for pride nor for restricting educational opportunities to the most able. As Comenius vividly put it, "there is no exception from human education except for non-humans."[20]

18. *GD* XXIV:2-3. For Comenius, God is to be sought in and through the natural world. These elements of seeking therefore not only explain piety, but also draw erudition and virtue up into it. For what follows, see also *GD* XXIV:25 (xvi) and XXIII:1.

19. For more detailed discussion of Comenius's idea of wisdom, see Smith, 1998.

20. *Pampaedia* II:30. On these points see *GD* IX:2-5; XVI:24; XXIX:2(ii); also Reents, 1992.

These are but a few of the consequences of his vision of authentic humanity for his general educational ideas. It is now time to return to our more specific question: What effect did this vision have on his views about language teaching? In our judgment, several clear points of contact can be made between Comenius's understanding of the human person and his reform of second-language education.

Language and Lordship

Consistent with Comenius's understanding of the human task is his view of language as a domain in which human lordship and stewardship are to be responsibly exercised. Languages, in his view, are to be deliberately cultivated as instruments to be used to the benefit of humanity and the glory of God.

Humanist educators of Comenius's day focused exclusively on Latin as the language of culture and erudition. Comenius rejected this emphasis, insisting that no vernacular language is incapable or unworthy of being cultivated. Neither is any vernacular language innately inferior to classical languages. If the latter appear to be superior, it is because they have been consciously cultivated for longer periods of time, and "if any language be obscure, or insufficient to express necessary ideas, this is the fault, not of the language, but of those who use it. . . . No language, therefore, need lack words unless men lack industry."[21]

We find in Comenius, then, a Christian affirmation of the diversity of languages that echoes themes already developed in the first two chapters of our study. For him, the cultivation of vernacular languages was a necessary part of the human task of tending creation. His understanding of the human task before God thus opened the way for an educational interest in nonclassical languages and a consideration of the pedagogy appropriate to learning them.

Given the diversity of languages and the need for peace, as well as the related need to spread the gospel abroad, this task, as he saw it, also in-

21. *GD* XXIX:14. It is clear from the paragraphs preceding this statement and the one following it that the cultivation intended is not primarily an increase in ornateness or sophistication, but in the capacity for making universal knowledge accessible to everyone. Cf. Polák, 1972; Přivratská, 1983.

volved using educational means to overcome the suspicions, separations, and hostilities that accompany diversity. Universal Christian education was to lay siege to the "stupidity" of "hating a man because he speaks another language, because he thinks differently, because he is less well educated."[22]

This general vision was subdivided into two aspects. On the one hand, some international medium of communication would be needed, for which Latin was an obvious but replaceable candidate. On the other hand, time should be given to teaching and learning the vernacular languages of neighboring countries. Instruction in these tongues should take place prior to any study of the classical languages in which the erudite were so interested. The improvement of language teaching thus took its place as a strategic part of the general improvement of human affairs, which was always Comenius's central aim.[23]

Words and Wisdom

Comenius did not merely offer fresh educational theories; he also put them into practice in highly successful language textbooks. These books represented a significant departure from the traditional language texts of the time, which contained simplified passages from classical authors. In contrast, a basic requirement of Comenius's pedagogy was that words and images of what they represented appear side by side. Thus, his textbooks were filled with pictures of objects and activities drawn from all areas of life. He decried the tendency in traditional classrooms to treat vocabulary items in isolation and to emphasize their form rather than the content they expressed. Such an emphasis on form, he insisted, could only result in empty eloquence and an erudition separated from virtue and piety, not in authentic wisdom. Words must be returned to the world, the arena of human responsibility, and not merely studied for their own sake.[24]

However, a simple enumeration of everyday objects and events was not enough. Comenius believed that particular facts must always be placed

---

22. *Panegersia* XI:22, cited in Sadler, 1966, 183.
23. *GD* XXII:1, 9. Cf. Banovitch, 1971, 111.
24. E.g., *GD* XXII:1.

in the context of a vision of the whole. Although he admired the rising emphasis on empirical science, he felt that the empiricists, with their accumulation of individual facts and observations, tended to lose sense of the wholeness and meaning of reality. Textbooks, he insisted, should "reveal the connection between things as they exist in themselves and flow from one to another."[25]

Comenius consistently expressed this two-faceted conviction in his language teaching textbooks. He did not select content for merely pragmatic reasons, but instead composed his textbooks with short chapters presenting, as parts of an ordered whole, the nature of God and of humanity, the world of nature and the sciences, arts and crafts, social realities, moral themes, and comparative religion — in short, erudition, virtue, and piety.[26] Every book was to impart wisdom. For Comenius, language teaching and learning were not a specialized set of techniques, separate from the broader curriculum. If the curriculum was to promote life lived in God's image, then all of its parts had to work harmoniously; language teaching, too, had to contribute to the three basic goals he had established.

One aspect of Comenius's conception has been almost universally incorporated into today's language texts. His advocacy of turning to the world of things and everyday human activity in the pages of language textbooks has been hailed as a revolutionary breakthrough and constitutes the norm today. The second aspect of his thinking has not made its way into modern textbooks as clearly. They do not as consistently reflect Comenius's concern for the whole, and therefore for the themes of virtue and piety.

Professionalism and Piety

Obviously, Comenius's blueprint for language education requires linguistic competence of the teacher. Such competence is necessary if the teacher is to provide an appropriate model of the language to be learned. Going further, he specified that the teacher must teach in a way that is sensitive to the particular stage of learning reached by each pupil as well as to the spe-

25. *Panorthosia* XXII:33, cited from Comenius, 1993.
26. Cf. Geissler, 1959, 100-101, 118. Comenius referred to the *Orbis Pictus* also as *Lucidarius* (Bringer of light) (Geissler, 111). Contributing to these three basic goals is in fact a precondition for inclusion in the Comenian curriculum; *GD* XVIII:8; XIX:52.

cific features of the pupil's mother tongue.[27] In keeping with Comenius's grounding of authentic human living in the imitation of God, imitation of models plays an important role both in his language pedagogy and in his general theory of education. Accordingly, imitation of the teacher's linguistic model plays an important role in Comenius's view of language learning.

However, for Comenius, the teacher models more than linguistic ability and sensitivity to the context. One implication of his insistence on not separating words from a wider sense of the whole and from the world is that *the teacher also models a particular vision of the world and a particular attitude toward others.* Even when modeling items of language for the purposes of language learning, the instructor is not concerned purely with words. The teacher displays a certain manner of speaking, a particular way of relating to others, and also says something about the way things are in the outside world. The educator's speech in class is not to consist merely of empty words; both a Christian view of the world and a Christian ethic of communication are to be modeled in the classroom.[28]

The language teacher must therefore, according to Comenius, be an individual of excellent moral integrity and profound piety.[29] These virtues are not the same as those admired by classical authors, of whom Comenius writes: "The spirit with which they fill their readers must be very different from that of Christ. . . . Christ teaches self-abnegation, they teach self-love. Christ teaches us to be humble, they to be magnanimous. Christ demands meekness, they inculcate self-assertion."[30] In short, the foreign language teacher has to model the virtues of Christ.

There is another reason why teachers should display virtue. Co-

---

27. See Caravolas, 1993, 156; *GD* XVII:27(iv). Children of different nations are to be taught Latin differently because of variations in their native grammars. While Comenius at times talks of method as universal and uniform due to the common nature of humanity, details such as this one reveal an accompanying concern for accommodating the differences between learners. Cf. XIX:53, where Comenius goes so far as to state that each mind is different and thus requires different methods.

28. A concrete example of this dimension of teaching is given at the start of chap. 8.

29. Caravolas, 1993, 152; Geissler, 1959, 145; Murphy, 1995, 157-59. Cf. *Pampaedia* VII:4: teachers should be "pious, honourable, serious, conscientious, industrious, and prudent . . . and utterly devoted to God," which means "that they should have God as a partner."

30. *GD* XXV:19(iii).

menius insisted that the learning process be easy and pleasant for the learners. This goal, however, could not be realized unless teachers inspired love, admiration, and confidence in their students, instead of cultivating the atmosphere of fear and coercion that prevailed in the classrooms of the day.[31]

Parrots and Statues

Comenius's emphasis on the interdependence of reason and sense experience is reflected in many details of his language pedagogy. In keeping with his criticism of rationalism, he rejected the deductive, rule-based approach that preceded him, with its heavy stress on mastering grammatical form, in favor of a broadly inductive approach in which exposure to examples precedes rules. Since words and things belong together, no language should be learned from a grammar. Thus in Comenius's textbooks the use of pictures, an innovation designed to cater to the senses, is of pivotal importance.[32]

While Comenius underscored the value of imitation, he did not advocate meaningless memorization. Reason has a role to play in the learning process, and comprehension must precede memorization, "for it is men we are forming and not parrots."[33] Sense experience needs to be guided and placed in a coherent context, and here the teacher has a formative role. Reason, action, and linguistic expression are to develop side by side. Thus Comenius regarded expression and communication as important factors in the learning process. He also dropped hints concerning the value of dialogue: "If the pupil is to be merely silent, you will not succeed in making him attentive, much less proficient."[34]

31. *GD* XVII:15-16.

32. *GD* XXII:11-12; XVI:19(iii). The emphasis on communication is in keeping with Comenius's emphasis on the communicative nature of God, whom we are to imitate.

33. *GD* XXII:3; cf. XVI:37(I); XVII:28(iv). Cf. Murphy, 1995, 177.

34. *Analytical Didactic* 24, cited from Jelinek, 1953. In a description of the learning process in *GD* XXVII:7, Comenius places communicative activity before analysis ("the processes of exact thought"): "The internal senses should acquire the habit of expressing in their turn the images that result from the external sensation, both internally by means of the faculty of recollection, and externally with the hand and tongue."

Language learning should thus follow a careful process of gradation in which the teacher guides but the pupil, in contrast to the passivity of the traditional model, is continually active in mastering new knowledge. The autonomy of the learner is not set over against the authority of the teacher; giving attention to the agency of both student and teacher is not understood as a potential power struggle. The learning process is rather shaped by the conviction that *both* are responsible bearers of God's image in terms of reason, virtue, and piety. This sense of shared responsibility informs Comenius's conception of appropriate pedagogy, which holds that "man is not a block of wood from which you can carve a statue . . . he is a living image, shaping, misshaping and reshaping itself."[35]

It would be out of keeping with Comenius's theory and practice of education not to note that a third agency is at work as well. In addition to teacher and learner, he asserts the relevance of God's co-agency in the educational process: language learning requires concerted effort, but "God will also help if implored."[36]

Games and Gardens

With his educational reform, Comenius wanted studying to become an enjoyable experience for pupils. However, one innovation that caused friction between Comenius and some of his fellow educators was his insistence on the positive value of pleasure and play. It was not incidental, but essential to his educational scheme, that learning should proceed pleasantly, and that play and enjoyment should be an important part of it. In the language lesson, "the intelligence as well as the language of boys should preferably be exercised on matters which appeal to them."[37] In keeping with this recommendation, Comenius provided language teaching materi-

---

35. *Analytical Didactic* 24. Cf. Banovitch, 1971, 117, 119; *GD* XXII:7 and XIX:44: "he who cannot express the thoughts of his mind resembles a statue, and he who chatters without understanding what he says, resembles a parrot." Comenius's pedagogy is to be distinguished both from rule-centered rationalist approaches and from approaches focused on mimicry and memorization to the exclusion of description and analysis. Banovitch (1971, 115-16) notes that he was critical both of predecessors who overemphasized the role of grammar and of those who neglected it.

36. *Methodus,* cited in Caravolas, 1993, 151.

37. *GD* XXII:7.

als in the form of dialogues and plays to be acted out; he also encouraged competitive activities. The notion of play does not for him connote randomness or aimlessness, but embraces both spontaneity and order, and so forms a purposeful part of the educative process.

This way of thinking is in harmony with his characterization of piety as having ultimately to do with enjoyment of God and with God's delight and enjoyment (recall that Comenius saw piety as embracing knowledge and virtue and thus the whole process of education). The description of both the ideal person and the ideal school as "gardens of delight" for God makes the connection between learning, play, and piety explicit. The prayer that prefaces the *Pampaedia* further connects in moving fashion divine and human play and pleasure:

> Do thou, everlasting wisdom, who dost play in this world and whose delight is in the sons of men, ensure that we in turn may now find delight in thee. Discover more fully unto us ways and means to better understanding of thy play with us and to more eager pursuance of it with one another, until we ourselves finally play in thy company more effectively to give increasing pleasure unto thee, who art our everlasting delight! Amen.[38]

The play of God and of humanity in the world, the person's delight in God, God's delight in his image bearers, the learner's delight in learning — these currents of joy flow into one another in Comenius's vision of the world made new. The "gate of tongues unlocked" was to open into a "garden of delight," pleasing to learners and Lord alike.[39]

38. *Pampaedia*, introduction, 6. Cf. Geissler, 1959, 103-11.

39. Compare the following words from the *Labyrinth of the World and the Paradise of the Heart* (cited in Murphy, 1995, 146): "The godly have not only simple peace within them, but also joy and pleasure which flow to their hearts from the presence and feeling of God's love . . . for how can anything be otherwise than sweet and joyful to a man who possesses this divine light within him through the spirit of God." Given that the aim of Comenian education is godliness, the idea that pedagogy should aim at sweetness and joy in learning is an appropriate corollary.

Lessons for the Present Day

We observed at the beginning of chapter 1 that the idea that the Bible has anything to do with foreign language learning can seem odd at first sight. We also pointed out early in chapter 2 the paucity of discussion within or outside the church concerning the ways Christian faith and foreign language learning have intersected. Even Comenius, a towering figure in the history of foreign language education, who emphasized constantly the inseparability of faith and learning, has often been interpreted in recent times as if his genuinely educational ideas had to be detached from his theological concerns. Such an approach fails to get at the reason for the "profound unity and . . . extraordinary coherence" that characterize his approach to language teaching.[40] Our present-day tendency to separate the elements in his thought that, in his own view, belonged so closely together has inhibited the investigation of questions we are seeking to reopen in this book.

What, then, have we done so far? We have suggested that there are biblical themes that can meaningfully inform Christian reflection on foreign language education. We have gone on to review the lives of several men living in various periods of history whose works, in various ways and with varying emphases, echo those biblical themes. We have explored the thought of Comenius, which provides perhaps the best example to date of a profound interweaving of Christian conviction and pedagogical innovation, and which has contributed significantly to the subsequent shape of foreign language education in the Western world. By now, we trust, it has become clear that to ask about the relationship of Christian faith to foreign language education is not to pose an empty or meaningless question.

What should also be clear by now is that biblically grounded convictions do not leap straight from the pages of the sacred text into the classroom in a way that stands outside of history. What we have sampled in the last two chapters is an ongoing endeavor in different times and places to understand foreign language education in the light of Scripture. The individuals surveyed have drawn upon their Christian faith in varying ways. In the remainder of this book we do not aim to simply copy these past approaches, which inevitably bear the marks of their historical settings. We do, however, wish to carry forward in our present-day context, with our

40. Caravolas, 1993, 155.

own particular emphases, the broad project of understanding how faith relates to language learning. We turn, then, from the pages of history to our contemporary calling as foreign language educators.

PART II

AIMS:
EMBRACING THE STRANGER

CHAPTER FOUR

Strangers and Blessings

> If I speak a foreign tongue
> With near-native pronunciation
> With impeccable grammar
> And a rich idiomatic vocabulary,
> But have not love. . . .
> If I have sophisticated discourse strategies
> And intercultural competency,
> But have not love . . .
>
> After 1 Corinthians 13

In the summer of 1994, I (Barbara Carvill) taught a course in foreign language methodology to Chinese teachers of English in Chengdu, the capital of the province of Sichuan. One weekend Chinese officials arranged a bus tour to the countryside to visit the gigantic Buddha of Leshan. There were about thirty-five Christian teachers from North America on the bus.

The day was going by pleasantly enough until, as we were riding back along a very narrow road through a village, an approaching tractor loaded high with bales of straw and driven by a young Chinese man squeezed too close to the bus. The bales struck the bus and smashed all the windows on the driver's side, covering the passengers with shards of very sharp glass. Although many of us had multiple cuts, nobody was seriously hurt. Those who were not harmed helped the injured passengers out of the bus and bandaged their wounds.

While first aid was being attended to, our Chinese guide led the young tractor driver along the line of Americans and made him look at every injury he had caused. With tears in his eyes he mumbled something as he went along, probably an apology. Then we waited for the police to come.

In the meantime, however, more and more townsfolk gathered and huddled around the culprit. They were debating some issue, but we didn't know what the point of contention was. After a while, our tour guide came over to tell me that the driver of the tractor did not feel forgiven. I assured her that we were fine and that she should tell him not to worry. But, our guide insisted, what he wanted to hear was a word of forgiveness directly from the mouth of an American, and not through the interpreter.

After making sure all injured members of our team were actually ready to forgive the fellow, I, the team leader and the only person in the group who could speak a few words in Chinese, looked in vain for an appropriate expression in my Chinese textbook. I found phrases for all kinds of occasions, but *forgiving someone* was not listed. Therefore I had to ask our Chinese interpreter for the appropriate expression, which I quickly learned by heart. Then I went to the huddle of people gathered around the culprit and, looking the young man in the eye, repeatedly spoke my memorized phrase with great intensity and conviction. Enormous relief came over the frightened face of the driver, and the folk standing around shook my hands with gratitude.

We learned three things from this incident. First, Chinese buses do not have safety glass! Second, we Americans act very differently in such situations. When we are involved in traffic accidents, we exchange insurance details and avoid talking to the other party for fear of jeopardizing our insurance claims. These Chinese villagers, on the other hand, did not reduce the relationship between victim and perpetrator to a merely legal one. Instead they acted in a way that resonates with Christian convictions concerning reconciliation and forgiveness. This cross-cultural encounter made us aware of some highly questionable features of our own North American practices. And third, the textbook had not prepared us well. It obviously did not count *forgiving someone for wrongs done* among the essential language functions a foreigner might need.

These insights, which grew out of a dramatic cross-cultural encounter, lead into the topic of the present chapter. They point to a need for teachers to ask themselves the following questions: By what criteria do we select what is worth teaching and learning? Is, for example, expressing forgiveness in the target language as important as voicing a complaint? What values lead us to teach the one but not the other? Further, what does such a choice imply about the kinds of persons we want our students to be when they are abroad? And, on a more general level, how should teachers working in Christian educational contexts respond when students ask how the language they learn in class equips them to act as Christians in a foreign country?

This chapter sketches an exploratory answer to such questions. It first proposes a general formulation of the aims and purposes of foreign language education in the light of the biblical themes explored in chapter 1. Then it examines in greater detail the nature of one of those aims.

Guests and Hosts

According to the biblical account we presented in chapter 1, cultural diversity is blessed by God and marred by evil. The proper response to this state of affairs is neither a naive, romantic celebration of cultural diversity nor a fatalistic acceptance of racism, tribalism, and nationalism that excludes, dominates, or kills others and thus sabotages God's vision of nations working shoulder to shoulder with each other. Thus Christians believe that nationalistic wars, "final solutions," and "ethnic cleansing" do not represent the last word about global multicultural and multiethnic reality. Jesus Christ, they insist, came to *redeem* all nations, not to abolish their diversity. Accordingly, God promises a day when peoples from all tribes and nations and languages will come together to worship and enjoy a life of shalom, of peace and justice.

Christians are not, however, to wait idly for this final day, but are to be coworkers for the coming kingdom, which is comprehensive and complex and involves all aspects of the creation. Foreign language education, too, is called to play a role in this cosmic story. But it will only do so if it is grounded in and grows out of a biblical vision for reconciliation, for justice and peace among nations. It must be shaped by respect for the other as an image bearer of God; it must be eager to hear the other; and it must be driven by love for God and for one's neighbor. In the light of these biblical themes, we propose *that foreign language education prepare students for two related callings: to be a blessing as strangers in a foreign land, and to be hospitable to strangers in their own homeland.*[1]

Students who become strangers[2] in a foreign land are called to be a blessing to the locals by speaking in the locals' tongue, by listening to their stories and sharing their own, by asking good questions, by comparing and contrasting, by learning from them — in short, by using the special freedom and responsibility an educated stranger has in the host country for being a loving presence. Similarly, students also are called to become good hosts to the foreigner or alien in their own land, to receive the stranger graciously, and to practice a kind of hospitality that is a blessing to both the guest and the host. Both callings, we propose, make up the very heart of foreign language education.[3]

The remainder of this chapter seeks to explore some crucial dimensions of the first calling: *to be a blessing as a stranger*. Chapter 5 will focus on the second calling: *to be hospitable to strangers*.

What Is a Stranger?

In a famous article on the subject, Georg Simmel points to the paradoxical nature of the stranger, who is marked at the same time by both distance and closeness. People far away are not strangers; they are simply unknown to us. They become strangers to us only when they enter our world and our group. "[B]eing outside it and confronting it," according to Simmel, "[the stranger's] position in this group is determined essentially by the fact that he has not belonged to it from the beginning, that he imparts qualities to it which do not and cannot stem from the group itself."[4] The stranger's spe-

---

1. See also Carvill, 1991a; Carvill, 1991b.

2. For the purposes of our discussion, we will use "stranger" in a broad sense that includes the concepts of sojourner, visitor, tourist, and traveler. When we speak of "strangers" or "foreigners," we imply that these persons are temporarily in a cultural context where their mother tongue is not spoken and where they interact with native speakers of the host country with varying levels of linguistic proficiency.

3. The German distinction between *Bildungsziele* (goals of general, broad formation that include the ethical and spiritual dimensions of education) and *Lernziele* (specific instructional objectives) is helpful in our context. In this chapter we are exploring the *Bildungsziele* of foreign language education.

4. Simmel, 1950, 402.

cial position in the host culture, being simultaneously outside and near, will be an important aspect of our discussion. As we shall see, it gives the stranger both a particular freedom and a special responsibility toward the people of the host country.

Members of the host culture may receive strangers with either hostility or friendliness. That is to say, they may either feel threatened by strangers and therefore may distance themselves from them, denying them social space, or they may welcome them with open arms, embracing and engaging them. If educators are to prepare students to be strangers in a foreign land, they must teach them about both the tribulations and joys of that role.

The Tribulation of a Stranger

Instead of painting travel abroad only as a blissful experience of cultural enrichment, teachers should also prepare their students for the difficulties involved in being a stranger in a foreign land. For instance, teachers could say to their students:

> As a foreigner, you and your history will be unfamiliar to the people of the target country, who most often will be only mildly interested in your origins. Your identity will be reduced only to what you are at the moment you face them. You will not feel known by them. You won't count. You'll be lost in the midst of people who are and feel at home, who are bound to one another in an intricate network of relationships, who have a different language from your own, a different history, and different aspirations. Their values, tastes, and assumptions will be foreign to you. You won't fit. As a stranger, you'll never know beforehand whether you'll be welcomed or met with studied indifference, aloof tolerance, or even cold hostility. Sometimes the very fact that you are, say, an American or an Arab may cause ill will toward you, and all kinds of positive or negative stereotypes may be projected onto you. Often the bewildered, shocked look of the locals will tell you that you've committed some unforgivable social blunder. You'll feel lost and powerless. People won't laugh at your jokes and you won't "get" theirs. You won't be able to blend in. Furthermore, when shopping you won't know the actual value of the merchandise you're buying, and thus, you'll never be sure if you're being exploited or treated fairly. And as a woman, you can't afford to

trust the eager helpfulness of young men. Worst of all, everybody will speak so rapidly at you and past you that you just won't understand.

In her landmark study of the lot of the stranger, Julia Kristeva[5] describes the foreigner's loneliness and suffering, which he or she often masks with an armor of cheerfulness in order to cover up a deep inner wound of humiliation. However, foreigners are not, Kristeva asserts, only victims. They themselves often display an angry arrogance that despises the puny narrow-mindedness of the locals.

Even if strangers learn the language of the host country, according to Kristeva, true communication is fraught with difficulties. Without social power and roots, the strangers' speech lacks authority, and no one listens to them. Cut off from their mother tongue and not mastering the new language, foreigners may become altogether mute. And when they do speak, "lacking the reins of the maternal tongue"[6] and unaware of the impact of their words, they are capable of saying the most outrageous things, including accidental obscenities. Kristeva's view, in summary, is that genuine communication between the stranger who has left home and the native who has remained at home seems almost impossible.

Given these hardships, students may well ask their teacher why anyone even wants to go abroad and become a stranger. There is both a spiritual and educational response to this question, and students deserve to hear both.

First and foremost, being a stranger does not mean to be altogether forsaken and alienated, but instead to be specially bonded to God. God did not desert his people in Egypt or during their Babylonian captivity. Reinhard Feldmeier makes the point that, in contrast to classical pagan views, the biblical view of being a stranger always implies an existential, covenantal relationship to God.[7] This primary relationship frees us from *ultimate* dependency on our location and culture. Moreover, since the founding and spreading of the church, Christian strangers belong to a worldwide community of believers, the global community of the saints. Thus they, our students included, will never be strangers in the deepest sense of the term. It is important that they experience the rigors and suf-

5. Kristeva, 1991.
6. Kristeva, 1991, 31.
7. Feldmeier, 1992, 53.

fering of being, so to speak, "in Egypt." However, doing so also carries with it an unexpected spiritual blessing: it provides them with the opportunity to learn in a unique way that they are in God's special care.

Revelatory Culture Clashes

The second reason why it is good and necessary to acquaint students with the difficult aspects of being in a foreign country is educational. Often the stranger unintentionally violates cultural norms and causes misunderstandings. Students abroad, too, may find themselves in embarrassing, sometimes painful situations resulting from their ignorance of key attitudes or customs prevailing in the foreign country. Such potential problems should not deter them from going abroad, however. Instead, teachers can prepare learners to profit from such incidents by showing how cultural clashes can illuminate the different assumptions, values, and unconscious behaviors prevalent in the host country, and thus can provide rich insights into both their own culture and that of their hosts.[8]

An episode involving Germans in the United States illustrates this point. Surely every language teacher has stories like this to tell.

In the summer of 1996 a German woman and her nineteen-year-old son visited an American family in a well-to-do suburb in southern California. On the morning of the first day of their visit the German guests were home alone, since their American hosts were at work. After breakfast the young man, a contemplative sort who loves to take walks, decided to scout out the neighborhood. After a long stroll he returned home. Not long afterward, two policemen appeared at the front door to protect the woman

8. Classroom activities for reflecting on cultural misunderstandings were developed already in the seventies. *Cultural minidramas* (Seelye, 1993) simulate misunderstanding, and *cultural assimilators* present conflict situations with multiple-choice questions about the possible reasons for miscommunication (Omaggio Hadley, 1993, 396). They are examples of what Geertz (1973) calls a "thin description of culture"; i.e., they work with very generalized stereotypes and universal pronouncements about the national character. "The whole process [of interpretating one cultural assimilator] takes about three minutes"! (Seelye, 1993, 163). More activities of this sort can be found in Brislin, 1986; Caroll, 1990; Storti, 1994; Seelye and Seeley-James, 1995; for a Christian perspective see Henning, 1993. Kramsch (1993) advocates a "thick description" (Geertz, 1973) in which the personal perspective and worldview of the students play a constitutive role in the interpretation of miscommunication.

inside (his mother!) from the potentially dangerous young man who had just entered through the back door.

When the son stepped from the kitchen into the hallway to see what was going on, the two policemen drew their guns and ordered him to surrender. By the time the police had checked passports and the misunderstanding had been cleared up, the frightened son had learned that in the United States of America young men may jog freely, but may not take leisurely walks alone through a wealthy neighborhood, especially not on a workday morning. If they do, they will appear very suspicious, and watchful neighbors will alert the police.

Experiences like this may be unpleasant and unsettling, but they are salutary wake-up calls to the reality of otherness: taking a walk, assumed in Germany to be innocent behavior, can be seen as suspicious in the United States.

Students who go abroad should expect such incidents. Upsetting though they are, they can also be blessings, for they force strangers and locals alike to reflect on the cultural context and the many historical and social reasons that cause such incidents. In doing so, they promote comparing and contrasting the two cultures.

The Pedagogical Challenge

But how can teachers help students experience the hardships of being a stranger when they are learning a foreign language in their home territory, in the safety of a classroom, with the target culture far away, and with very little or no possibility of interacting personally with the native speakers of the target country?

Some experiences of what a stranger goes through can actually be lived out in the foreign language classroom. Rather than making language practice as safe and pleasurable as possible, it is good from time to time not to shield students from situations in which communication breaks down and learners become voiceless and frustrated over not being able to express in the foreign language what they want to say. At such a moment, the teacher must step back and reflect with the class on what just happened, why it happened, and how the students felt.[9] Students have to expe-

9. Kramsch also advocates this kind of "meta-talk" (1993, 246).

rience and accept that such breakdowns in communication are common for strangers in a foreign land. They have to develop strategies for handling such crises in the target language and a willingness to continue communicating beyond the breakdown.

It is well known that many wretched experiences foreigners have are not solely the result of their deficient verbal skills (both Germans in the incident described above were speaking English very well), but also stem from different cultural values and practices. Therefore, preparing students for the role of stranger necessarily requires a kind of language training that both centers on the cultural mores of the target country and makes students increasingly conscious of their own cultural values and practices.

For instance, students should be asked to spell out their own stereotypes of the target country and its inhabitants; they should also be led to understand the stereotypes people of the target country most likely will have of them. In addition, they should learn about the stereotypical expectations locals have of strangers, and what happens when strangers fulfill or ignore such expectations. For example, Chinese expect American hotel guests to tip, although tipping is not customary in the People's Republic of China. If the American visitor knows about this cultural difference and does in China as the Chinese do, he or she disappoints the hotel personnel acquainted with American customs. The issue then becomes, should an American tip the Chinese busboy or not?

Students will not be good strangers in the host country if they are not familiar with matters of etiquette on a verbal and nonverbal level. Reading the epigraph of the present chapter against the grain, we need to stress that to be filled with love and goodwill toward the people of the target country is essential but not sufficient. The stranger also needs to know the lingual, social, and cultural codes of the host country, if love and goodwill are to be received as intended and not as an involuntary offense.

The educational challenge, however, goes beyond providing students with real, virtual, or vicarious experiences of a foreigner's hardships. This is only the first step. The second step is more significant. The kinds of strangers our students are called to become are able *to understand and articulate* in the target language the reasons for intercultural misunderstandings and breakdowns.

To this end, teachers will model and practice with students how to analyze and interpret such experiences. They will ask learners to compare and contrast social norms and practices in the host culture with those in their own.[10] If, for instance, the encounter between the young German and the California police were analyzed in class, factors like the high crime rate among young males in the United States, the American institution of *neighborhood watch,* and different German and American assumptions and traditions having to do with taking a walk *(spazierengehen)* would surface in the discussion.

Students also need to practice how to discern and evaluate the spirit at work in any given cultural practice in order to answer this evaluative question: Does this spirit destroy the fabric of human life and creation, or does it heal, and affirm the goodness of life? Students who in their foreign language training develop thoughtful intercultural and spiritual discernment and can articulate it in the target language are in a position to bring a gift of real value to their hosts.

*   *   *

Thus far we have attempted to develop several pedagogical reasons for acquainting students intimately with the possible tribulations of being a stranger in a foreign culture. But what about the joys they can experience?

In exploring the positive aspects of being a stranger, we will first talk about the joys of learning a new language and then explore three gifts a carefully prepared, thoughtful foreigner can bring to the host culture: seeing what locals themselves do not see, hearing what they do not hear, and asking good, probing questions. Naturally, students first need to learn their hosts' language if they want to offer these gifts.

10. Excellent examples for this kind of intercultural analysis can be found in Kramsch's study (1993). So far the most extensive and thorough presentation of how to teach and assess intercultural competence has been written by Byram (1997), who adds intercultural competence to the five competencies that make up communicative competence: linguistic competence, discourse competence, actional competence, sociocultural competence, and strategic competence (Macintyre et al., 1998). For Byram, intercultural competence comprises factual *knowledge* about the culture, an *attitude* of "curiosity and openness," and two major *skills:* the "skills of interpretation and establishing relationships between aspects of the two cultures and . . . skills of discovery and interaction" (1997, 33). See also Krumm, 1995.

The Joy of Learning a New Language

The process of learning and practicing a new language can be very gratifying in itself. One can derive great pleasure in making strange sounds, in savoring the texture of new words and phrases, in learning quaint idiomatic expressions, and in ordering and viewing reality in new ways. In short, one can experience gratifying joy in acquiring a new language and in seeing a new world unfold through its use. Learners have the chance to become children again, with their typical fascination with and delight in new words. They may be impressed by the previously unknown complexities and intricacies of both their own language and the language they are learning.

Unfortunately, it also happens over and over again that bright-eyed, eager pupils, who at the outset were so enthusiastic about learning a new tongue, soon lose interest and become bored and resistant. Apparently our foreign language classrooms sometimes lack some of the qualities of the "garden of delight" Comenius envisioned. How can we work against the onset of such boredom?

Perhaps we could begin by modeling and emphasizing basic convictions about the nature and purpose of what we are doing when we study foreign languages.

Learning a new language is a joyful gift one gives to oneself and to the other. By studying the language of the host country, one says to its people: "I want to meet you, to connect and communicate with you; I want to hear your voice; I want to know what it is like to be you in your culture. I've already started to walk toward you; I've gone through some of the rigorous and demanding discipline necessary to acquire your language; and I've begun to learn about your ways. Even though my steps in your direction are clumsy and faltering, I'm on the way, eager to engage you. I'd like to participate in and learn from the many different conversations carried on in your culture." Calvin Seerveld is right when he asserts that "to learn a different language is an act of love."[11]

A recent movie by a Cameroonian filmmaker[12] portrays the eminent Dr. Albert Schweitzer as a stranger who did not love enough. Though the Schweitzer depicted in the film had lived and worked as a medical doctor

11. Seerveld, 1997.
12. *Le Grand Blanc de Lambaréné,* by Bassek ba Kobhio, 1995.

in Lambaréné for more than three decades, he had been too tightly imprisoned in his colonial arrogance to receive and learn anything from the Africans. "You can only give, but not share," an African woman says to him near the end of the film. "You know German, French, English, Greek, Latin, and Hebrew, but in all the years you've been with us you've made no effort to acquire our language." By failing to learn his hosts' language, Schweitzer had withheld from them a precious gift: the joyous gift of love.

Brokenness and Communication

Acquiring a new language means learning new verbal symbols that refer to a cultural reality mostly unknown. It is only natural that language learners bring their own values, expectations, and assumptions into an unfamiliar context, and work out of their own setting as they try to explain themselves to speakers who do not know their cultural background. Since these learners are struggling with a verbal and cultural code whose rules they have not mastered and whose implications escape them, the result of their attempts to communicate will often be misunderstanding. They and their native dialogue partners construct meaning differently.

Does this mean that real understanding between strangers and native speakers cannot occur? Is Kristeva right in suggesting that language cannot bridge the gap between strangers and the indigenous inhabitants of the host country?

We believe that Christians need not be as pessimistic as many postmoderns are about the likelihood of genuine communication. It is obvious that our finitude makes the modern ideal of perfect transfer of meaning unrealistic and that our brokenness continually gets in the way. Yet we do share with the other the common gift of humanity, and, working together, we can learn, correct, refine, and redefine our messages until we understand and feel understood. The Chinese tractor driver mentioned above did, after all, finally get the words of forgiveness he needed, and the California police did ultimately apologize for their behavior after the misunderstanding was cleared up — and then engaged in a cordial exchange with the German visitors about crime rates in the United States and Germany, gun control, and the drug culture. Such a collaborative construction of meaning, however imperfect, should be received with gratitude.

The Gift of Seeing

The kind of strangers we want students to become will be wide-eyed and present in the foreign place. Their senses will be keenly open, and they will notice all sorts of details in this new culture. They will delight in the unfamiliar and the strange around them. They will be curious, inquisitive, and alert, and will experience the unfamiliar world with fresh, childlike eyes, a world that has gone little noticed to the locals themselves because it has become so utterly familiar. They will discover and revel in differences between the new culture and their own, be they in food, in use of public space, in nonverbal communication habits, in bathing customs, in cutlery, or even in doorknobs.

The distinction Erich Fromm makes between *looking* and *seeing* is helpful in this regard. As tourists, many people tend too easily to look but not to see. For the present, they merely take pictures of interesting sights, hoping to do the seeing later. As Fromm writes, "Taking pictures becomes a substitute for seeing. Of course you have to look in order to direct your lens to the desired object. . . . But *looking* is not *seeing.* Seeing is a human function, one of the greatest gifts with which man is endowed; it requires activity, inner openness, interest, patience, concentration."[13] When attending to the visual dimensions of the foreign culture, the language educator should train students in the kind of active, open, patient, and concentrated seeing Fromm talks about. Practicing attentive, respectful seeing will not only deepen the visual abilities of students, but will also stimulate their interest in verbalizing their discoveries in the target language. One helpful activity for practicing comparative seeing is to have students analyze sections from films or TV shows from the target country without sound. Such an activity also provides a motivating and meaningful context for acquiring vocabulary, since the students will want to name, compare, and contrast what they have seen.

This kind of seeing rewards not only the students but also the inhabitants of the host country. What a gift students can give to them when they are able to describe their observations and discoveries in the target language! Students' attentive curiosity and loving visual intensity may even inspire the natives to see their own surroundings with *new* eyes, and to be filled with a sense of gratitude and joy for what they have at home —

13. Fromm, 1974, 343.

things great and small to which they have grown indifferent. To inspire such seeing and such gratitude would be a blessing indeed.

Of course, the culture of the host country may also have sad, distressing, lamentable aspects to which many of its citizens have grown callous. But there, too, the stranger can be an agent of blessing by pointing humbly to blind spots and inconsistencies, thereby helping the locals see themselves more honestly. One example will suffice as illustration.

When Germans visit the United States, they are often shocked by what they see as an ostentatious display of the American flag on houses and garage doors, in schools and in churches. They interpret this phenomenon as dangerous chauvinistic patriotism, because they bring their own experience with the German national flag to bear on what they see in the United States. They look at the "Star-Spangled Banner" with the eyes of a people once part of a destructive political system that misused national symbols. The uncomplicated, naive, proud patriotism many Americans express when they raise the flag in their private or public spaces is very foreign to the German who remembers the catastrophe of the Third Reich.

Thus, when Germans criticize the use of the American flag, they perceive it in terms of their own historical experience. A dialogue between Americans and Germans about the meaning and significance of their respective national flags might lead to helpful clarification. Germans may learn that, for Americans, the flag on their garage door might not necessarily signify that the United States is number one in the world, but rather may represent the flag raiser's thankful acknowledgment that there exists, despite all the fiercely defended individualism one finds in the United States, one national symbol that transcends all ethnic, social, and racial differences. Such dialogue could encourage Americans and Germans alike to look afresh at the meaning of national symbols and their understanding of national identity. In this case, it might help the Germans realize that not all patriotism is aggressive; it might also open American eyes to the fact that idolatry of the flag can be destructive. Such a dialogue would surely be an intercultural blessing. In highlighting and questioning the familiar, the stranger brings a gift — the gift of another vision, another perspective, which comes from the outside. As Mikhail Bakhtin writes,

> In the realm of culture, outsidedness is a most powerful factor in understanding. It is only in the eyes of *another* culture that foreign culture reveals itself fully and profoundly (but not maximally fully, because there

will be cultures that see and understand even more). A meaning only reveals its depths once it has encountered and come into contact with another, foreign meaning: they engage in a kind of dialogue, which surmounts the closedness and one-sidedness of these particular meanings, these cultures.[14]

The Gift of Questions

Obviously, the ability to enjoy what is different, to be intrigued by what is strange, and to cultivate a playful and aesthetic openness to what is foreign is a prerequisite strangers must bring to the foreign country if they are to be thoughtful people whose seeing has depth. As foreigners, our sensory awareness and attentiveness are intensified. So is our need to understand linguistic or cultural phenomena that do not make sense to us because of our different outlook on life, different values, and different norms and ways of doing and interpreting things. As foreigners, we live in a permanent state of hermeneutical alert.

For instance, an American student of Spanish who had learned that *bomba* means "bomb" was astonished to hear his Costa Rican host tell him while pointing at his old car, "Voy a llevar el auto a la bomba."[15] The student wondered quietly about the violent method of automobile recycling in Costa Rica. When half an hour later the owner of the car came back with the same car, the student asked him why he had changed his mind. To his surprise he found out that the Costa Rican had gone to the gas station for gasoline and had no intention of having his car blown up. In Costa Rica, a gas station is called "pump," a meaning of *bomba* that was unfamiliar to the student.

Such a "hermeneutical crisis" can be pleasurable, because it gives the foreigner the right to ask questions. To be sure, strangers have little social power, but they do have the privilege of asking the people of the host country to interpret and clarify. A new culture does not fully reveal itself without questions. Without questions one does not hear the voice of the other. Questions are verbal tools for use on the stranger's quest into the foreign culture. They are a sign that he or she takes initiative and responsibility for meeting

14. Bakhtin, 1986, 7.
15. "I'll bring the car to the bomb."

and understanding the locals and their ways. Therefore, one important curricular goal in language instruction is to teach not only the linguistic but also the cultural competency to ask good questions that get at the underlying meanings, values, and commitments of the target culture.[16]

Questions addressed to the people of the host country will, of course, reveal the stranger's assumptions and perceptiveness — and sometimes his or her ignorance. Kenneth Chastain relates the following incident:

> During a trip to Hungary I encountered a hostile reaction to a question some American travelers had asked. "Do you know Jesus?" may be a commonly-understood question among Christians in the United States, but it was obviously misunderstood by the Hungarians, who were living at that time under a Communist regime. "What do they think?" they asked heatedly, "Do they think we are heathens who have never heard of Jesus?"[17]

Sometimes the stranger's questions can reveal an abysmal ignorance of basic historical data. In 1992 an American college student in Spain for the first time asked a forty-year-old gentleman on whose side he had fought in the Spanish Civil War! At other times such questions can reveal a condescending, ill-informed conception of how people in progressive Western societies live, as when American high schoolers ask German exchange students whether Germans have refrigerators. Obviously, questions come with some risk. At worst, they may reveal downright appalling ignorance or offensive stereotypes, and thus may become insults that break off communication.

Good questions, on the other hand, can unlock doors. They can show that a foreigner has thought himself or herself into the new context, that he or she respects the native host as a human being created in God's image. Good questions try to get at the historical context and the multiple causes of present phenomena. But questions cut both ways. Foreigners will not only be asking; they may also have to answer for their native country and, maybe for the first time, will be expected to speak with authority about their own culture. Under that pressure they will become aware of how little they actually know about their native land and how precarious it is to make general pronouncements about it.

16. See also Carvill and Westra, 1999.
17. Chastain, 1991, 3.

If their own questions are to be helpful, students also need to learn which historical events have marked the host country's recent history, so that they can ask appropriate questions of the appropriate age group. Good questions can become a blessing. They can create an occasion for the native to talk about subjects in which his or her compatriots are no longer interested (for example, war stories), but which need to be told. Good questions may move the locals to explain themselves in new and healing ways. As a result, the foreigner will have the privilege — or the burden — of sharing in the tale. Foreign language programs must prepare students for such occasions and must teach them how to show and express empathy, what to say and what not to say when native speakers share their grief.

Good questions may not allow for easy answers; in fact, some questions may have no answer at all. But they may initiate important and productive cross-cultural dialogue. In Bakhtin's words, "We raise new questions for a foreign culture, ones that it did not raise itself; we seek answers to our own questions in it; and the foreign culture responds to us by revealing to us its new aspects and new semantic depths."[18]

Clearly, questions of this caliber are gifts and blessings the stranger brings to the foreign country. For this reason, the importance of practicing questions in the classroom cannot be emphasized enough. Students must develop much more than the linguistic and sociolinguistic ability to form contextually appropriate interrogative sentences. They must develop *an ethos of questioning* that shows that they belong to the kind of "hearing" people we talked about in the first chapter.

The Gift of Listening and Hearing

The stranger who reaches out with questions must listen attentively for answers. The typical role of the thoughtful stranger in a foreign country is that of listener. Listening is a complex and intricate skill that cannot be analyzed in detail here. Simply put, the message one hears is the result of a creative, interactive process between what the listener takes in and the linguistic knowledge and cultural assumptions he or she brings to the aural text.[19]

18. Bakhtin, 1986, 7.
19. For more details see Omaggio Hadley, 1993.

But the core of the gift of listening and hearing involves more than developing good linguistic and cultural listening skills; the stranger must also "have ears to hear."

Perhaps the Chinese character for "to listen" can clarify the concept. The character *tīng* consists of five elements that separately stand for *ear, eye, you, undivided attention,* and *heart.* Thus this character gives an image of attentive listening, with one's ears and eyes focused on the other, while hearing with the heart. Strangers who listen in this manner, motivated by respect and love, will be enriched by what they hear, and misconceptions they may have brought to the conversation will be corrected.

Understanding the other too quickly, however, might actually do the other an injustice. As Z. D. Gurevitch points out, we all tend to "understand" before we even listen.[20] In cross-cultural dialogue we tend to assume that the other is not significantly different from us, and that the differences we do notice can be explained in terms of our frame of reference.[21] But instead of integrating the other into our own conceptual framework, it is crucial, Gurevitch suggests, to be able to *not* understand:

> The ability to not understand is the ability to recognize and behold the other (or the self) as an other. In a moment of not understanding, what had been considered "understood" is relinquished as mere image. . . . When the other is perceived as strange, he or she is liberated from the image that one has projected onto the other's experience from the center of one's self. The other then emerges as an independent and "distant" phenomenon.[22]

To cultivate the ability to not understand actually is to respect the otherness of the other and may lead to a point in a communication at which we shift "from the centered self to the perspective of the other."[23] We do not reach the goal of cross-cultural understanding when we understand and explain the other merely as a cultural product, but only when the process

20. Gurevitch, 1989.
21. Nicolas Shumway discusses, for example, how difficult and maybe even impossible it is for both teacher and students to understand the cultural values of the Spanish *conquistadores* from the vantage point of the secular, unheroic postmodernism of the 1990s (Shumway, 1995).
22. Gurevitch, 1989, 163.
23. Gurevitch, 1989, 194.

of communication leads us to experience the other as a subject, a center of consciousness different from our own. In other words, we achieve that goal only when we encounter and cherish the person from a different culture as a responsible, responsive person made in God's image.[24]

At this point, one implication of the aim of foreign language instruction we are proposing emerges clearly: if we strive to prepare students for the role of strangers, who can bring a blessing to the people of a host country, we do not want to train them to get as close as possible to the unattainable model of the *native speaker*.[25] Doing so would actually defeat the purposes of cross-cultural communication, which include bringing another vision to the host culture, learning from each other, and enriching and correcting each other. In order to bring a blessing, the stranger may not "turn native" and discard his or her cultural identity,[26] for then he or she would lose the potential for performing a "fermenting function."[27] As Bakhtin stresses, when developing an understanding of a foreign culture, one must *not* forget one's own homeland and merge completely into the new culture:

> Of course, a certain entry as living being into a foreign culture, the possibility of seeing the world through its eyes, is a necessary part of the process of understanding it; but if this were the only aspect of this understanding, it would merely be duplication and would not entail anything new or enriching. *Creative understanding* does not renounce itself, its own place in time, its own culture; and it forgets nothing. In order to understand, it is immensely important for the person who understands to be *located outside* the object of his or her creative understanding — in time, in space, in culture. For one cannot even really see one's own exterior and comprehend it as a whole, and no mirrors or photographs can help; our real exterior can be seen and understood only by other people, because they are located outside us in space and because they are *others*.[28]

24. Cf. Joldersma, 1999.

25. For a thorough and convincing critique of the questionable ideal of becoming the *native speaker* in foreign language instruction, see Meyer, 1995; Byram, 1997; and Kramsch, 1998b.

26. In light of this goal, the popular practice of giving learners foreign names needs to be reconsidered.

27. Alois Wierlacher speaks about the "fermentive Funktion" a stranger may have in a culture (Wierlacher, 1990).

28. Bakhtin, 1986, 7.

The Blessed Stranger

So far we have proposed that foreign language education is obligated to train language learners to become thoughtful strangers, that is to say, kind, educated, and informed persons with a sense of cultural identity who, by their open, curious, and humble way of seeing, questioning, and listening, bring a blessing to the host country.[29]

But that is not the whole story. As a stranger, one not only gives but also receives. The foreign culture, with its practices and institutions, its arts, literature, and folk traditions, its traumas and triumphs, also enriches and expands the stranger's outlook and view of the world. Experiencing how another people lives out its human calling before God, whether faithfully or unfaithfully, stimulates foreigners to reflect on their own practices and, as a result, may change the way they view their own culture.

Though we will explore this theme in more detail in the next chapter, we conclude this chapter with one example of such a change. The following is excerpted from the diary of an American college student of Spanish who spent three weeks of voluntary service in the Dominican Republic where she, together with other students, assisted native teachers in Christian schools established for the children of Haitian sugarcane cutters.

Friday, January 10. I have never traveled outside of the United States before, so I wonder what it will be like to be in a foreign country. Our professor warned us at the pre-departure meeting that instead of transplanting our American culture and ideals to people in the Dominican Republic, we should try to become "a little bit Dominican." I dismissed her words in favor of an energetic discussion with my classmates about beaches on the tropical island.

Still Friday. After eight hours, two layovers, and countless complimentary bags of peanuts, I have arrived in the Dominican Republic. What a rude awakening! At the airport, pushy men

---

29. In view of this educational aim, class trips to the target country that imitate tourist excursions might need to be reconsidered and reorganized to include components of voluntary service, whereby students can offer their talents, goodwill, and helpfulness in small ways as gifts to the host country.

run off with my luggage, demanding a tip in return. By the time I collect my suitcase and my sanity, I am sweating profusely in the heat and humidity.

The guest house where we are staying may be nice by Dominican standards, but it would rate one star at best in the U.S. Needless to say, it offers no television, unreliable electricity, and a shower that's barely a cold trickle. Even that sounds pretty good right now. As I fight off exhaustion, I wonder how I can become a little bit Dominican when all I can think about is going home.

Monday, January 13. In Los Alcarrizos, I am filled with dismay as I see the classroom in which I will be tutoring young school children for the next two weeks. The strong smell of burning garbage and raw sewage greets me as I check around for rats and other rodents. I make a mental note to keep my feet off the floor as much as possible.

I feel I've been trapped in a rerun of *Little House on the Prairie*. One teacher is responsible for several grades in this classroom. As she works with one group, the other students are to copy lessons off the chalkboard into their notebooks with stubby little pencils.

My partner and I nervously begin our lesson with a small group of first graders. We fumble our way through shapes and colors in Spanish, then move on to the alphabet. We hold up flash cards with vowels, but the students don't show a glimmer of recognition. Discouraged, we discontinue the lesson and decide to read stories to them. I wouldn't trade anything for the looks of wonder as I read to them the Spanish translation of *Curious George*.

Monday, January 20. I am a few minutes into the lesson with the first graders when I make a stunning discovery. These children have remembered every concept we reviewed on Friday! This is a big change from last week, when they couldn't remember concepts we had discussed five minutes earlier. I tell the children how proud I am of their hard work, and they squirm with delight.

I am exhilarated; in a small way I have made a difference in the way they learn. At the same time, I am sad, because these students have potential that will probably never be developed. High school and college are financially impossible for so many of them. I am determined to make the rest of this week a valuable learning experience for the students. I may not be able to change their living condition, but maybe I can help them see that learning is important and can even be fun.

Wednesday, January 22. I am watching a chapel service at the school. The students, other volunteers, and village people clap and sing praises to the Lord with enthusiasm. The other volunteers and I do our best to learn the words of the songs. Suddenly the teacher who is leading the service calls my name. I play dumb and pretend not to understand. But of course, the only person in the entire village who speaks English happens to be standing right next to me, and she translates the leader's request. I look helplessly at my Calvin College classmates, who look relieved their names weren't called.

I offer the world's shortest speech in Spanish, thanking the teachers and students for their hospitality and sharing their faith with us. I receive smiles and a round of applause. It suddenly hits me that these people don't care that I'm not a great public speaker, that my hands are trembling, and that I have hopelessly mangled several Spanish verbs.

What matters to them is that I have made a genuine effort to open up to them. They know I have traveled a long way to be with them and to help them learn. They know I have struggled to adapt to their culture. That's what they applaud as I stand in front of them with tears in my eyes. And that, I think, is what my professor meant by becoming "a little bit Dominican."

Tuesday, January 28. As I strap myself into the seat of the airplane for the trip home, I think of the school children I have worked with and wonder if they realize we aren't coming back to study with them and teach them games like duck, duck, goose. Are they angry with us for coming into their lives for such a short time, only to leave and never return?

As the plane rises, the Dominican Republic gradually disappears from view, but it will never disappear from my mind. I think about returning to life under the gray winter sky of Grand Rapids. But I am not the same person I was eighteen days ago. I have become "a little bit Dominican."[30]

30. This diary by Marybeth Voss was quoted by Edna Greenway, who accompanied this group of students to the Dominican Republic (Greenway, 1994). It also appeared in the *Banner*, April 19, 1993.

CHAPTER FIVE

Hospitality to the Stranger

[I]f there is any concept worth restoring to its original depth and evocative potential, it is the concept of hospitality.

Henri Nouwen

[H]ospitality is not only an ethical virtue but an epistemo-logical one as well.

Parker Palmer

Sur notre terre, c'est connu, il y a deux catégories d'êtres humains: les Français et les étrangers. Les Français parlent tous français. Les étrangers, étonnament, ne parlent pas tous le même étranger. Certains, pour nous compliquer la tâche, parlent même le français.

Pierre Yves Ruff, *Au-delà de l'identité*

The early encounters of Christopher Columbus and his men with the inhabitants of the Caribbean were riddled with misunderstandings that at times bordered on the farcical. For instance, on one occasion Columbus wished to converse with a group of Indians who had approached his ship in a canoe, but was unsure how to encourage them to come nearer. He came upon the idea of having some of his men dance to the rhythm of a tambourine on the foredeck of his ship. He presumed that when the Indians saw such festivities, they would surely come closer to see what was going on. The result was not quite what he had anticipated. As soon as the music and dancing began, the Indians dropped their oars, covered themselves with their shields, and began raining arrows on the Europeans.[1]

Given the gap in language and culture between the two parties, it is not surprising that misunderstandings occurred. Particularly interesting, however, in Tzvetan Todorov's account of Columbus's journeys, is the author's awareness that attitude in cross-cultural communication is as important as ability.[2]

Columbus himself was polyglot: he spoke Genoese, Latin, Portuguese, and Spanish. Nevertheless, when approaching the Indians, he assumed either that they had no genuine language of their own and had to be sent to Spain to be taught to speak, or that their language was basically the same as his, only spoken badly. Accordingly, in spite of openly acknowledging in his journal that he did not understand their language, he nevertheless recorded detailed interpretations of what they had said. Thus, after one encounter with the Indians he wrote in his diary, "I do not understand their language," but then added later the same day that they had told him about a nearby place "of vast extent, great commerce, richly provided with gold and spices, visited by great ships and merchants."[3]

Such feats of interpretation apparently were based on Columbus's tactic of listening for vocabulary items that sounded like words from his own language and then reading into them things he wanted to hear, especially concerning the proximity of riches. It is his curious claim to understanding, despite his admission that he did not know the new language, that led Todorov to conclude that communication failed not just because of ignorance, but because of attitude: Columbus was not really

1. Todorov, 1983, 32.
2. For what follows, see Todorov, 1983, 14-33.
3. Todorov, 1983, 31.

interested in what the Indians had to say; he was more concerned with fitting their words into his own preconceptions. As Todorov himself puts it: "In Columbus's hermeneutics human beings have no particular place."[4]

Columbus's failings as a stranger abroad are obviously relevant to chapter 4, in which we explored the theme of bringing blessing as a stranger. Perhaps even more interesting at this juncture, however, is the parallel Todorov draws between Columbus's negative attitude toward the Indians and developments in Spain, where, in 1492, the Moors were defeated in the final battle of Granada and the Jews were expelled from Spanish territory.[5]

It is this kind of linkage that points us to the theme of the present chapter. We do not leave behind who we are simply by traveling to a new context. Our ability to be a blessing as a stranger abroad is profoundly linked to whether our basic attitude to cultural difference at home is one of hospitality or exclusion.

In recent decades postmodern discussions have pointed out how Western civilization and modern rationality have been treating strangers, or "others." The West, postmoderns argue, has either dominated, appropriated, or assimilated foreigners, thus divesting them of their otherness.[6] We need to reckon with this accusation when we teach about other cultures. Our educational challenge is to educate students to welcome the

---

4. Todorov, 1983, 33.

5. "The year 1492 already symbolizes, in the history of Spain, this double movement: in this same year the country repudiates its interior Other by triumphing over the Moors in the final battle of Granada and by forcing the Jews to leave its territory; and it discovers the exterior Other, that whole America which will become Latin. We know that Columbus himself constantly links the two events" (Todorov, 1983, 50).

6. Julia Kristeva's study (1991), for instance, offers what may be the most disenchanting portrait of the lot of foreigners in Europe. In this book she sketches images of foreigners, exiles, and immigrant workers and their legal and social status throughout Western history. Strangers need to be welcomed as strangers, she says, because they bring a valuable lesson for those who have psychoanalytical eyes to see: Strangers make locals aware that within everyone lives a stranger, a nonrational ego, an inexplicable, mysterious, wordless self with whom each of us will have to wrestle and come to terms. Strangers mirror our own strangeness and thus play an important role in any culture. In Kristeva's view, the acceptance of the *stranger within* will lead to the acceptance of the *stranger out there*. Welcoming or excluding the stranger in society has much to do with one's own honest self-knowledge and self-acceptance, Kristeva reminds us.

other, the stranger, and to build cross-cultural connections that have the well-being and flourishing of the other at heart.

The thesis we intend to explore here is that, in addition to preparing students for their role as strangers, foreign language educators are called to develop in them the ability and resolve *to be hospitable toward strangers.* Such ethical and attitudinal formation may well be more lasting than linguistic proficiency, which will dwindle later in life if not activated.[7] Not all foreign language students will have the opportunity to go abroad and use their language skills in the target country. However, even if they never leave their home country, the time and effort teachers expend in helping them develop an attitude of hospitality to the stranger will not have been wasted.

Traditionally, neither encouraging the practice of graciously opening one's home to guests one already knows nor showing hospitality toward strangers has been an explicit instructional goal in the school curriculum. Perhaps hospitality is practiced and modeled in the homes from which students come,[8] and it may now and then be preached in the churches they attend, but for the most part, schools place very little emphasis on teaching it. Yet, the cultivation of a hospitable attitude and disposition toward strangers and their culture is an important dimension of a young person's education and therefore deserves disciplined attention. Foreign language education can play a substantial role in this process.

Therefore, in this chapter we will explore *hospitality to the stranger* as an overarching metaphor and spiritual virtue in foreign language education. Intercultural competence,[9] we propose, must be informed by a spirit of hospitality and a loving, welcoming disposition toward the foreign language, the foreign culture, and its people.

---

7. In the American *Standards for Foreign Language Learning* one can find a similar hope. "Even if students never speak the language after leaving school, for a lifetime they will retain the cross-cultural skills and knowledge, the insights, and the access to a world beyond traditional borders" (1996, 24).

8. The Greek Orthodox Lambros Kamperidis writes, "In my childhood, at Christmas dinners, a place was always reserved for the stranger and wayfarer. A few days later, on New Year's Eve, a slice of St. Basil's bread was set aside for the stranger. Even if not physically present, a stranger occupied a special place in the household" (Kamperidis, 1990, 5).

9. As defined in Byram, 1997, and Byram and Fleming, 1998.

Hospitality as Metaphor and Virtue

Many theorists have explored the role of metaphor in educational thinking in recent years.[10] Metaphors are not simply colorful figures of speech or rhetorical decorations; they help us see differently by illuminating one thing in terms of another. They shed special light on a subject and bring into focus dimensions and features otherwise unclear or even unnoticed. A metaphor is more suggestive than definitive, and has expansive explanatory power. It guides, shapes, and organizes our views, practices, and choices in a certain direction. As Erazim Kohák states, "Metaphors . . . shape the context of our experience as a meaningful whole, deciding in the process not only what is primary and what is derivative, but also who we ought to be and how we ought to act."[11]

Each of the guiding metaphors familiar in education, such as, *transmission, nurture, cultivation, production,* and *liberation,* forms and patterns in particular ways the teaching and learning process and its curricular choices. It makes a difference whether we think, for example, of foreign language learners as plants to be cultivated or as production sites with measurable input and output. Metaphors orient our ways of teaching and provide coherence and meaning. We live and teach by metaphors.

In addition to metaphor, scholars have also shown recent interest in the relationship of spiritual virtues to learning. Mark Schwehn argues that a basic set of spiritual virtues, typically developed within the context of religious commitment and community, is integral to healthy learning.[12] Charity and justice, for instance, enable us to read others as we would have them read us. Humility encourages us to be open to correction and to persevere with difficult subject matter and texts, instead of dismissing them as boring or irrelevant. Focusing on these virtues is not, Schwehn insists, simply a matter of adding ethical behavior *alongside* learning. Such virtues should *inform and shape* learning: "To 'teach' these virtues means first to exemplify them, second to order life in the classroom and throughout the academic community in such a way that their exercise is seen and felt as an essential aspect of inquiry."[13] Both of these wider discussions are relevant

10. See, e.g., Beavis and Thomas, 1996; Block, 1992; Lakoff and Johnson, 1980; Munby, 1986; Ortony, 1979; Sacks, 1979; Soskice, 1985; W. Taylor, 1984; Thornbury, 1991.
11. Kohák, 1996.
12. Schwehn, 1993.
13. Schwehn, 1993, 60.

to the present study. Hospitality to the stranger is both a spiritual virtue and a fruitful metaphor for foreign language education.

We will begin our exploration of the relevance of *hospitality to the stranger* in language learning by focusing on the nature of hospitality itself. We will then explore its relevance to cross-cultural encounters in the foreign language classroom.

The Practice of Hospitality

Hospitality, a virtue common to all human cultures, implies the gracious sharing of a meal with a stranger and often includes giving shelter. The host creates a space where non-members of a group can feel temporarily at home.[14] Often with lavish generosity she or he presents only the very best and bestows special honor and protection on the guest. A bond is created between host and guest, so that the guest will want to return the hospitality sometime in the future. In festive moments of shalom, while giving and receiving hospitality, humankind overcomes the fear of the stranger who could be a potential enemy and celebrates communion in the midst of differences.[15] Christine Pohl aptly defines hospitality as "a practice that integrates respect and care."[16] The host cares for the well-being of the guest whose dignity as a human person she honors and respects.

In the first chapter of this book we showed how Israel was called to be a blessing to the stranger in its midst and to love the alien as a neighbor. In the New Testament, extending hospitality to strangers is not just a thoughtful, generous, or polite act that marks Christians as kind human beings. It is much more. As we have already seen, according to the words of Jesus in Matthew 25, extending hospitality to the stranger is a matter of life and death — eternal life or eternal death. Welcoming strangers fulfills the command to love God and to love one's neighbor as oneself.

In many passages in the Old and New Testament, strangers who are received hospitably turn out to be divine messengers — sometimes God himself or Christ — bringing a life-giving message. In Christian hagiography,

14. Murray, 1990, 17. Murray refers here to Durkheim's *Professional Ethics and Civic Morals* (1958), where hospitality is seen in the context of rights and group membership.

15. Cf. Hiltbrunner, 1972.

16. Pohl, 1999, 69.

stories abound of saints who gave refuge to the most unsightly and unlikely people, only to discover that they had welcomed God. "God is always using the stranger to introduce us to the strangeness of truth," observes Parker Palmer.[17] Christ becomes visible, real, and present among us in the guest we welcome. This deep mystery makes Christian hospitality unique.[18]

Granting hospitality is also an act of thankful remembrance of God's love for and protection of aliens and strangers throughout history (Deut. 10:18-19) and a foreshadowing of the feast of God with all nations at the end of time (Isa. 25:6-9). At this banquet each culture and nation will bring its unique gifts, and together all nations will praise God in rich diversity and splendor. This eschatological vision clearly has implications for the here and now — both in the way we treat strangers and in our attitude to cultural diversity.

The practice of hospitality lies close to the center of a Christian's life before God. "To be moral is to be hospitable to strangers," states Thomas W. Ogletree in his work on Christian ethics.[19] Welcoming the stranger is not an option; it is a central dimension of being human, since God has given humankind the "gift of and call to connection,"[20] that is to say, the ability and the command to love one's neighbors. We are to welcome with kindness those who do not belong, those who are not at home in our country, including those who have come from other cultures and do not speak our language.[21] All are God's image bearers. John Calvin's admonition to his xenophobic contemporaries in his sermon on Galatians 6:9-11 is still worth hearing today: "If there come some Moor or barbarian, since he is a man, he brings a mirror in which we are able to contemplate that he is our brother and our neighbor: for we cannot abolish the order of nature which God has established as inviolable."[22] In a world with increasing economic integration, an international labor force, and great social mobility across national boundaries, hospitality is a virtue much in need.

17. Palmer, 1983, 74.

18. For a very detailed and rich cultural history of hospitality in major world religions, see Bonet-Maury, 1959.

19. Ogletree, 1985, 1.

20. Olthuis, 1993, 160.

21. Recent voices in the field of missiology propose hospitality to the stranger as an alternative to Western missionary practices of the past, which often were shaped by a colonizing mentality. See Koyama, 1993, and Gittins, 1994a.

22. Quoted in Pohl, 1999, 65.

Xenophilic Hospitality

An obvious question arises here: Is the biblical call to hospitality really a fitting metaphor for the kind of hospitable welcome we propose for the foreign language classroom, where students are supposed to learn a language, not how to practice charity? After all, Jesus was concerned about hospitality for poor sojourners, for travelers at risk without protection, for people who needed shelter and food. Surely, that emphasis is not generally appropriate to foreign language instruction.

We would like, for the purposes of this discussion, to distinguish between two types of hospitality. There is, on the one hand, the *diaconal* or *Good Samaritan* hospitality illustrated in Matthew 25.[23] Most likely, the modern language classroom will not normally serve as a stage for welcoming strangers in distress. But there is also *xenophilic*[24] hospitality, which, like diaconal hospitality, involves the kind reception of the foreigner as an image bearer of Christ, as *imago Dei*. However, unlike its diaconal relative, xenophilic hospitality is motivated by the eagerness to receive strangers first and foremost because they come from another nation and culture. With this kind of hospitality we graciously invite a foreign guest, a foreign tongue, foreign ways into our homes, lives, minds, and hearts.

The emphasis in foreign language education, we suggest, should be on the cultivation and practice of xenophilic hospitality. Our goal should be to nurture students in such a way that they look forward with openness and curiosity to strangers, and joyfully welcome the enrichment and change their visits bring for both hosts and guests.

23. This helpful distinction is developed by Fuchs, 1988, 257. The adjective "xenophilic" is our coinage. In medieval Europe two separate tracks of hospitality developed. On the one hand, monasteries looked after the local poor and the needy travelers. When the numbers of the poor were very large, the care offered was often "distant and relatively anonymous." Wealthy ecclesiastical or aristocratic houses, on the other hand, offered lavish hospitality to the traveler or visitor of high standing in order to cultivate and maintain power and influence (Pohl, 1999, 48-51). See also Murray, 1990, 46. Our distinction between xenophilic and diaconal hospitality does not imply this medieval separation between rich and poor. Nor do we see xenophilia in the negative way Todorov uses this concept (Todorov, 1991). He sees in xenophilia a fascination with issues of other cultures as a way of escaping social responsibility in one's own culture. See also Bammer, 1995.

24. "Xenophilic" from "xenophilia," love for the stranger, specifically here love for the linguistically and culturally other.

Hospitality — a Metaphor for Education

Viewing education in terms of hospitality is relatively new. Furthermore, the limited currency this metaphor has gained has been mostly within the context of Christian religious education.

Early on, crucial impetus for seeing the significance of hospitality for education came from Henri Nouwen, who presented his vision of Christian ministry and seminary education as an exercise in hospitality.[25] In a number of his writings Nouwen laments the absence of this Christian virtue in a world filled with hostility and with estrangement from self, neighbor, and God.

As a remedy for the widespread authoritarian spirit in educational institutions, Nouwen envisions the relationship between teacher and student in a new light. The teacher, as host, he writes, "is called upon to create for his students a free and fearless space where mental and emotional development can take place."[26] As good hosts, teachers need to value, affirm, and deepen the life experiences of their guests, the students. But this process will take place in both directions. "[S]tudents," Nouwen insists, "are not just the poor, needy, ignorant beggars who come to the man or woman of knowledge, but they are . . . indeed like guests who honor the house with their visit and will not leave without having made their own contribution."[27]

Although Nouwen's focus on student self-esteem and self-expression reflects the educational ideals of the early seventies, his view is relatively balanced. Not only does he advocate that teachers welcome their students in a nonauthoritarian manner; he also encourages them to articulate clear boundaries and positions, and not to hide their convictions. In Nouwen's view, students who do not hear their teachers express *their* convictions will never become aware of *their own* values and commitments.[28]

25. Nouwen, 1972, 49-57.
26. Nouwen, 1986, 86-97.
27. Nouwen, 1986, 89.
28. Nouwen, 1974, 15. Thomas H. Groome follows in Nouwen's footsteps when he points to hospitality as a virtue of the teacher of religion. As the most appropriate attitude of the educator, hospitality requires not only deep empathy with the learner viewed as pilgrim, but also a welcoming psychological and intellectual humility on the part of the teacher, that is to say, her willingness to relinquish "epistemic privilege" (Groome, 1988, 17).

Whereas Nouwen and others[29] advocate that teachers of religion cultivate hospitality primarily in order to create a conducive learning and teaching climate, Susanne Johnson,[30] who also reflects on religious education, goes further.[31] For Johnson, hospitality creates a place where differences meet and where power relationships are transformed. The host, who has cultural power in the home, opens that home to the stranger who is without power. In the act of being hospitable, the host, to a certain degree, becomes the 'servant and, at least for the duration of the visit, the guest takes center stage. "Hospitality in its deepest sense," Johnson writes, "is a willingness not only to receive the stranger, but also to be changed and affected by the presence of the other, not only personally, but also institutionally, curricularly, and politically."[32]

In brief, for critics like Nouwen and Johnson, a commitment to hospitality serves as a corrective to deficiencies in contemporary education. Hospitality creates both a welcoming pedagogical climate for teachers and students and a special place where conflicts can be aired in mannerly, respectful dialogue.

To the best of our knowledge, hospitality has not yet been claimed as a key metaphor for foreign language education. By proposing the metaphor of xenophilic hospitality, we do not intend to focus our discussion solely on the teacher-learner relationship[33] or on personal encounters between foreigners and students inside and outside the classroom, although these are very pertinent aspects of the topic. *Hospitality to the stranger* will serve primarily as a *metaphor for the way both teachers and students understand and interact with otherness.* In other words, it is our conviction that hospitality must shape the spirit and manner in which learners welcome, acquire, and respond to the foreign language and culture.

29. Palmer, 1983; Vogel, 1991; Seymour, Crain, and Crockett, 1993; Cooper, 1996; Russell, 1996.

30. Johnson, 1993.

31. Johnson uses the metaphor of hospitality to propose a middle position in the ongoing debate between neoconservatives and postmodernists about America's cultural identity, a debate that focuses on this question: Should North America continue to cultivate its traditional Eurocentric character or become a bona fide pluralistic, multicultural entity?

32. Johnson, 1993, 348.

33. This aspect has been explored in an exemplary way for the Christian foreign language classroom by Pederson, 1992.

To Be at Home and Not to Be at Home

The full implications of thinking of foreign language education in terms of granting hospitality will become clearer in later chapters. At this point we will focus on what happens to our cultural identity when we learn a foreign language. For this we will take a closer look at various salient aspects of hospitality. Hospitality obviously implies having and caring for a home. It also involves both opening that home to others and being open to receiving from them. We will consider each of these aspects in turn.

To begin with, a host must have a home, or at least some place he or she can share freely with a guest. As Nouwen notes, "Nobody can be a good host who is not at home in his own house."[34] To have a home, in terms of our discussion, means, among other things, to belong somewhere, to accept one's roots in a particular culture. The national culture with its subcultures gives its members a *cultural* identity (which does not encompass all that we are!) and a language that connect them to members of their communities, to their ongoing conversations, stories, history, traumas, and dreams.

Whether we function as host or as guest, we do not come as blank slates. We have already been shaped and given a cultural identity by where we came from. Nor should this identity be seen simply as something to be escaped from or risen above. Instead we are called to cherish and love what is wholesome in our home, our culture, our traditions; we are to cultivate it and delight in it with gratitude for God's good gifts to us.

Some readers will object that our picture of "home" is too cozy; at the very least, our talk of home will certainly raise some postmodern eyebrows. In the postmodern view, the very claim to a home that provides security and centeredness (as well as power) has, throughout history, driven others away, making them marginal or homeless.

Could these postmodern critics be right? Instead of insisting on traditional concepts of home, wouldn't it be much more realistic and less dangerous to affirm the "radical homelessness" of postmodernity[35] and to

34. Nouwen, 1974, 24.

35. Postmodernity, writes Brian J. Walsh, can be described "as a culture of radical homelessness. We can no longer be at-home in the world, first because we recognise that any notion of the home is merely a social construction. Second, we are confronted with the violence of our social construction vis-à-vis other people in the world

see humans as nomads, as drifters and wanderers, "attached to no home and always separated from father and mother"?[36]

We think not. We agree with those critics of postmodernism who insist that, in spite of the sinful exclusions perpetrated by traditional views of home, the fact remains that everyone yearns to be at home somewhere. To have or to want a home is normal, human, and good. We concur with Brian Walsh, who argues that "the primordiality of both memory of home and expectation or hope of homecoming is constitutive to human life and foundational to culture-forming."[37]

Here lies a basic difference between practicing hospitality and simply abandoning any hope of ever really being at home. Hospitality implies not only having a home, but also welcoming others within it and taking responsibility for maintaining it in a welcoming state.

Simply throwing one's home open without serving as host is not enough. Giving notice that the house is vacant and available to anyone who cares to use it is not hospitality. Neither is it particularly hospitable to pretend one's home is perfect and to ignore the presence of disrepair that could harm the guest. Along with our gratitude for the gifts we have received from our culture, we are to face up to its evils. As hosts, we are called to lament and grieve what is inhuman, unjust, broken, and destructive in our society. We also must acknowledge both our own participation in those evils and our own unsuccessful or halfhearted attempts at righting the wrongs around us. Listening to the guest's perspective may make us want to change some aspects of our home that, until then, had seemed normal to us. This, too, is part of what it means to have a hospitable home. We are to both accept and take responsibility for who we are.

Furthermore, it goes nearly without saying that, for hospitality to be possible, our home must not become our private castle in which we take refuge from foreigners and strangers. Students with xenophobic tendencies consider their "homes," their cliques or gangs, defensive fortresses providing power and identity. Given this view, anything and anybody foreign becomes a threat to be warded off. As Zygmunt Bauman remarks,

---

whereby home for one group of people is homelessness for others. And third, the very environment in which we live is now polluted to the point where it is becoming inhospitable to us" (Walsh, 1998, 8-9).

36. M. C. Taylor, 1984, 156.
37. Walsh, 1998, 9.

[A]ll xenophobia, ethnic or racist, all positing of the stranger as an enemy and, unambiguously, as the outer boundary and limit to one's individual and collective sovereignty, has the idealized conception of the secure home as its sense-giving metaphor. The image of the secure home transforms the "outside of home" into a terrain fraught with danger; the inhabitants of that outside turn into the carriers of threat — they need to be contained, chased away and kept away.[38]

In contrast, the biblical message tells us that to be at home is a gift given by God, to be used not for safe separation from others, but instead as a blessing to strangers. "A true homecoming," Walsh notes, "is possible only if the security of home is extended to the vulnerability of the other, if the safety of the familiar is extended beyond the boundaries of home to the unfamiliar, the alien."[39] Hospitality, then, is our grateful Christian response to God's gift of a home. Like all true gifts, a home does not belong entirely to the one who received it, for it bears the mark of the Giver, who wants us to share it with others.[40]

Hospitality also implies that the stranger not only will be greeted, but also will be given loving attention. The stranger not only will be fed and given drink; his or her voice also will be granted space. His discomfort will be met with concern, her stories will be heard and responded to. The

38. Bauman, 1995, 135. This quotation is Bauman's summary of Phil Cohen, *Home Rules: Some Reflections on Racism and Nationalism in Everyday Life* (London: University of East London, 1993).

39. Walsh, 1998, 19.

40. There are less idealistic views of hospitality that concentrate more on the power of the host as the master of the house. Yet, a potentially paralyzing dilemma arises from this emphasis. For Jacques Derrida, for example, the host has to give to the guest, but he is compelled to limit this gift in order not to lose the mastery of the house. Thus, true hospitality is impossible, according to Derrida, since it demands an act of excessive giving through which the host would lose his property and power. Hospitality is only beyond hospitality. John D. Caputo summarizes Derrida as follows: "Hospitality is what is always demanded of me, that to which I have never measured up. I am always too close-fisted, too ungracious, too unwelcoming, too calculating in all my invitations, which are disturbed from within by all sorts of subterranean motivations — from wanting to show off what I own to looking for a return invitation. I am never hospitable and I do not know what hospitality is" (Caputo, 1997, 112). Such a view is telling as a confession of our need for grace, but to regard hospitality as inherently out of reach is to deny the possibility of that same grace. Understanding our home as a gift for sharing rather than as a possession to be mastered eliminates Derrida's dilemma.

fact that those stories may be new and different enriches, rather than threatens, the host's task.

Of course, the host is obliged only to listen, not to ape the stranger or to agree with his or her every word. Offering hospitality does not mean the host has to try to become identical to the guest; in fact, to do so would be to forfeit the possibility of mutual enrichment. It does, however, require a spirit of openness. All of us have experienced the difference between homes where we are merely greeted with carefully measured civility and those in which we are genuinely welcomed, where there is authentic give-and-take. Maintaining a hospitable attitude means that we receive the representative of the target culture graciously and with love, and that we make space within ourselves for the stories and experiences he or she brings us from that culture.

This view of hospitality offers a different angle on a dilemma we commonly encounter in discussions on foreign language learning: How do we simultaneously maintain our own identity and conform to the language and culture we are learning? Muriel Saville-Troike offers a vivid example of this dilemma in the following description of the plight of a Japanese woman learning English: "One of [the woman's] professors told her that she shouldn't bow to American professors, because that wasn't considered appropriate. This professor was trying to teach her a sociolinguistic rule in English. She was crushed. 'I know Americans don't bow,' she said, 'but that's my culture, and if I don't do that, I'm not being respectful and I won't be a good person.'"[41] The professor's reaction highlights this dilemma. His response risked not respecting a cultural need deeply embedded in this Japanese student. Being hospitable means both affirming our own cultural identity and, at the same time, giving the stranger, the other, a loving, welcoming space in which she can be who she is.

Who Shall Be Host?

That one does not have to be wealthy or highly cultured to offer hospitality is an important lesson students must learn, especially those who come from economically depressed homes.

Some years ago I (David Smith) was involved in Christian outreach to international students at the University of Marburg. One day, while

41. Quoted by Kramsch, 1993, 44.

making my rounds, I found myself in the room of a student from South Korea who had recently arrived in Germany. The Korean's room was small, boxlike, and bare, and all he had to offer his guest was black coffee. I have a strong dislike for the taste of coffee, but this student's eagerness to offer such hospitality as he could was so apparent that I accepted it without comment and did my best to down the drink.

Even though the Korean student was living in substandard accommodations in a foreign land and had little to offer, he still displayed a hospitable spirit. The response to the call to be hospitable need not depend on being totally at ease in one's cultural home or believing that one's home is wonderful, perfect, and opulent. No matter how much or how little we have, all of us are to practice intercultural, xenophilic hospitality.

In light of this call, one cannot help but note the sad state of American primary and secondary education, where fewer than 35 percent of all students learn a foreign language.[42] The situation in Christian schools is no better. The message the educational world involuntarily gives pupils when it does not require them to learn a foreign language goes something like this: "You belong to the intellectually and socially powerless; you are not going to the university; you won't go abroad. You don't need to listen to the voice of the stranger. You don't need to learn a foreign language. You have nothing to give foreigners and nothing to gain from them."

Looking for Guests

It is not necessary to wait until one achieves a high level of proficiency in the target language before reaching out to the stranger. A Spanish professor in Texas, with its high population of Spanish speakers, provides a good example.

This teacher required her introductory Spanish students to spend half an hour per week with resident Spanish speakers in a nearby retirement home. The students practiced the topics of conversation and the types of questions they were to ask beforehand, and after each visit they

42. According to 1994 enrollment statistics in American public (state-funded) schools, 33.04 percent of all students in grades seven through twelve learn a foreign language. Only 16.2 percent of all students in grades seven and eight, and not even half (42.2 percent) of all students in grades nine through twelve, are in foreign language courses (Draper and Hicks, 1996).

handed in the results of their conversations. Thus, once a week a busload of American college students was eagerly awaited by a hall full of older people, many in wheelchairs, who were only too ready to talk about the weather, their health, and their families.[43] Similarly, the students also looked forward to these weekly visits with their elderly partners. Furthermore, these experiences in the retirement home helped motivate them in their study of Spanish and, in many cases, gave their attempts to learn the language an element of downright delight. They discovered that, even at the beginner's level, their clumsy attempts to communicate and to reach out to the stranger resulted in meaningful human encounters.

Not all schools are able to employ such creative means for developing language skills. In some cases, even if native speakers of the target language live in the area, the educational institution will not allow students to leave the classroom, or else will make the logistics for doing so forbiddingly complicated. In such situations native speakers should be invited into the classroom and welcomed hospitably. Such personal encounters with native guests present precious opportunities both for practicing the linguistic skills of hospitable communication and for challenging narrow stereotypes students may have about representatives of the foreign culture.

Being Truthful as Host

When inviting the foreigner and the foreign culture into their world, students soon will realize that some aspects of their own culture are good and can be affirmed and presented to guests with confidence. At the same time, these student hosts must also become aware of the destructive, unjust, and unhealthy features of their society. It is critical, for instance, that they get to know the larger tragic drama of the twentieth century and the role their nation played in it and how this same history was experienced and interpreted in the target country.

As students become acquainted with the traumatic events of the twentieth century, they need to see how the insistence on ethnic, racial, or ideological purity turns tribes and nations into hateful, self-righteous peo-

---

43. For logistical reasons the university students could not invite the elderly people into their homes. But notwithstanding, it was a beginning, and a genuine personal encounter was made possible by the effort.

ple ready to kill those human beings they label inferior, worthless, or simply "other." Christian students must learn that, at times, even believers, whatever their nationality, have failed to welcome strangers, and instead have committed atrocities against them, often in the name of God.[44] "Our coziness with the surrounding culture," writes Miroslav Volf, "has made us so blind to its many evils that, instead of calling them into question, we offer our own version of them — in God's name and with a good Christian conscience."[45] On the other hand, it is equally important that students learn that throughout history, Christians also have offered hospitality and have received the stranger kindly in the name of God, even at great personal risk and cost, whether during the monastic culture of the Middle Ages, during the persecutions of the Third Reich,[46] or, more recently, in the *sanctuary* movement in the United States. Students should learn that granting hospitality in inhospitable times can be a political act, or, as Pohl puts it, "an act of resistance and defiance, a challenge to the values and expectations of the larger community."[47]

To put it briefly, if we are to receive the foreigner, the foreign language, and the foreign culture with a respectful, kind, and truthful spirit, we must develop both a proper appreciation of our own culture and a critical distance from it. Chauvinistic, ethnocentric hosts do not practice good hospitality. They insult or humiliate their guests.

Kulturkunde in the Third Reich

A telling example of such an inhospitable attitude can be found in the way schools taught foreign language and culture in Nazi Germany. In addition to promoting military and economic aims, the motive for teaching English and French in German schools during the Third Reich was to cultivate in students an uncritical pride in and love for Germany — and hatred for

---

44. For instance, 80 percent of the population of Rwanda claims to be Christian. Rwanda was considered the African country with the strongest charismatic revival (Martin, 1995, 1).

45. Volf, 1995, 197.

46. See for instance on the NACFLA website (http://www.spu.edu/orgs/nacfla/) the work of Marilyn Severson on teaching the French Resistance or the work of hospitality during WWII in Le Chambon by French Calvinists as described by Hallie, 1979.

47. Pohl, 1999, 62.

non-Germans. Germans needed to know the language and culture of their enemies in order to defeat them more easily.[48] The teaching of culture[49] in foreign language instruction was intended to create in pupils a militant attitude, and thus to prepare them for war.[50] As one telling document proclaims,

> We do not want to get to know England or France per se. We only want to use them as a means to get to know and to love Germany. . . . We do not want to make an effort to understand the other; we rather want to understand ourselves. . . . Culture is not, as it once was, something that connects people. No, it actually separates people and groups them into friends and enemies. Under certain circumstances [the teaching of] culture creates animosities.[51]

In Nazi pedagogy, the only purpose served by learning a foreign language was to establish German superiority and to legitimize the rejection and exclusion of strangers.

Students obviously need to learn how to cultivate both gratitude for

48. See Lehberger, 1986.

49. *Kulturkunde,* understood mainly as the study of the racial makeup of a nation.

50. "Allgemeine Ziele des neusprachlichen Unterrichts sind:

1. Weite Verbreitung der Kenntnis fremder Sprachen zu Nutzen von Wirtschaft, Heer, Marine, auswärtiger Politik und Propaganda.
2. Bewußte Kenntnis fremden Volkstums, um durch Vergleichung das eigene Wesen deutlicher zu erleben.
3. Verständnis für Geschichte, Staatsaufbau und Rassenzusammensetzung fremder Völker, mit denen wir in Berührung kommen müssen, Rückspiegelung auf unser Staatsleben.
4. Möglichkeit der Verständigung und Einwirkung auf das Ausland.
5. Begründeter Stolz auf das eigene Volkstum."

(Hüllen, 1979, 203, quoting Siebert.)

51. Our translation of "Wir wollen . . . nicht England und Frankreich um ihretwillen kennenlernen. Wir wollen durch sie nur Deutschland kennen- und liebenlernen. . . . Wir wollen uns auch nicht so sehr bemühen, andere zu verstehen, als uns selbst zu verstehen" (Münch, quoted by Hüllen, 1979, 207). "Kultur ist also nicht, wie es früher hieß, etwas die Völker Verbindendes, sondern geradezu etwas Völker Trennendes, ist eine *Freund-Feind-Gruppierung,* also unter Umständen etwas Feindliches" (Rudolf Münch, "Doch noch Kulturkunde" [1936], quoted in Hüllen, 1979, 214).

and critical distance from their cultural home. Their ultimate loyalty, after all, does not belong to their ethnic or racial makeup or their national culture, but to the One who is God of all cultures and all nations. It is ultimately this allegiance that transcends home as a source of power and identity and makes possible the freedom and openness to create a hospitable space for welcoming the stranger.[52]

Whom Shall We Invite?

I (Barbara Carvill) once asked a teenage friend of my daughter how she liked her French teacher. "He isn't too bad," she said, "but we can't stand it when he presents EVERYTHING French as cool and way better and more sophisticated than our American culture!"

It is understandable that many teachers — above all in settings like the United States, where foreign language is not a compulsory subject — try to make their language programs attractive by presenting everything the target culture has to offer as admirable and praiseworthy, thus perpetuating the romantic notion that all that is different and foreign is good. We are called to be good hosts, but should we invite every stranger, willy-nilly, into our home?

Every host knows that there are good guests and bad. Some we tolerate with concealed but fervent hopes for their early departure, for they damage and rupture the fabric of the home and leave little sense of blessing behind.[53] Other guests leave a feeling of enrichment, of new life.

52. Volf, 1995, 198; Volf, 1996, 40.

53. In the popular play *Biedermann und die Brandstifter* (The Firebugs) by Swiss author Max Frisch (Frisch, 1958), the Biedermanns open their home to three strangers, ruthless criminals from hell, who shamelessly misuse the hospitality offered them. They not only plan to set fire to the house, but also manipulate their hosts into collaborating in their own destruction. But the heart of the problem lies within Biedermann himself, since his hospitality runs no deeper than good middle-class manners do. He lives a lie and has not faced the fact that he is a criminal himself, and that he is "at home" with a bad conscience. Consequently, he lacks the moral integrity and strength necessary to throw the three bandits out. Instead of giving, he is being taken, and in the final scene he even hands the criminals the matches so that they can burn down his house. "Create in us a pure heart," we might pray as a response to this play, "because a pure heart will give us the strength of moral discernment and prevent us from practicing hospitality foolishly and from inviting devils unaware."

They offer a fresh perspective and tell stories the host has not heard before.

In a similar vein, language teachers must consider carefully which aspects of the foreign culture they should welcome into the classroom. What criteria will guide their choices?[54] When designing a curriculum, they must discern thoughtfully the spirit of foreign cultural practices and ask whether such practices are potentially destructive to the home, to the self, to one's neighbor, to human community, to the environment. They also will ask whether the materials they want to introduce do justice to the stranger as a human being made in God's image — and as a stranger. We expect to welcome the genuine other in the classroom, not a compatriot in foreign guise.

An example will illustrate this point. Out of fear that Western ideas would undermine communist ideology, English textbooks formerly used in the People's Republic of China contained a variety of stories about Lenin and Karl Marx, as well as many fables and moral tales, taken from around the world, that extolled communist ideals. The calculated intent of the textbook editors obviously was to instill communist virtues in the Chinese students learning English. Thus the English-speaking stranger presumably being embraced really was no stranger at all, but a Red Chinese moralist in English clothing.

In short, the teacher needs to be a wise and circumspect gatekeeper at the welcoming open door of the foreign language classroom. This does not mean that every stranger invited in must be clean, mild mannered, and easy to be with. Some of the materials the teacher chooses may be perplexing and troublesome for the students, and not easy to embrace.[55] The crucial question, however, is whether what the teacher has chosen helps students practice hospitality. That is to say, will it invite openness and curiosity and develop a kind spirit? Will it encourage students to treat the aspect of culture under consideration with respect, not judging too

54. For sound insight into this complex issue see Henning, 1993; Takalo, 1994; and Takalo, 1997.

55. Dwayne Huebner remarks: "The stranger, the alien, the enemy — anyone who is different than I am — poses an unspoken question to me. In fact to both of us. The question is why am I as I am, and why is she as she is? Her life is a possibility for me as mine is for her. And in the meeting of the two of us is a new possibility for both of us. . . . Differences . . . are invitations to be led out, to be educated" (Huebner, 1985, 464).

quickly but *hearing* first and *evaluating* later? Will it motivate students to compare and contrast? Will they be enriched and challenged by it? Will students, as a result, embrace the other and otherness?

Hospitality and Embrace

In his essay "A Vision of Embrace: Theological Perspectives on Cultural Identity and Conflict,"[56] Miroslav Volf develops a useful image for any encounter with the other: the act of embracing. Volf uses this image in his reflections on conflict in multicultural settings, on what it means to love one's enemy, and on how to bring about reconciliation. For our study of xenophilic communication across cultures and languages, Volf's exploration of the embrace as an essential category of Christian social action is very helpful. It draws together and highlights the main points we wanted to make in this chapter.

The stranger we "embrace" in foreign language education is, in the broadest sense, the language and culture of a people. We attempt to teach and learn a foreign language not merely as a linguistic system, but as a medium of communication used by human beings made in God's image, and we see a foreign culture as shaped by responsible personal agents. Communication across cultures is not just for exchanging information, for wanting to sell or buy, for having pleasure, and the like. Our motives in engaging the "other," as we shall see in the next chapter, should always be guided and inspired by the more fundamental aim of cross-cultural communication, namely, to build hospitable and kind relationships and good human connections through which people enrich and bless each other, having the well-being and flourishing of each other at heart.

Volf introduces the concept of the embrace as follows:

> In an embrace I open my arms to create space in myself for the other. Open arms are a sign that I do not want to be by myself only, an invitation for the other to come in and feel at home with me. In an embrace I also close my arms around the other. Closed arms are a sign that I want the other to become part of me while at the same time I maintain my own identity. By becoming part of me, the other enriches me. In a mu-

56. Volf, 1995.

tual embrace, none remains the same because each enriches the other, yet both remain true to their genuine selves.[57]

In short, when we embrace, we open our arms and show that the other is welcome. That is to say, we do not close ourselves off; we neither exclude the other nor act indifferently; instead, we invite the stranger in.

In the context of this study, the embrace means that we do not want to remain monolingual, monocultural beings. Native English speakers, whose mother tongue is the *lingua franca* of our world, indicate with their open arms that they are ready to abandon their attitude of linguistic superiority and walk humbly the long and arduous road of learning the tongue of another people.

But we open not only our arms; we open our minds and hearts as well; we shed our haughty airs and create a welcoming space for the other. Opening our arms to embrace implies an attitude of childlike expectation. Without an initiative of goodwill toward the stranger and the trust that something precious is going to come about through this encounter, cross-cultural communication in the name of hospitality will not happen.

Obviously, the eagerness to embrace makes us vulnerable. Things may not turn out as expected. As Cornelius Plantinga, Jr., puts it,

> A person willing to embrace is a person who is not worried about preserving a false dignity that depends on perfect decorum. An embrace is often awkward and funny: your glasses clatter together, you have a false start when figuring out whether it will be right to right or left to left; you are very different in size, etc. Similarly, the person who undertakes to learn the language of the stranger has to be willing to make mistakes, make false starts, cause amusement to the native speakers — all in open, free, good humor. The idea isn't, first of all, to get an icy, controlled correctness, but to join hand and mind . . . with someone who is delightfully other — and to smile at each other a lot in the process.[58]

The hospitable embrace provides an image for meeting the other without domination, fusion, subjugation, or indifference, tendencies we will explore in more detail in the next chapter.

57. Volf, 1995, 203.
58. From a personal note to Barbara Carvill.

But not all embraces are hospitable. A strangling bear hug, for instance, is not a hospitable act, but rather "a devouring embrace that takes the other in until there is nothing left of 'them' but us."[59] Zygmunt Bauman, following Freud, describes such an essentially xenophobic reception of strangers as *phagic,* and the other extreme, the exclusion of the other, as *emic:*

> The phagic strategy is *inclusivist,* the emic strategy is *exclusivist.* The first assimilates the stranger to the neighbours, the second merges them with the aliens. Together, they polarize the stranger and attempt to clear up the most vexing and disturbing middle-ground between the poles of neighbourhood and alienness — between "home" and "abroad," "us" and "them." To the stranger whose life conditions and choices they define, they posit a genuine "either-or:" conform or be damned, be like us or do not overstay your visit, play the game by our rules or be prepared to be kicked out from the game altogether.[60]

In a hospitable embrace we dare to encounter the other in a place of give-and-take and of transformation. In Volf's words: "In an embrace, the identity of the self is both preserved and transformed, and the alterity of the other is both affirmed as alterity and partly received into the ever-changing identity of the self."[61] Thus, as we have stressed repeatedly, to acquire the language of the stranger does not entail the loss of one's own cultural identity or the adoption of the stranger's identity. At the same time, however, when we learn to speak and write with foreign words and to hear and understand strangers' voices and their stories, we do not stay unchanged. We receive a gift, a blessing from the stranger we embrace.

This gift and blessing may not always be easy to accept. The act of receiving it often involves a difficult and unsettling process of accepting the otherness of the stranger and of being questioned and challenged by commitments, values, and views that conflict with our own.

But if we can nonetheless cultivate an attitude of hospitable openness and loving respect, a kind of "double vision"[62] may develop within us:

59. Bammer, 1995, 47.
60. Bauman, 1995, 180.
61. Volf, 1996, 143.
62. Volf, 1996, 213.

the ability to see a conflictual issue not only from our own perspective but also with the other's vantage point in mind. By listening to the stranger and by being seen and mirrored in the other, we may modify our own views and take a fresh, critical look at the quality of our own commitments and traditions. In this process we are enriched by the gift of the stranger. Our cultural identity is no longer monochromatic, and through hospitable connection with the stranger we develop a "spacious heart."[63]

Thus, embracing the stranger brings us both *enrichment* and *correction*.[64] We need this correction to overcome our own cultural arrogance, which leads us to see the other not as truly other but just as an imperfect version of ourselves. We need the creative ferment the stranger brings into our lives. We need to hear and enter into both the joys and the sorrows of the other culture. It is important that we learn about the historical reasons and causes that led to present miseries. If we in these ways truly embrace the stranger, we will both rejoice and lament with him or her, and in so doing will become aware that we are all part of a common, broken humanity in need of redemption. At the heart of hospitality is the embrace.

Conclusion

In his book *The End of Education* Neil Postman laments the absence of direction and meaning in many schools today and stresses the importance of "a transcendent, spiritual idea that gives purpose and clarity to learning."[65] Without an overarching teleology or narrative shaping education, Postman argues, we lack ideals, purpose, continuity, and hope for the future.

What we have tried to develop in the last two chapters addresses Postman's concerns. We have attempted to show that *being a blessing as a stranger* and *practicing hospitality to the stranger* are rooted in an overarching narrative central to the biblical message and the Christian life. We believe these ideals can provide purpose for and meaning in the learning of a new language. They offer criteria and guidance when curricular and pedagogical decisions have to be made for the foreign language classroom.

In a TV interview on the topic of southern hospitality during the

63. Gundry-Volf and Volf, 1997.
64. Volf, 1996, 213.
65. Postman, 1995, 5.

1996 Olympic Games in Atlanta, an African-American woman talked about how much she enjoyed welcoming and helping people from many different nations who came to the games. She concluded her comments by saying, "I think my arms have become wider." We do not know whether this woman spoke with any of the foreign visitors in their own language; yet, in the process of figuratively, and maybe literally, embracing total strangers, something happened: the arms of her heart grew wider.

What if students, after having studied Spanish, French, German, or Chinese in school or at a college or university, could say, "My heart, my mind, my arms have become wider. Through cross-cultural encounters I have learned to listen to God's call to welcome and embrace what was foreign to me, and it has made me a richer person, a person ready to share that richness with others"? Or, echoing the refrain from the college student's diary quoted at the conclusion of chapter 4, "I have become a little bit Dominican"?

CHAPTER SIX

For Profit, Pleasure, and Power?

The time: several years ago. The setting: a sunny summer afternoon in a small town in England. I (David Smith) am teaching German (or at least so I fondly believe) to a class of sixteen-year-old students in a state-maintained school. Some sadistic genius has designed our classroom for maximum exposure to the afternoon sun and minimum ventilation. It is warm and the class is sluggish.

One of my students, let's call her Cheryl, has her birthday today and is even less motivated and less cooperative than usual. She has received from a male admirer a gift of some rather striking bright red satin lingerie, which she holds up for those behind her to see. Surprisingly enough, this display proves to be somewhat distracting to the predominantly male rear third of the class, and I ask her to put it away. Her countermove is to ask the age-old question: "Sir, why do I have to learn German? I'm leaving school in a few months and I've already got a job at the corner shop; how many Germans do you think I'm going to serve?"

Once again I find myself on the defensive. Cheryl has not only asked *that question;* she has even preempted the work-hard-now-and-you'll-get-a-job-later reply. Why indeed? Why struggle to teach a foreign language to members of a community that exhibits so little interest in it? Instead of trying to teach it to all students, why not simply send those who need a foreign language for specific purposes to specialized language schools? Feeling my grip on the situation to be in danger of slipping, I go for the because-you're-in-my-classroom-and-I'm-in-charge ploy. Cheryl subsides into inactivity, and I'm left again with a feeling of dissatisfaction, knowing that I have not answered the question. I evaded it.

Naturally, students are not the only ones who challenge foreign language instructors to justify what they are doing. Unlike, for example, teachers of mathematics, foreign language educators rarely have the luxury of simply taking for granted that their subject is a necessary and secure element in the curriculum. The traditional belief that foreign language learning was justified because it developed mental discipline and cognitive agility has long since eroded. Since then an uneasy discussion has been under way as to what else foreign language learning might be good for. The psychological threshold provided by the new millennium has only intensified the discussion.[1] Foreign language educators find themselves repeatedly having to make a case to colleagues, parents, and students for what they have to offer.

In the last two chapters we proposed an overarching rationale for foreign language education that is grounded in the Christian themes we explored in chapter 1. This rationale focuses on our attitudes to difference, our ability to be open to others, and the ethical dimension of our relationships with strangers.

It also became clear toward the end of chapter 5 that none of the goals we suggest can be taken for granted. The document we cited from Nazi Germany shows that it is eminently possible to engage in learning other languages and cultures without love, without the desire to bring blessing or to offer hospitality. There is no automatically guaranteed connection between simply learning something of another language or culture and relating ethically to that culture. Nor should Nazi Germany be thought of as an isolated example in this connection. Are not linguistic and cross-cultural skills often used today mainly for propaganda or raw economic exploitation? Even the motives for learning the language and culture of others can be basically self-centered.

With this basic awareness in mind, the present chapter will explore a range of motivations commonly advanced for foreign language education. Our intention here is not to simply pit the rationale we have outlined against its alternatives, and then to argue that the latter are wrong. Instead, we will suggest that each motivation surveyed needs to be placed in the kind of broader ethical context we have sketched if it is to heed the biblical

---

1. See, e.g., Matter, 1992; Rivers, 1993; G. R. Tucker, 1993.

call to love the stranger. Rather than rejecting these justifications outright, we will suggest that, while all of them have a measure of validity, each also is open to Christian objections if it becomes the overarching justification for a foreign language program and is not responsive to the more basic call to love our neighbor.

Three Basic Questions

We will respond to various notions of what foreign language education is all about with three simple assumptions and three related questions in mind. The first assumption is that, as we go about our educational tasks, we work with an implicit or explicit picture of the kind of person we would like to see leave our classroom. We seek to have some effect, however slight, on the learners who pass through our care; we want them to develop in a certain direction. The first question, then, is this: What kinds of persons do the proponents of varying motives for doing foreign language learning want their students to become?

Our second assumption is that it is not adequate to view language learning simply as a self-enclosed end in itself, something that can take place without reference to an outside world or to the speakers of the language studied. As foreign language educators, we are, among other things, enabling learners to come into some kind of relationship with speakers of the target language. The second question, then, is: What kind of relationship to members of the target culture do advocates of these different motives have in mind?

Our third assumption is that sharing a world with fellow humans who are created in God's image and who are linguistically and culturally diverse has something to do with the reason for making foreign language learning part of education. The time-honored human habit of dividing the world into members of our culture on the one hand, and lesser beings of inferior importance on the other, is not, as we have seen, consonant with a Christian worldview. This leads to the third question: Does the motive under consideration honor the stranger as one created in God's image, as one who hopes, thinks, suffers, trusts, and weeps, and whose sighs and laughter are just as audible to God as our own?

These three simple questions will constitute a basic yardstick against which we will assess the strengths and weaknesses of various motives for foreign language education. To repeat: What kind of person does each motive aim to engender? What kind of relationship to the foreign culture and its speakers does it promote? Does it do justice to the stranger as an equal, made in God's image?

The Entrepreneur

The first kind of foreign language graduate we will consider is the entrepreneur, a familiar figure on the contemporary scene.[2] A recent article by G. Richard Tucker titled "Language Learning for the Twenty-First Century" clearly illustrates some of the main features of the entrepreneurial rationale for foreign language instruction.[3]

While Tucker laments the pervasive monolingualism of English-speaking North America and the modest success of its efforts at foreign language education, the future, he insists, looks bright. The signing of the North American Free Trade Agreement (NAFTA) will, in his view, provide powerful social and economic incentives for governments, parents, and students to take foreign language learning seriously. As a result, they will invest more resources in language teaching, will develop new learning technologies, will carry out more research, and thus will produce a workforce with greatly enhanced international competence. Given this promising new situation, every language teacher, it seems, will sit under her own vine and fig tree.

The central purpose of language learning in this heady vision is quite clear: to give the workforce the essential skills for grasping new economic opportunities for both the individual and the nation. Equipped with the necessary language tools, workers will be able to secure jobs and conduct business more efficiently and profitably than ever before. Quite obviously, the kind of teaching and learning implied by this view focuses on the "proficiency" and "competence" that can lead to "efficient exchange" between nations.[4] It is clear, given these objectives, that pragmatic economic values

2. An earlier version of the material in this chapter followed Todorov in referring to the "profiteer" in this connection (Todorov, 1993). Despite the qualifications that were added, some took this to reflect a view of all economic activity as sordid. Such a view is far from our intentions.

3. Tucker, 1993.

4. Tucker, 1993, 166-67.

will assume the leading role in shaping the content and delivery of the foreign language curriculum.

Tucker's article is an example of what one might call the "any messiah will do" syndrome. The core of his argument seems to be concerned less with pedagogical matters than with the idea that economic changes will finally give status and recognition, and therefore resources, to foreign language learning. Foreign language educators, wearied by the long struggle to find ways of convincing an uninterested, monolingual society that their beleaguered corner of the educational enterprise is worthwhile, now will find signs of hope in economic developments that presumably will bring nations closer together. Tucker also is convinced that "the cumulative impact of international political and economic developments during the last several years will at long last motivate parents, educators, and policy makers to explore the development and implementation of innovative language education programmes."[5]

It is this promise of new, improved programs that most likely makes the entrepreneurial approach appealing to foreign language educators. Not that teachers, by and large, actually believe that the fundamental purpose of what they do is to be found in its economic value; it is rather that traditional, more idealistic motivations seem to cut little ice with parents and learners, not to mention governments. With the arrival of NAFTA, the European Community (which has generated identical rhetoric on the other side of the Atlantic), or any other move toward economic integration across national borders, a messiah appears to have come. Finally we have a tool for persuading parents to urge their offspring to enroll in our courses. Finally our students have a good reason to work hard at them.

We do not suggest that the economic motivation for language learning is wrong, or even base and ignoble, compared to the lofty benefits of a liberal arts education. Economic well-being is important, and a Platonic disdain for honest labor is far from Christian. Work is a good and necessary part of life before God, not a kind of accidental cancer on creation, and the ability to earn a living from acquired skills surely is an important and desirable outcome of foreign language study. The entrepreneurial motivation is an important aspect of foreign language education.

But our acceptance comes with qualifications, for such a motivation confronts us with a key question we raised at the beginning of this chapter.

---

5. Tucker, 1993, 167.

What kind of relationship with speakers of the target language is implied in this entrepreneurial justification for language learning?

Most proponents of this view see this relationship as basically competitive. Tucker, for instance, claims we need foreign language competence so we can "compete effectively in the commercial world of the 21st century."[6] Given this perspective, cultural and sociolinguistic understanding becomes a kind of intelligence gathering that allows us to keep pace with competitors. After all, if we fall behind, we jeopardize the potential profit to be gained in our dealings with the other. Children are sometimes exposed to this competitive imperative already at an early age: a publicity brochure for a BBC French course for children of preschool age to twelve proclaims that "in the international world our children will compete in . . . a second language will be essential. Vital for competing with polished peers."[7]

However, business activity can and should take place within the horizons of ethical concern for the well-being of everyone and everything concerned: the workforce, the community, the trading partner, and the environment. Cross-cultural business encounters should be informed by the drive not only to compete but also to serve. Yet can we even imagine an official document encouraging foreign language study primarily so that we can better attend to the needs of others, and only secondarily because it will increase our ability to meet our own economic needs?

This deeper concern is often missing in rhetoric that pictures the one whose language we are learning either as an economic resource (cheap labor or potential consumer in overseas markets) or as a competitor. All too often champions of the entrepreneurial position give the impression that ultimately we learn foreign languages in order to be set over against the other as rivals. What place is left for humility, service, or compassion in a world where the most proficient make the greatest profit?

In short, the entrepreneur has a valued place, but cannot furnish the overall guiding vision for foreign language education.

6. Tucker, 1993, 166.
7. BBC leaflet, not dated.

The Persuader

This focus on business negotiations leads us to the persuader, who reaps from language study an increased ability to convince others to adopt a particular point of view. This persuasive intent may, of course, have economic grounds, as when one engages in business negotiations, but it might also be motivated by a range of other reasons, as can be seen in the following excerpt from a U.S. government document titled "Strength through Wisdom: A Critique of U.S. Capability." This report of the President's Commission on Foreign Languages and International Studies deplores the "scandalous incompetence" of Americans and states:

> Nothing less is at issue than the nation's security. At a time when the resurgent forces of nationalism and of ethnic and linguistic consciousness so directly affect global realities, the United States requires far more reliable capacities to communicate with its allies, analyze the behavior of potential adversaries, and earn the trust and sympathies of the uncommitted. . . . In our schools and colleges as well as in our public media of communications, and in the everyday dialogue within our communities, the situation cries out for a better comprehension of our place and our potential in a world that, though it still expects much from America, no longer takes American supremacy for granted. . . . The President's commission believes that our lack of foreign language competence diminishes our capabilities in diplomacy, in foreign trade, and in citizen comprehension of the world in which we live and compete.[8]

The issue here is clearly broader than economic gain; it now includes a focus on winning others over, or being forearmed in the face of their hostility. Central to the document's concern is the need to win allies and maintain a position of strength and security in a threatening international environment. In this context, cultural and rhetorical dimensions of language learning take on greater importance than they had for the entrepreneur, but once again we see the other cast as a rival — albeit now for ideological reasons, and not on economic grounds. The rationale for learning a language is either to persuade the other to assimilate and support one's own ideas or to gain security in the face of the other, who is considered a threat.

8. Perkins, 1980, 11-12.

111

It would, however, be a mistake to see the persuader in a negative light only. After all, it is naive to suggest that we live in a world where it never will be necessary or appropriate to convince other peoples or individuals to change their course of action. One need not believe in American supremacy — or identify the American way of life with the kingdom of God — to recognize that persuasion has its rightful place in both international and interpersonal relations.

Moreover, learning a foreign language for the purpose of converting unbelievers may well be the most popular rationale for many Christian educators. Thus, training for evangelism, which involves persuading others that the gospel is true, is frequently offered as a central justification for language study in Christian schools. Although we do not believe this motive provides the most basic reason for foreign language learning, we find it valid, grounded, as it is, in the long history of language education and Christian mission, a theme we surveyed in chapter 2. Though secularists may frown at the very thought, we find nothing odd or inappropriate in seeking to communicate to others a truth that has set us free. We are convinced that, in this context too, persuasion has its rightful place.

However, the goal of effective persuasion, when taken as the dominant motif, can very easily lead to relationships based on domination. When such a dynamic prevails, one side arrogantly asserts that it alone has the truth and the other is totally bereft of it — which means in turn that the other, not oneself, must undergo the humbling process of learning.[9] Christian missionary endeavor itself has been far from immune to this temptation, which runs directly counter to the idea of hospitality. In short, we suggest that an interest in persuasion, though a valid ground for language learning, can become dangerous if taken as the overarching metaphor outside of a context of love for others.

The Connoisseur

The connoisseur, unlike the entrepreneur or the persuader, is not bent on material gain or personal power. Instead, connoisseurs are enthusiasts seeking spiritual edification, that elevation of the soul that comes with the mastery of another language and the experience of another culture. Their

9. Compare our discussion of Paul's comments from 1 Corinthians 14 in chap. 1.

112

basic ground for language learning is humanistic, a term encompassing at least two emphases: the cognitive-cultural and the affective.

The first emphasis draws on the venerable tradition of humanistic learning, the ennobling contact with all that is highest and best in the manifold intellectual and cultural traditions of humankind. Whether we think of Rabelais, Rilke, or Calderon; French cheeses or Spanish wines; German castles or Mayan ruins, this humanistic motif thrives on immersion in the riches of the foreign culture. Gaining these riches is what gives learning a foreign language its impetus and goal. I (David Smith) know a connoisseur, a medical doctor by profession, who once seriously propounded to me his theory that every now and then, when the human race is in danger of sinking into cultural degeneracy, God sends us a genius like Jesus, Michelangelo, or Goethe to call us back to the true life of high culture. Foreign language instruction for this kind of connoisseur is the doorway to ennobling experiences culled from the world's cultures, and thus a part of education into true humanity.

The second variety of connoisseur, with roots in humanistic psychology, focuses more on the inner enrichment one can achieve through self-expression in the new language. As Gertrude Moskowitz puts it, "Some of the purposes of using humanistic communication activities to teach foreign languages are to improve self-esteem, to develop positive thinking, to increase self-understanding, to build greater closeness among students, and to discover the strengths and goodness in oneself and one's classmates."[10] Here true riches are found not abroad, but within. Foreign language study is a pathway to self-discovery and self-esteem, a new tool each individual can use to explore his or her inner world. Thus, the connoisseur of emotional experience joins the connoisseur of cultural experience.

It seems at first blush that the culture-loving connoisseur may represent a more humane emphasis than either the entrepreneur or the persuader. Here is someone genuinely interested in the foreign other. Instead of wanting to make a profit from the other or replace the other's ideas with her own, this connoisseur is quite prepared to be enriched by the foreigner. Her basic attitude is one of appreciation, and often she is motivated to move beyond dilettantism to a serious engagement with another culture.

There is something appealing about the second type of connoisseur as well, and the focus he represents also has a certain measure of validity.

10. Moskowitz, 1982, 20.

After all, self-discovery surely is an important part of learning, and for many students who come from a variety of different cultural backgrounds, such self-discovery may well involve exploration of another language and culture. While Christians will question Moskowitz's contention that foreign language study can lead to a discovery of one's own innate "goodness," surely broadening personal horizons and gaining self-confidence and self-knowledge are important goals of language instruction.

Despite their unquestionable value, however, neither set of humanistic emphases represented by our two types of connoisseurs adequately addresses the critical issue of relationship. Even though either of these connoisseurs might and often does establish good relationships with members of the target culture, building such relationships does not seem to be a central educational objective in this humanistic view of language study. Instead, its primary emphasis seems to be on the personal experience and personal gain of the individual learner.

That emphasis prompts several questions. Is the culture-loving connoisseur of the first variety as eager to explore the street-level hopes and tragedies of the foreign country as he is to revel in its highbrow treasures? Is he willing to learn about the world of the Algerian immigrant in Paris, the unemployed Turk in Germany, and the exploited miner in Chile — or do concerts, poetry, and art museums claim virtually all of his time and interest?

And what about our second type of connoisseur? Is the self-actualizing learner of the humanistic classroom as willing to share the challenging burdens borne by speakers of the target language as she is to explore her own emotional well-being? If so, why do descriptions of such classrooms so often stress the student's voyage of inner discovery while paying little attention to the world outside?[11]

In sum, we deeply appreciate the connoisseur's delight in the joys of exploring a new language and culture. However, where this vision is dominant, there is a danger that the basic attitude will still be one of profiting from the other. The basic attitude pervading the connoisseur's language study will be akin to that of the entrepreneur, for both are interested in personal profit. The only question is whether that profit will be measured by intellectual, cultural, or emotional gain, or in the growth of a bank account or stock portfolio. For the connoisseur, the other may basically be a

---

11. See Smith, 1997c.

provider of gratifying or edifying experiences. The central emphasis on self-enrichment may result in little more than a kind of intellectual or emotional tourism, rather than a genuine concern for the other.

The Tourist

There is, of course, a brand of tourism much more popular than the one the sophisticated connoisseur practices, a tourism that has spawned a whole industry of "learn Spanish in two days or your money back"–type publications. In our judgment, this second brand of tourism too, like that of the connoisseur, ought not be dismissed. After all, it will be as tourists that most language learners make their first real forays into cross-cultural communication.

Still, when compared to the serious matters of making money, winning arguments, and attaining true humanity, the concerns of the tourist seem much more casual — and often quite superficial. Todorov describes the tourist as "a visitor in a hurry who prefers monuments to human beings."[12] Because vacations are short and getting to know people takes time, the typical tourist is drawn by the sights, curiosities, and local color that can be captured on film for later digestion. The language requirements for these quick visits tend to be restricted to the demands of small-scale transactions and activities that smooth one's path in the foreign country: booking into hotels, tipping waiters, buying pizza and cokes, reading road signs, and cashing traveler's checks.

Although foreign language proponents sometimes advance tourism as a reason for language learning, it rarely takes center stage in educational discussions. The reasons for the reluctance to make it central are not hard to find. To be sure, tourism is a normal, valid activity, and there is nothing wrong with relaxation in the midst of the serious business of life. Seeing parts of the world that lie beyond our everyday horizons and mingling with people we would not normally encounter can in itself bring significant pleasure and enrichment. Not infrequently, the tourist's first stay in a country is the beginning of a much deeper connection to, appreciation of, and even love for the foreign culture and its people.

Despite the enjoyment tourism affords, however, it is quite another question whether concern for people's pleasure in their leisure time pro-

12. Todorov, 1993, 342.

vides adequate justification for investing the nation's time and money in foreign language programs, especially if the high-speed, low-cost courses sold on the pages of glossy magazines are as effective as they claim to be. If these courses do in fact deliver what they promise, it would be far less bother to simply provide them free of charge, and then allow students to learn on their own the language they will need on their vacation.

Curiously enough, despite teachers' reluctance to appeal to tourism as a ground for language learning, its influence in foreign language curricula is obvious. Although foreign language study is most often justified in public discussion in terms of the production of entrepreneurs, many curricular materials seem designed in the main to produce tourists. Thus students often spend a great deal of time learning how to ask questions like "How do I get to the bus station?" or "Do you have a single room for three nights?" or "How much are chicken and fries?" In short, many texts seem bent on teaching students what one colleague once cynically referred to as "how to fill your belly abroad."

This restricted orientation to the needs of tourists also falls short in another regard: it serves to reinforce the predominance of certain languages over others. For example, serious British tourists will tend to learn French and Spanish, languages useful to them while on holiday, but not Hindi or Urdu, even though a large Indian or Pakistani immigrant population may be living in their own immediate neighborhood.

Finally, however, if we are to properly analyze tourism as a justification for language learning, we must once again deal with the key issue of relationship. What is the tourist's basic relationship to the stranger?

Tourism, like business, is ultimately shaped by our attitudes toward others. It can be a springboard to deeper exploration and connection, but it can just as easily become one more arena for the expression of self-centeredness. Todorov speaks to this point in his remarks about "impressionists," whom he defines as highly perfected tourists whose first interest is in "the impressions that countries or human beings leave with them, not the countries or the peoples themselves."[13] While the impressionist may exhibit interest or even wonder when face-to-face with the foreign culture, "he himself," Todorov insists, "remains the sole subject of the experience."[14]

13. Todorov, 1993, 345.
14. Todorov, 1993, 345.

Zygmunt Bauman concurs with Todorov, pointing out that, for many tourists, everything foreign is expected to remain obediently unthreatening, and that the tourist industry caters to the needs of visitors by providing a harmless, pleasurable experience:

> In the tourist's world, the strange is tame, domesticated and no more frightens; shocks come in a package deal with safety. This makes the world seem infinitely gentle, obedient to the tourist's wishes and whims, ready to oblige; but also a do-it-yourself world, pleasingly pliable, kneaded by the tourist's desire, made and remade with one purpose in mind — to excite, please and amuse. There is no other purpose to justify the presence of that world and the tourist's presence in it.[15]

This mentality frequently is accompanied by an unconcealed resistance to what is foreign. Thus many British visitors to Spain are happy to enjoy the sights and the sun as long as the hotel serves fish-and-chips and they don't have to interact too much with Spaniards who can't speak their language.

In summary, tourism may be a pleasant and valuable pastime, but by itself it will not suffice as a primary rationale for learning a foreign language.

The Escapologist

Compared to tourists who will only risk an occasional foray into the unknown before returning to the comforting familiarity of a home they never entirely left behind, escapologists have a radically different goal. For them, foreign language learning is a jailbreak out of what Eric Hawkins calls the "monolingual prison" of ignorance and prejudice.[16] Escapologists see freedom and "the autonomy of the individual"[17] as the purpose of education. What we encounter in this view is a particular vision of liberal education in which individual emancipation is a primary goal, and cultural locatedness is construed as an obstacle to achieving that goal.

---

15. Bauman, 1995, 96.
16. Hawkins, 1989, 29.
17. Hawkins, 1989, 29.

The escapologist's approach points to the fact that we all grow up with the limitations imposed on us by having been socialized into a particular community, a particular set of values, a particular language. Achieving rational autonomy requires transcending those limitations, escaping from our cultural straitjacket, and setting out for more universal realms. According to Hawkins, "the person who has never ventured outside his own language is incapable even of realizing how parochial he is — just as the earthbound traveler who has never journeyed into space takes the pull of gravity for granted as an unalterable part of the scheme of things."[18] Schooling can offer some compensation for what Hawkins refers to as the learner's draw in "the great parental lottery," and can begin to lead the student toward a more critical and rational perspective.[19]

Foreign language learning is thus important, Hawkins argues, because "perhaps the best apprenticeship for wisdom is practice in making apt comparisons. Informed choice . . . builds on apt comparison and is the essence of judgment."[20] Montaigne, writing in a similar vein, once advocated that we "rub and polish our brains by contact with those of others,"[21] a recommendation in tune with Hawkins's argument. In contrast to that of the connoisseur, the escapologist's goal is not so much to immerse himself in another culture as to gain a loftier vantage point from which his own vision is less clouded by the limitations of language and culture.

The pattern of our critique is probably familiar by now. This justification, like the others surveyed, represents a partial truth in need of a wider ethical context. There clearly is much good in the claim that looking through more than one window on the world can bring a broadened vision and a more informed capacity for judgment.

However, the ideal the escapologist espouses is often basically individualistic; its goal is not connection with others, but enhanced autonomy for oneself. Others are important not for their own sake, or for the perspectives they bring, but for the added leverage they give in a personal quest for autonomy. The escapologist gives the impression he or she is looking for freedom from outside shackles, not for the bonds of committed relationship.

18. Hawkins, 1989, 32.
19. Hawkins, 1989, 30.
20. Hawkins, 1989, 30.
21. Cited in Todorov, 1993, 351.

The Revolutionary

The revolutionary can perhaps be seen as an escapologist with postmodern leanings. The revolutionary finds the purpose of foreign language learning in its contribution to a critical pedagogy that can free learners from the dominant discourse of their community. Learners are to become actively critical of the values and assumptions that surround them, not least those of the entrepreneur and persuader.[22]

At the same time, the revolutionary is skeptical about the achievement of rational autonomy, one of the escapologist's goals, since she is acutely aware of the cultural and political meanings that not only shape us from without but are part of our own inner world. The very words we utter are steeped in the formative power of our cultural context; we have, after all, learned them from others and taken over the meanings assigned them by others. To the revolutionary, life in an ideologically laden world is a continuing fight to somehow find and establish one's own voice in a language already charged with socially created meanings.

Thus for Claire Kramsch's critical foreign language pedagogy (discussed further in chapter 9), the classroom is a place of struggle and power games, of tension between the individual voice, the voices of one's culture, and the voices of the foreign culture. As she puts it, "the goal is not a balance of opposites, or a moderate pluralism of opinions, but a paradoxical, irreducible confrontation that may change one in the process."[23] This process of confrontation with conflicting voices is to bring about conscientization, the process of making learners aware of the dominant assumptions of their native culture so that they can begin to critique and transform its values.[24]

To be sure, Kramsch notes, the learners will always remain outsiders to the foreign culture, since their knowledge will inevitably be colored by the shaping force of their own cultural context. The God's-eye-view is forever out of reach. Nevertheless, an encounter with another culture may provide enough gravitational pull, or rather enough unsettling conflict of perspectives, to distance students sufficiently from their own culture, to make them feel a little less at home in the world they have always taken for

---

22. Cf. Kramsch, 1986.
23. Kramsch, 1993, 231.
24. See Freire, 1996.

granted. Learners are thus left in a "third place" between cultures, like migrants with no certain home.[25]

Kramsch's work is insightful and thought provoking, and we warmly affirm certain of its emphases. For example, gaining a critical perspective on the values of the culture that surrounds us is one of the aims of Christian education, which seeks to avoid being conformed "to the pattern of this world."[26] We discussed in chapter 1 some of the implications of the fall for our attitude to cultural diversity. One such implication is that we should not feel totally at home in a culture that contains evil as well as good, and that we may need to be confronted with the perspectives of outsiders in order to see ourselves in a more critical light. And in chapter 5 we discussed the salutary educational potential of culture clashes that the student encounters as a stranger.

In terms of relationship to the other, however, it is not clear that the revolutionary's point of view signifies real progress. Kramsch presents communication as a matter of irreducible conflict, and the foreign culture, as she sees it, seems to provide raw material for critical pedagogical purposes having to do primarily with the transformation of one's own culture. Moments of genuine connection with others do occur, but the "life-changing dialogues" she describes are "miracles," "leaps of faith," "epiphanies," and therefore beyond the reach of pedagogical processes.[27]

The picture Kramsch paints seems somewhat reminiscent of an eccentric record collector interviewed a few years ago on TV, whose favorite pastime was playing five or six records simultaneously. He admitted that the result was mostly cacophony, but described with enthusiasm the rare but beautiful moments of harmony that emerged from time to time.

In summary, it seems to us that, if we use a model of communication in which our voices are in irreducible conflict with the voices of others and confrontation is both method and goal, love for our neighbor is threatened. As we view it, the danger inherent in the revolutionary's position is that the other will simply get a supporting role in the power struggles that are somehow to bring about liberation from and for our own culture. As we have previously indicated, we see the role of the other in significantly different terms.

25. Kramsch, 1993, 233-57; for more detailed discussion see Smith, 1997b.
26. Rom. 12:2.
27. Kramsch, 1993, 2; Kramsch, 1995d, x.

Profit, Pleasure, and Power

No doubt much more could and should be said about each of these visions of foreign language education, and perhaps others could be added. For now, however, enough ground has been covered for us to make two general observations.

First, like most educational paradigms, these six alternative views are rarely found in pure, mutually exclusive form in classrooms. Educational reality is usually more of a mix, with discernible dominant tendencies. We surmise that most teachers entered the profession as connoisseurs, while many of the textbooks they use seem designed for tourists. When challenged by students and parents, on the other hand, they frequently appeal to the motives of the entrepreneur. Perhaps most teachers at present are connoisseurs claiming to train entrepreneurs — and in fact producing tourists.

Second, as we have been careful to point out, each orientation we have examined has hold of some part of the truth. Each carries some validity in the total endeavor of foreign language education. Nowhere have we claimed that the entrepreneur, the persuader, the connoisseur, the tourist, the escapologist, and the revolutionary will never achieve good relationships with speakers of the target language. An educational framework, in and of itself, can neither guarantee good relationships nor exclude their possibility.

We do, however, believe that where any one of these six models becomes the dominant motivation for a program of foreign language education, there is a built-in drift toward certain modes of relating to others. These modes can be described in summary as having to do with profit, pleasure, and power. We learn a foreign language in order to *profit* from it, whether by getting ahead in the job market, by competing more successfully in business, or by making intellectual and cultural gains. We learn a foreign language for our *pleasure,* whether in discovering our self-worth and growing in confidence, or enjoying a poem, a meal, or a stroll through an open market. We learn a foreign language for *power,* be it to persuade others to become like us or to escape or transform the confines of our upbringing.

Each of these motivations carries some validity. What is missing in all of them, however, is a strongly or overtly developed concern for the speakers of the other language as *people,* valuable in themselves. As we try

121

to justify learning to know other languages and cultures in a context where the appeal is constantly made to basically selfish motives, it is tempting to fall into the same pattern. All too easily we can find ourselves in the situation described by Todorov, where, in spite of all the apparent interest we might show in other languages and cultures, "the Other is caught up in a pragmatic relation; he is never the goal of the relation."[28]

Therefore, we are convinced that, if these various goals of foreign language learning are to contribute to the total educational effort in a constructive way, they must be rooted in the kind of wider vision we are proposing in this book. The spirit that informs these goals matters a great deal.

The callings to be a gracious host and a sensitive stranger point us beyond profit, pleasure, and power, while not canceling them out. If business interactions and tourist visits are carried out within an ethical context at whose heart are a concern for the well-being of the other and a desire to leave behind a blessing, then the other is no longer simply a rival or an object. If learning the other's language and gaining breadth of cultural knowledge are oriented toward being able to hear the other's stories, and giving the other space to be human, then our efforts are grounded in a purpose beyond self-enrichment. If we obey the call to seek our neighbor's good, we will use power to build up the other rather than dominate him — or to enhance our own self-empowerment. If heeded, the biblical call to bring blessing as a stranger and to practice hospitality could place the familiar justifications for foreign language education in a new and more life-giving light and could provide a challenging corrective to our tendency to place learning about others in the service of self.

It should be clear by now that we are not working from a naive assumption that an extended experience of foreign language learning will of itself produce enlightened peacemakers with open hearts toward the stranger. Student attitudes can be deeply ingrained and very resistant to change.

That fact should not deter us, however. After all, less controversial goals, such as fluency or accuracy, face similar challenges. Although our best efforts to achieve these objectives do not unfailingly turn every student into a fluent, accurate user of the target language, we do not therefore write these goals off as hopeless. Instead, we engage in ongoing discussion,

28. Todorov, 1993, 343.

research, and revision to find out whether there are better ways of achieving them than those we currently use.

When we consider affecting attitudes toward the stranger, it seems that the most helpful question we can ask is not "Will this strategy prove to be a holy grail that transforms all of my students?" — for it won't. We should rather ask, "What kinds of pedagogical choices will contribute most toward achieving the goals of being a good host or stranger, and which choices, however well entrenched and familiar, are likely to subvert them?" While pedagogy alone will not guarantee Christlikeness, it can constitute either a significant encouragement or a hindrance in our classroom efforts to work toward it. Our responsibility is to determine which of these two results our teaching strategies produce.

It is important to note that each of the six motivations sketched above has left its imprint on foreign language education. Each has led to distinctive choices and priorities among the wide range of possible educational contents and instructional strategies. Thus the tourism emphasis has focused on short exchanges of information and economic transactions, and the interests of the connoisseur center on literature or the language of emotional self-expression. Followers of humanistic and critical pedagogy also have developed markedly different ways of teaching. It seems to us to follow quite naturally that, in a similar way, a focus on our callings as strangers and hosts could also leave a particular imprint and could lead to distinctive educational practice.

This connection between basic visions of the meaning and purpose of foreign language education and the content and pedagogical strategies employed will be the focus of Part III. In that final part of our study we will explore the implications of the perspective we have proposed for course content and for pedagogy. We will use case studies of the ways emphasis on the connoisseur and the revolutionary have shaped pedagogy to investigate whether our Christian approach might make any difference in the day-to-day practices of the classroom. Finally, we will offer some examples of teaching activities designed with Christian emphases in mind.

Before we look in more detail at classroom practice, though, a final anecdote may help show the importance of attending to the basic perspectives on the world that shape our teaching.

A number of years ago, I (David Smith) became friends with Jed, who had begun attending my church. His house was an interesting experience: its downstairs rooms were a combination of motorcycle workshop and bikers' meeting place. On the occasions we met there for prayer and Bible study, various friends of Jed would drop by.

One particular evening we were joined by a wiry youth who introduced himself as Sprog. Sprog was dressed from head to foot in a fetching combination of khaki and motor oil. He was a thoughtful conversation partner. As we chatted, we got onto the subject of schools.

Sprog did not have particularly fond memories of his school days, which had been prematurely interrupted when he was expelled. He summarized his educational experience in approximately the following words: "The teachers taught me that life was all about the survival of the fittest, but when I stole stuff from the stockroom they threw me out."

I would hazard a guess that teaching "survival of the fittest" did not appear in the mission statement of Sprog's school. I don't know whether any of his teachers ever used the term as such. But his lasting memory was of an education that, whether implicitly or explicitly, taught him that life was a competition to get ahead. He saw it as quite inconsistent that he should then be penalized for behaving accordingly.

Sprog's analysis of his experience suggests that the overarching ethos we set for educational practice is of considerable importance, and that it might teach more than we think. It suggests that guiding goals do make a difference.

Was Sprog right?

PART III

PRACTICE:
IMPLICATIONS FOR THE CLASSROOM

CHAPTER SEVEN

Images of Others, Images of God:
The Content of the Foreign Language Course

When we teach, we are always implicated in the construction of
a horizon of possibility for ourselves, our students and our
communities.

Roger Simon

*Imagine you are a teenage Martian attending the Martian equivalent of a
school. You have just begun to learn about Earth and its inhabitants, and
your teacher has given you some homework. You are to gather information
and then write a description of what a human being is, and what he or she
typically does. You train your transporter beam on planet Earth, and by some
strange quirk of fate all it is able to pick up is a textbook from a foreign language course. This text will have to form the basis of your essay. What could
you be expected to glean from it? What are you likely to write?*

*   *   *

This scenario may belong to the realm of science fiction, but the issue it
highlights is very down-to-earth. Which image of the stranger does the
content of our foreign language course present? What picture of the foreign culture do learners get from the materials they use in language class?

These questions are related to a basic theme we have been following

127

throughout this study. Christians believe all humans are made in the image of God. Strangers, too, have lives shot through with spiritual and moral significance. Strangers, too, are creative, reflective, and sinful; they wrestle with the challenge of making responsible choices; they too experience the blessings and sufferings of a fallen world.

Do our educational materials reflect this basic reality? Are the strangers who walk the pages of the textbook or speak from the cassette or television screen in our classroom merely consumers with shallowly materialistic agendas, or do they hope, fear, suffer, rejoice, believe, or pray like the rest of us? In sum, what vision of life is conveyed by the images of the stranger found in our language lessons?

These concerns are related to more established questions we commonly ask of educational materials, particularly about their portrayal of gender, ethnic groups, and socioeconomic classes. Researchers continue to fine-tune their methods of analysis in order to detect and measure biased representations in each of these areas.[1] Texts that exclude certain perspectives are routinely criticized for their potential to distort the vision of learners by presenting a restricted, and therefore skewed, picture of the world. Christian educators also have begun, at least on a limited scale, the same kind of analysis, asking not merely what the texts claim to teach, but also about other messages they convey by their choice and organization of materials and their presentation of subject matter.[2]

Inquiring into the general view of the world implied in a textbook is particularly pertinent in the foreign language classroom. As learners begin to explore a foreign language and culture, they encounter familiar areas of learning in a new context. They learn to tell time anew. They learn again about numbers, houses, transportation, and food. They learn new forms of personal interaction, new norms for carrying on conversations. They encounter others they have not met before and observe various aspects of their way of life. Having already learned an immense amount about their own social world, they now begin to explore various aspects of the new culture of the stranger.

However, course materials often focus more on the needs of the visiting tourist than on the world of the stranger. Often the tourist's world is defined by immediate survival requirements, leisure activities, and prag-

1. Cf., e.g., Rifkin, 1998.
2. E.g., Van Brummelen, 1994a.

128

matic transactions: paying for services, asking for directions, securing help in case of emergency, and the like. It is a world that is often virtually bereft of any spiritual significance.[3]

A telling example of this tourist approach appears in the eighth lesson of the German college textbook *Modern German*.[4] The reading selection "Besuch in Mainz" (visit in Mainz) describes how American college-age students get a room, orient themselves to the city, and wander the streets of Mainz for an afternoon. Led by an imaginary tour guide, they pass the castle, the cathedral, and several museums without showing interest in these places or the desire to enter any of them. After dinner they go to a movie. The next day they change traveler's checks in a bank, shop in various big department stores, and write postcards home. The following morning they are off again by train. During this day-and-a-half stay they have beer or coffee at the railway station, dinner and wine in some hotel, and a meal in a Yugoslavian restaurant. Unfortunately, however, the text says nothing about the importance of Mainz today; ignores its most famous citizen, Gutenberg; and gives no hint of the religious and political significance of the city during the past two thousand years. Contact between the travelers and the citizens of Mainz is limited to inquiries about hotels, directions, restaurants, and shopping places. One wonders how these American students are enriched by staying in Mainz and what they will write home about the significance of their stay in this city.

The reading section "Besuch in Mainz" does not model how one is to be a good stranger in a foreign country. It is not conducive to promoting the basic goals of foreign language education we developed in Part II. To be sure, the student visitors to Mainz are learning some practical skills tourists need, but they dispense very poorly, if at all, the gifts strangers can

---

3. Cf. Byram, 1989, 8-23. Byram comments that due to the emphasis on transactional skills, "the development of pupils' personality, their capacity for empathy, their understanding of others' experience, emotions and rationality are in danger of being ignored" (13). We need reminding, he urges, that "there are other needs which must not be forgotten, arising from the fact that we are teaching children and contributing to their education" (12). Neuner and Hunfeld suggest that course content should be drawn from a wide range of basic areas of experience, including existential experiences such as birth, death, and being in the world, ethical principles, and religious orientations (Neuner and Hunfeld, 1993).

4. Vail and Sparks, 1992, 432-44.

bring. They do not really see anything, they do not open doors through questions, and they do not listen to the voices of the people of Mainz.

This example shows the importance of asking certain questions of curricular materials before we begin working with them in our classes: Does the content and the way the content is patterned sustain our basic educational goals or not? Are the values and beliefs they reflect in tune with Christian faith?

Questioning Course Content

The first and most obvious features of the content of foreign language texts that may trouble Christian teachers are individual items of content. Horoscopes, for instance, are frequently used in association with learning the future tense, and at least one textbook included a page of instructions for palmistry.[5] Christian teachers are likely to object to such use of superstition with occult overtones, and to wonder why this material is included when more orthodox and wholesome expressions of spirituality are generally notable by their absence.

The inclusion of content items that are offensive to Christian teachers and/or learners is sometimes a point of contention, but it is a relatively superficial one, since it can be solved by simply removing or skipping over the offending page.

However, the problem of *absences* in the text, of dimensions of human experience that are *not* addressed, is a more fundamental concern. This issue has to do not merely with a particular portion of text that is contentious, but with the way material is *organized* to highlight certain aspects of life in the foreign culture — and to underplay others. Any textbook writer has to select a limited amount of material from the boundless possibilities she could have included. She will emphasize some things and pass lightly over others — or ignore them altogether.

A basic question Christian foreign language teachers will want to ask about most course materials is why religion and the vocabulary of faith are so often conspicuous by their absence. Why is the presence of religious belief and practice in the foreign culture rarely acknowledged beyond the level of learning the names of a few religious holidays? Why are women

5. Jury and Peck, 1987, 8, 11.

and men of faith often invisible in portrayals of the target culture, even when that culture has been shaped in significant ways by religious belief and practice? Depictions in textbooks, audiocassettes, and videos may include church buildings and the names of certain festivals, but how many people do students encounter in course materials who regard faith as a significant dimension of life? For how many of the characters who inhabit the pages of their textbooks does religious belief make a real difference when choices must be made?

Cultures cannot be adequately understood without reference to the influence of faith on their development. Nevertheless, foreign language courses often underplay this aspect of the target culture. Take, for instance, the *Harris Committee Report*,[6] which set up the framework for the National Curriculum for Modern Foreign Languages in the United Kingdom. The report included an example of how to structure an extended sequence of materials based on the study of a country. It appears from the examples in the report that the important features of a given country are geography, food, economy, history, and art, along with tourism and the media.[7] Are we to assume that faith and spirituality are relevant only to our own Christian subculture but are not woven into the fabric of life in the target culture? Learners could be forgiven for drawing this conclusion from many of their course materials.

One might object that such matters are too difficult for learners to tackle in a foreign language, at least until they attain a high level of proficiency. If they struggle to ask directions to the hotel, how will they cope with discussing the meaning of life? However, arguments based on the complexity of the language needed to deal with issues of belief have little weight. After all, attending to the presence of faith does not necessarily imply engaging in high-level theological discussion. And when it comes, for instance, to describing a person's morning routine, in many languages "I pray" is actually less complex than "I get up."

Neither will it do to point to the widespread secularization of modern Western cultures as a reason for ignoring the presence of faith. Consider, for instance, the important role religion plays in cultural contexts within Francophone and Hispanic countries. What more often seems to be at work in building course materials is the secular perspective of their au-

6. DES/WO/HMSO, 1990.
7. DES/WO/HMSO, 1990, 41-42.

thors, or a desire to avoid controversial material.[8] In other words, the reality of the stranger's context does not prove decisive in the selection of cultural elements to be included in textbooks, but rather the author's and the publisher's point of view — or perhaps their fear of controversy. Whatever the reason, the stranger's faith is effectively held at bay.

Frameworks of Meaning

But the mere absence of references to the spiritual dimension of life is only one way authors neglect its significance. They may also structure their texts in a way that offers little space for faith-informed reflection. That is to say, the content of a foreign language course may reflect certain basic patterns that narrow and limit the image of the stranger presented.

Take, for instance, common attitudes to the public and the private sectors of society or to work and leisure in Western liberal democracies. The organization of many foreign language course materials seems to reflect a basic Western tendency to divide life into a public world of work and economic transactions on the one hand, and a private world of leisure on the other.[9] The first sphere has to do with services rendered and money changing hands; the second is structured around the centrality of personal preferences.

When foreign language textbook writers adopt this Western schema, learners gain expertise in using public transport, paying in restaurants, or exchanging currency when in a foreign country. They also learn to express their preferences about food, music, entertainment, and sporting activities.[10]

But how would the spiritual dimension of the lives of people in the target culture fit into this basic Western dichotomy of public and private?

8. In the United States, with its strong tradition of separation of church and state, the inclusion of religious themes in textbooks is especially touchy. For American textbook writers, excluding religion from educational materials often takes precedence over doing justice to the religious dimensions of the foreign culture.

9. Cf. Marshall, 1988.

10. The Harris report, mentioned above, proposes asking students to "research and evaluate the layout of a town and plan the siting of (e.g.) a leisure centre or a large industrial complex" (DES/WO/HMSO, 1990, 42). Clearly this kind of activity prepares students mainly for their roles as tourists and entrepreneurs.

Would there be room for issues having to do with religious convictions? After all, faith does not fit comfortably into a vision of public life focused on commodities changing hands. Nor is it simply a matter of private preference on a level with choosing cake over ice cream. And how do concepts such as following a calling or serving others fit into the work-leisure dichotomy? Where will there be opportunity to consider work as joyful service to others, or prayer and shalom as relevant to our labors, or ethical questions that might challenge our leisure activities?

In short, if this Western dualistic framework implicitly determines the arrangement of materials in a foreign language course, it will be extremely difficult to do justice to the complex interconnections between what people in the target culture believe, hope for, or worship and other key aspects of the lives they live. As a result, a significant part of the stranger's being will be closed off from view.

One might also look more closely at the way a given textbook portrays the public world. What, for instance, is the range of tasks and occupations in which members of the target culture are engaged? Does it include only commercially oriented activities, or does it also focus on charitable activity? And what about the text's vocabulary? How much of it relates purely to consumer goods, rather than, for instance, to our natural surroundings or community values?

Thoughtful teachers should ask similar questions about the kinds of interaction and experience included in the functional syllabus underlying the text. Why do teaching materials so commonly offer the vocabulary and phrases to show *dissatisfaction* in the foreign setting — to complain that the towels were damp in the hotel room or that the meal was too slow to arrive in the restaurant — and so rarely pay attention to how one can *encourage* or sensitively praise someone in the target language?

Or consider the relationship between repentance and forgiveness. Learners are quite commonly taught to express regret in the foreign language, so they can apologize for being late or for forgetting their homework. It is far less common for the language of forgiveness to be practiced in the classroom, or even included in the common functions, as Barbara Carvill found out during the incident in China described in chapter 4. Why are students taught how to apologize, but so rarely how to forgive?

And what about the role money plays in the textbooks? Do people treat it exclusively as something to purchase goods and services with, or do they include the possibility of giving it away? A popular activity for prac-

133

ticing the conditional is to set up a hypothetical situation: If someone gave you a million dollars, what would you buy? This exercise assumes that the role of money is to give access to goods. I (Barbara Carvill) decided to change the exercise. For an oral German exam, I asked students to prepare an answer to the following question: If you were given a million dollars, how would you give it away? Most of the students found a variety of good causes for their donation, and it was interesting for me to find out what they considered worthy of financial support.

Others, however, without noticing it themselves, had great trouble donating the whole amount. They first mentioned the brand names of expensive German cars they intended to purchase. One student admitted he had real problems giving the whole amount away and that he wanted to keep at least a third for himself. He felt that the wording of my question manipulated him into doing more good than he was capable of. I appreciated very much his honesty and, at the next oral exam, changed the question to: "If you were given a million dollars, what percentage of the money would you keep, what would you do with it, and how much would you give away and to whom?" Facing these questions, students could more honestly examine the value of money in their lives and the extent of their altruistic disposition.

In summary, there are broader issues at stake when examining instructional materials for the foreign language classroom than whether the Bible is mentioned. We might well ask if materials focus primarily on the linguistic resources the learner needs in order to interact to his or her own benefit — whether to secure services, obtain goods, or navigate successfully — at the expense of giving attention to ways of being curious, open, and a kind and helpful presence in the target culture. We should also consider the frameworks of meaning that implicitly organize and make sense of the information presented about another culture and the lives of its inhabitants. If there are problems here, the text in question may not serve the educational goals of becoming a good stranger or a good host.

A Case Study

The questions raised above were posed in general terms, and could be followed up in more detail in relation to any specific text. An unusually in-

134

sightful example of an analysis of a particular textbook that raises Christian issues is provided by Clinton Schaffer's critique of the German first-year college text *Kontakte*.[11] In order to balance our general discussion of content issues with a practical example, we now look briefly at some of Schaffer's main points. Teachers not familiar with *Kontakte*[12] may find it helpful to consider the relevance of the questions Schaffer asks to a critique of textbooks for other foreign languages as well.

One feature of *Kontakte* evaluated by Schaffer is the cultural "portrait" section included in each chapter. He notes that the group of historical figures covered in these sections

> encompasses scientists and inventors, educators, artists and architects, social reformers and social scientists, poets, playwrights, and musicians. The spheres of theology, religion and (with the possible exception of Wilhelm von Humboldt) philosophy and politics, are not represented. . . . Considered individually, each person portrayed belongs unquestionably to the cultural pantheon of the German-speaking world. Viewed as a group, however, they chronicle a history that begins around 1800 and consists largely of the uninterrupted pursuit of technological advancement, artistic innovation, and social improvement.[13]

In other words, these sections, in Schaffer's view, convey more than mere cultural information; taken together, they seem to reflect a particular perspective on history and culture.

Schaffer goes on to examine possible grounds for the author's selection of these historical figures, after which he once again points to some of the key aspects of German culture the text excludes:

> It is difficult to assess whether this skewed vision of the past is based more on the assumption that students will identify more readily with Benz than with Bonhoeffer, or upon a tactical decision to avoid controversial events and individuals at all costs. What matters is the message that *Kontakte* conveys to students: that the history and culture worth knowing are those of the sanguine and secular modern era, from which

11. Schaffer, 1998.
12. Terrell et al., 1996.
13. Schaffer, 1998, 26.

the spiritual and even speculative dimensions have been cleanly and completely excised.[14]

Schaffer further argues that this cultural selectivity is not an isolated feature of the text. He sees the same pattern of exclusion in other parts of *Kontakte*: theology, for instance, is not listed in a graphic displaying the various academic disciplines, despite the sizable theological faculties of most German-speaking universities.[15]

Another of Schaffer's examples of exclusion and selectivity concerns the content of dialogues that, at least at times, he finds to be very shallow in their treatment of the religious dimension of human existence:

One of the book's earliest chapters presents, on facing pages, an interview activity dealing with character traits and a graphic from the German weekly "FOCUS" citing how young people from England, Japan, Germany and the U.S. assess their own attitudes and priorities (pp. 28-29). In the interview activity, "religiös" ("religious") is listed along with attributes such as "traurig," "freundlich," and "sportlich" ("sad," "friendly," and "athletic," respectively). For the student, in other words, the nature of being religious seems to have more to do with emotional or physical qualities than with actions or commitments.[16]

Nor does *Kontakte* do complete justice to the *FOCUS* materials cited. The follow-up questions provided in the text downplay the reference to religion in the original German article. According to Schaffer, "the graphic's reference to a statistic showing that German young people are second only to American youth in viewing themselves as religious is effectively ignored, or at least deemed an uninteresting topic of conversation."[17]

Some of *Kontakte*'s visual representations, Schaffer notes, show the same marginalization of religion. For example, in one of the test bank's line drawings, the church is displaced from the market square to the edge of the picture and is located "beneath a cloud of smoke spewing from an adjacent factory."[18]

14. Schaffer, 1998, 26.
15. Schaffer, 1998, 27.
16. Schaffer, 1998, 28.
17. Schaffer, 1998, 28.
18. Schaffer, 1998, 27.

Schaffer goes on to question the adequacy of the moral discourse of the text, which, he suggests, "remains at the level of winking at common foibles and lapses," making it "no great surprise that the verb 'lügen' ('to lie') is . . . absent from the book's glossary."[19] That same moral inadequacy is evident when readers are invited to "enjoy condemning" the opinions of a character whose portrayal "seems designed to evoke contempt rather than compassion," thus revealing "the short reach of *Kontakte*'s inclusive embrace."[20]

A similar shortcoming can be seen in aspects of the text's treatment of a pressing contemporary social problem in Germany. While Schaffer describes the efforts of the book to deal with issues of ethnic difference as at times "strikingly successful and thought-provoking," he questions the use of a somewhat stereotypical cartoon genre to represent real historical instances of anti-foreigner violence in Germany, suggesting that the cartoons found in the book leave behind the impression that such events belong in a simplified and fictional cartoon world.[21]

In highlighting these features and a number of other significant details found in *Kontakte*, Schaffer shows how Christian concerns can be relevant in identifying the patterns and omissions found in foreign language textbooks. Asking such questions may remind us that the content of the foreign language course is not simply a given. Someone has to design that content, which means that, among other things, the worldview of the designers, the perspectives and market interests of the publishers, and the perceived needs of students and teachers come into play.

Where a textbook is already in use, this kind of critical questioning of the values and beliefs encoded in it can provide an excellent learning opportunity if shared with the students using the text. Students who read the "Besuch in Mainz" text mentioned above could be given the following assignment: "What interesting aspects of Mainz and its history did the travelers miss completely during their short stay in Mainz? Visit the official website of Mainz to find out, and plan a different and longer visit." Or: "You have just asked a German about good places to eat in Mainz and you received a friendly answer. What else could you ask in order to get a sense of Mainz and its citizens?" (Possible answers: "Are you from Mainz?" "How long have

19. Schaffer, 1998, 28.
20. Schaffer, 1998, 29.
21. Schaffer, 1998, 31.

you been living here in Mainz?" "What do you like most about your city?" "What makes you proud to live in this city?" "In your opinion, what should a foreigner see in Mainz to get a sense of the spirit of the place?") *Kontakte,* or any other text, may be approached in a similar manner.

From Text to Hypertext

We have thus far focused our discussion of the content of teaching materials on the linear texts — textbooks, videos, audio recordings — which until recently have been the basic resources of the language teacher. However, in recent years the rapid development of computer technology has opened up new possibilities for language teaching materials, allowing students instant access to audio and video extracts, the ability to alter their speed and sequence and the level of help provided, and enhanced possibilities for recording their own utterances and comparing them with a native model. The learner's role now becomes more interactive. In addition to repetitive practice of grammatical items, computer software offers simulations of visits and adventures in the target culture, allowing learners to choose where to go and what to do next, and presenting them with situations that draw upon their growing knowledge of the target language and culture.

One feature of multimedia learning materials is their new way of organizing content. Instead of being presented with a text that is structured into chapters and follows a single linear sequence, learners now have access to a mass of material stored on a disk in such a way that it can be accessed in a multitude of ways, as they move from one item to another via a complex web of associations rather than in a set, preestablished pattern. These new possibilities thus seem to offer a way around the issues raised above concerning the worldviews communicated through the structuring of textbook content. Unlike a textbook, which in its linear structure imposes a certain view of life on learners, multimedia resources offer the possibility that each learner access and sequence the material differently, reorganizing it according to his or her own interests and values. Does this make the concerns of this chapter potentially obsolete?

There is no doubt that multimedia technology offers significant new possibilities to teachers and learners of foreign languages.[22] It does not,

22. Cf. Blake, 1998.

138

however, lessen the need for discernment when one considers the content of learning materials, and for at least two reasons.

First, multimedia resources, while impressive in their scope, are still finite, and they still have authors — "the subjectivity of the programmer is as unavoidable as that of the textbook author."[23] These new resources still represent a selection from a wide range of possible content, and continue to be marked by inclusions and exclusions. It will therefore still be pertinent to determine which aspects of human experience they cover and which they leave out in the range of materials they present to the learner for exploration. Moreover, as the sheer quantity of information and choices placed before the learner rapidly increases, the role of the teacher in helping the student select from and make sense of the flood of data becomes more critical.[24]

Second, the new way of presenting material can, when combined with certain content, communicate a worldview of its own. The following passage describes an interactive video disk titled *A la rencontre de Philippe* that was developed at the Massachusetts Institute of Technology as part of the Athena Language Learning Project. Claire Kramsch describes the disk as follows:

> [A] young Parisian named Antoine turns to the camera and invites the students to go with him to a café where they are to meet Philippe. As they arrive, the student witnesses a fight between Philippe and his girlfriend Elisabeth. Elisabeth is visibly angry. She suddenly gets up and storms out of the café shouting "J'en ai marre des parasites!" ["I am sick and tired of parasites!"]. In the following conversation between Antoine and Philippe, we learn that Philippe has been living for three months in Elisabeth's flat, that their relationship is a shambles, and that she has asked him to leave. . . . Philippe sits there looking rather gloomy, when he suddenly turns to the camera and asks the student to help him. This is the beginning of the involvement of the student who will help Philippe find a flat and a job in Paris and get reconciled with Elisabeth.[25]

Following this introduction, the learner responds to a variety of questions from Philippe and influences the course of events by choosing

23. Kramsch, 1993, 202.
24. Noblitt, 1995, 279.
25. Kramsch, 1993, 198.

from among several possible courses of action. The learner can become involved in the action in a variety of ways:

> He or she can type in and receive messages "on the telephone," ask for a re-run of portions of the film, for a transcript, for subtitles. Then, while Philippe goes to a job interview, the student can call up on the screen various documents: a plan of Paris, of specific districts, of newspaper ads that she circles; she can click on a specific quartier and the camera leads the student to the local grocery store, bakery, or real estate agency for inquiries; she can click again on a specific street and the camera goes and visits specific flats, leads her up the stairs and into the different rooms. No decision by the student is wrong, it just leads down a different path to a different ending.[26]

Kramsch's last comment seems particularly revealing. Far from creating an innocent medium in which questions of worldview become irrelevant, this resource seems to embody an existentialist outlook in which what matters is choosing for its own sake. This disk presents material dealing with relationships, employment, and life decisions, all in the context of a French character, a particular stranger, who wants to build a future. Yet Kramsch emphasizes that the message conveyed by the structure of the learning activities is that no one decision is right or wrong, but merely different from the others. But doesn't the life of this stranger mean more than a series of arbitrary choices with endlessly varied outcomes? Furthermore, if the choices are not right or wrong, merely different from others, will they or their effect on Philippe really matter to the learner?[27]

This is not to question the usefulness of electronic multimedia resources, or to suggest students should never encounter strangers in those materials whose values might diverge from their own. We do suggest, however, that responsible educational use of such resources will give attention to the framework of meaning and ethical significance in which the stranger appears and into which the learner is drawn. Students must be helped to become critically aware of the worldviews that have shaped the

---

26. Kramsch, 1993, 198.

27. As Kramsch asks, "how can we prevent the microworlds of the computer from becoming solipsistic playgrounds for the mind?" (1993, 202).

materials with which they interact, and of the ways they themselves are shaped by those materials.

Moving beyond the specific software discussed above, anyone evaluating such materials should, in our view, ask a whole series of questions. For example, what image of the stranger emerges when strangers become figures we can manipulate at random and the learner *constructs* their lives instead of attentively listening to them? How can teachers help learners discern that not all choices are equal and that not all information is equally significant? How can teachers help students find a sense of meaning for life in the array of words and images confronting them? We also need to ask which principled stances learners should adopt when they use multimedia. Such questions might open up fresh ways of exploring the ethical contours of relating to the stranger. For example, one guideline for students might be to avoid doing anything to the images of persons depicted in the materials that they would not do to living persons themselves.

However one answers questions like these, hypertext resources clearly cannot be regarded as innocent solutions to the weaknesses of textbooks. As James Noblitt puts it, "the problem of hidden epistemology is present in all media. . . . The educational challenge is to make sure that the student understands the medium."[28]

Restoring the Balance

We have been suggesting that a secularized perspective can lead to particular silences and distortions in the content of a foreign language course. This should not be taken to mean that we are for a moment advocating a textbook world where every character is a Christian, attends church, and embodies the height of moral virtue. To point out that faith and spirituality are often excluded from instructional materials is not the same as arguing that they should become the sole concern of our pedagogy. Nor does it mean that a text written from a Christian perspective should not be open to the same kind of scrutiny we urge on secular texts. Curricular materials written by Christians, after all, may also distort the image of the stranger. Our central concern is that the materials used in the classroom allow the humanity of the stranger to appear as fully as possible. This objective is not

28. Noblitt, 1995, 280.

achieved by excluding faith, but neither is it achieved by excluding the brokenness of another culture or the challenges believers in that culture face.

This plea for course materials that introduce the learner to the full humanity of the life of a culture leads to another complex issue. If Christians seek to design course materials that look at another culture through Christian eyes, how are they to distinguish between the eyes of faith and the eyes of their own cultural context? As I try to discover what is life-giving and what is problematic in another culture, how do I manage to distinguish Christian discernment from my own cultural perspectives and prejudices, since my particular way of following Christ is not culture-free?

We have no neat solution that would remove the complex difficulties and temptations inherent in understanding or teaching another culture. Two observations are, however, in order.

First, the position of the Christian is not inherently more difficult than that of anyone else. Christians do not see the world from a particular biased perspective while everyone else just sees it as it is. A secular perspective also will project its own expectations onto the culture it is observing, as Schaffer's examples illustrate. The difficulties in understanding another culture from within our own are shared by non-Christians and Christians alike.

Second, we have emphasized all along that loving attention to the other in a context of mutual giving and receiving should be at the heart of a Christian approach to foreign language education. Taking the implications of our faith seriously should predispose us to listen carefully to members of other cultures, rather than projecting our own values and ideas onto them. As Christian educators seeking to do justice to other cultures, we should supplement our own outsiders' efforts at description and understanding with careful attention to voices from within the foreign culture — especially voices of lament and celebration.

Listening to the laments expressed by natives of the target culture can help us discern which aspects of the culture reflect brokenness and thus cry out for healing. The problem is, if we resist portraying the foreign other romantically as only good and beautiful, and actually face the reality of sin, we risk standing in judgment and alienating our students from the very culture we would like them to learn to appreciate.

Attending to voices of lament from within the other culture can help us overcome this predicament. Many who voice such grief will be Christians. For example, we can focus on the lives of people such as Charles Péan, a French Salvation Army officer who worked tirelessly to get the penal colonies on Devil's Island closed down, or Jean Vanier, who responded to the inhumane treatment of sufferers of mental illness by inviting them into the Christian communities he founded in France.[29] Listening to such Christian protests coming from inside the foreign culture can both assist us in our efforts to approach that culture from a Christian perspective and challenge our own values and ways of life.

This approach also allows room for joy. Mourning with those who mourn, we can also rejoice with those who rejoice. We spoke in earlier chapters about the need for Christians to discern what is good in their own culture and to receive it gratefully. Hearing from Christians in other countries about the gifts for which they are grateful, the things they celebrate in their heritage, may not only add to our appreciation of their world, but also may give us a fresh perspective on our own. Perhaps the other's celebration will stimulate us to affirm our own culture; perhaps it will challenge us to change. In short, learning of the ways members of the foreign culture are working to bring about shalom, peace, and blessing can not only lead us to support their efforts; it can also shed light on our own path.

Questions to Consider

The points we have raised in this chapter are intended to illustrate that the content of a foreign language course, textbook, or syllabus is not innocent or neutral. This awareness is important when we consider foreign language education as an integral part of Christian education. The mindful Christian educator must be critically aware of inclusions, absences, and underlying patterns found in her instructional materials, and must find creative ways of correcting these absences and distortions or using them to sharpen students' insight into the nature of textbooks as value-laden human constructs.

Nor is the content of textbooks neutral in relation to our more specific proposal in this book: that hospitality to the stranger and being a blessing as a stranger are important motifs for foreign language education.

29. For units of French work on these topics see Baker et al., 1996a; Baker et al., 1998a.

Both the image of the stranger presented in course materials and the kinds of linguistic interaction with strangers included in the syllabus are relevant factors as we seek to make these motifs central to our teaching. On a more negative note, it should also be clear by now that just adding Bible verses or Christian texts to foreign language course materials in order to make them Christian will not address the issues we have raised.

With these concerns in mind, we suggest that a number of questions need to be asked of any curricular materials in addition to the familiar ones (Is the text appropriate for the learner's level of proficiency? Is the grammar presented clearly? Do activities and tasks do justice to different learning styles? Is the syllabus well sequenced by level of difficulty? etc.).[30] Ten additional questions a thoughtful teacher might ask when assessing course materials are as follows:

1. Judging by the content and approach of the textbook as well as its stated aims, which of the characters discussed in chapter 6 (the entrepreneur, the persuader, the connoisseur, the tourist, the escapologist, and the revolutionary) does it seem to promote? How much can it contribute toward encouraging learners to become good strangers and hosts?

2. How is the material arranged, and what significance does that arrangement have? For example, does the text show a divide between public/economic- and private/leisure-oriented worlds, or a sharp separation of the sacred from the secular?

3. How does the text present the humanity of members of the target culture? Do they fear, doubt, suffer, sin, hope, pray, or celebrate as well as work, shop, play, eat, and drink?

4. What is the range of human tasks and callings portrayed in the course materials? Which are missing?

5. What is the range and quality of human relationships among the people portrayed? Is an ethical dimension of communication or of human interaction in general in evidence? In what ways? How do people of different generations relate to one another?

6. Do the people portrayed ever face significant decisions involving more than issues of personal preference? How do they approach those decisions, and by what criteria do they make them?

30. Cf. Richards, 1993.

7. Do the teaching materials include any spiritual or religious dimension of the target culture or individuals? How does the text treat this dimension? Which aspects of it are portrayed or suppressed?

8. Do the instructional materials pay attention to marginalized members of the target culture? Do they incorporate any voice of lament for the broken aspects of that culture?

9. What does the text invite us to learn from the strangers it presents to us? Which of their stories are we asked to listen to? What do they celebrate?

10. How does the text treat the learner? Does it give opportunity for open-ended and personally invested responses to issues raised? Which of the learner's interests and motives does it appeal to?

Obviously, no course materials are perfect, but identifying their weaknesses is necessary if we are to point those weaknesses out to our students and discuss them. It can also show us in what ways we may need to modify or supplement our instructional materials if we, as Christian educators, want them to serve our purposes.[31]

Content and Pedagogy

In this chapter we have tried to illustrate some of the ways the content of foreign language courses may be open to examination from the standpoint of Christian belief. If this book were to conclude here, we would already have shown in part how a reflective Christian stance might make a difference in what goes on in the foreign language classroom. Yet our discussion would be woefully incomplete, and for at least two reasons.

First, even though the content of language courses is a crucial element in foreign language instruction, discussions in our field have typically been more preoccupied with questions of appropriate and effective *method* than with examinations of course *content*. Conversely, if our Christian exploration remains satisfied with questions about content and

---

31. One way of developing a wider range of resources would be to write to foreign nationals, including Christians, and ask them questions such as the following: Who are your heroes? What do you think is wrong in your society? What moral issues do you struggle with? What stories mean most to you? Who in your society do you think is doing something really worthwhile?

stops short of an examination of pedagogy, we are in a sense only charting the foothills of foreign language education. We have already asked whether Christian faith might affect content; now a second, inevitable and more challenging question remains: Could Christian beliefs have anything to do with teaching methods?

Second, if we revise content without reconsidering the teaching strategies that shape the ways it is made accessible and experienced by learners, we may end up subverting our own best intentions. Suppose we want to introduce a text in which a speaker from the target culture addresses some spiritually significant theme. Accompanying the material with a set of factual questions with right/wrong answers would offer the learner little opportunity to interact meaningfully with its substance. Changing content without changing pedagogy may achieve little.

A more extended example may help to make this point clearer. A few years ago, I (David Smith) spent some time developing a unit for learners of German about the White Rose, a group of German students who organized resistance against Hitler in Munich during the Second World War.[32] One of the activities I devised was based on a set of statements made by various people and the media around the time the key members of the White Rose were caught by the authorities and executed.

These statements reflected differing stances toward what the group had been doing and toward their execution. For example, a newspaper headline announced death sentences for treason; Sophie's sister asked why the task of opposing Hitler could not be left to someone else; and one of the condemned students commented at the execution that the members of the White Rose group would soon see one another again in eternity.

One of my aims in teaching this material was to bring students to reflect on the various stances and perspectives reflected in the different statements. In that connection, one of the tasks I assigned was to match each of the statements with the person who most likely had made it. I included in the exercise a brief description of each person's role in the drama.

When I tried out this activity with a class of fourteen-year-old learners, one of my most able students gazed at it for a while, then complained that she couldn't do it. I sat with her for several minutes, trying to discover where the problem lay. We quickly established that she understood all the language necessary to complete the activity; lack of comprehension did

32. This unit of work can be found in Baker et al., 1996b.

not seem to be the issue. However, after some minutes of puzzlement I realized she was looking for a linguistic clue that would show her which statement went with which description.

As I thought about her problem, it struck me that every time she had been asked to match items in her foreign language lessons, the decisions had rested on linguistic form. They had involved pairing a singular pronoun with a singular verb, two elements of a reflexive verb, or some other grammatically connected set of linguistic features. She had never been required to reflect on the meaning or personal significance of the phrases she had been asked to match. She thus expected this to be the required process whenever she was asked to link pairs of items in a foreign language lesson, and that expectation now defeated her attempts to do this new activity. As soon as I pointed out to her that this time there were no linguistic clues, and that she had to think about what the sentences meant and who might have said them, she was able to proceed and quickly complete the activity.

As a result of this experience, I was left with a fresh realization of how the habitual practices that made up my language teaching could not only enable learners to interact in certain effective ways with texts or utterances in the foreign language; they could also undermine their ability to get at the meanings expressed in those texts and utterances. In short, fresh content had shown up some unforeseen, negative side effects of my customary procedures, difficulties I would have to attend to for my pedagogical goals to be realized.

For both these reasons — the importance of method in discussions of language teaching and the interlocking nature of the relationship between content and pedagogy — a Christian exploration of language teaching must give attention to the question of appropriate pedagogy, which will be the focus of the next two chapters.

CHAPTER EIGHT

Faith and Method

To demand or preach mechanical precision, even in principle,
in a field incapable of it is to be blind and to mislead others.

Isaiah Berlin

One morning some years ago I (David Smith) was teaching French to a
class of fourteen-year-olds. We were practicing for the oral examination
that was to come at the end of the course. Part of our practice involved answering a range of personal questions, such as, where do you live? how old
are you? what do your parents do? One student was having difficulty re-
membering the word for an obscure parental occupation, which was not
an unusual problem. After all, one cannot expect that the lives of all students fit neatly into the basic range of vocabulary provided by foreign language course materials and examination syllabi.

I responded in the usual way, as I had been taught in my training and
had learned from working with colleagues in this, my first school. I suggested that for the purposes of the exercise the student supply the name of
any occupation that came to mind; after all, the examiner would not really
be interested in what this pupil's parent actually did for a living. He or she
would just want to hear a correct French phrase in order to evaluate it for
complexity, accuracy, and pronunciation. My response fit in with a
broader pattern of advice I had picked up as part of the professional wisdom of my craft. If, for instance, students were asked to design family trees

149

in the target language, beginning-level learners with particularly complex families were advised to simplify the facts for the purposes of the exercise. Such suggestions had never seemed problematic to me before; wasn't language practice the main purpose of what we were doing?

On this particular day, however, I began to feel uncomfortable with my response. I began to wonder whether the ethics of communication really mattered, even here in language practice, whether my concern for integrity in communication did not fit badly with the advice to simplify and change the facts if truth or accuracy are inconvenient. Wouldn't it be more in tune with my Christian convictions to teach students to wrestle with the language they were learning until they could express themselves with integrity?

When I shared these thoughts with colleagues, things got more complicated. My fellow teachers did not agree with me, and their objections forced me to do some more thinking. The first comment was that I was confusing artificial practice exercises with real communication. The examples of language use I was concerned with, they argued, were just role playing for the purposes of learning; to expect that they convey truth would be to apply a standard that was not only inappropriate but would expect too much of weaker learners. Their second comment was that I had no right to expect my students to honestly divulge personal information in the classroom if they preferred not to. Since both objections seemed to have substance, I began to wonder if my initial concern had been mistaken after all.

Further reflection, however, convinced me that my colleagues' first objection missed the mark, and for at least two reasons.

For one thing, we claimed in our school to be following a communicative model of language teaching. This meant, among other things, that when students used language in the classroom, their speech was to be as authentic as possible. That is to say, rather than concentrating on abstract, noncontextual exercises, their language use should consist of actual communication — or at least lifelike rehearsal for future communication. Was it not then inconsistent of us to appeal to the artificial character of our role-playing activities when we were challenged on an ethical issue? If it was genuine communication we were practicing, surely its ethical dimension should be reflected and addressed in our rehearsal for reality. After all, what attitudes toward communicating with strangers did we want to foster? Did telling the truth matter also when we were talking to foreigners, or only when we were speaking with members of our own language group?

Given our preference for accuracy over truth content, how were students implicitly learning to treat the stranger? Furthermore, if we regularly implied to pupils that the content of what they said did not matter, were we not sending clear messages that, in spite of our communicative ideals, we were not really interested in what they had to say?

These worries were strengthened by another consideration, one that grew out of observing the responses of students. I found with various groups of learners who had been advised to practice flexibility with the facts that, before long, one student or another would come up with the question, "It's okay to lie in French, isn't it?" I began to realize that, however sophisticated our rationale, or our distinctions between communication, rehearsal, and role playing, student perceptions were much more down-to-earth: they tended to focus on the content of a communicative activity more than on its form.

For instance, if I asked eleven-year-olds to do a class survey about pets, it was not uncommon for some of them to do so in their mother tongue and proudly present me with the results. *I* thought we were rehearsing phrases; *they* thought they were doing a survey to find out about the distribution of pets.[1] In a similar way, if I told students that the content of a language exercise was not particularly important, their conclusion was simply that it was okay to lie in the new language. It was all very well for me to have fine distinctions between role playing and real communication, but what if the students perceived themselves as lying? And isn't attending to the perceptions of learners an essential factor in finding out what our pedagogy actually achieves? In short, the first objection of my colleagues did not convince me at all.

The second, however, I found considerably more persuasive. With the family circumstances of learners seeming to become more complex as the years passed, what right did I as their French teacher have to ask them to talk in front of their peers about what their parents did, where or whether they went on holiday, or what their house was like? What if their father was in prison or their lack of economic wealth became a ground for scorn by materialistically minded fellow learners?[2]

---

1. For a description of a similar phenomenon, see Clayden et al., 1994.

2. Rivers voices a similar concern (1983, 109-10). Cultural background may also be a factor leading some learners to be reluctant to share personal information in the public setting of the classroom.

I felt the force of this concern for students' privacy particularly strongly. It reminded me of an incident a couple of years earlier, when I was training to become a language teacher. I had been asked to administer a standard oral test that included the question, "Do you have any brothers or sisters?" One of the students taking the test burst into tears when I asked her this question, and I discovered too late that her brother had been killed in an accident just a few days earlier. Her pain back then was one of the factors leading me now to wonder how a concern for truth could be coupled with the need to protect learners from intrusive, painful, or embarrassing questions.

During this rethinking process I discovered an article discussing some of these very issues. In a paper titled "The Nature and Role of Personalized Questions in the Foreign Language Classroom," Patricia Myhren suggests, among others, the following strategies for supporting a concern for truth telling:

- Use nonpersonal activities for practicing vocabulary and fine-tuning grammar.
- Avoid asking embarrassing questions — and allow pupils to refuse to answer any questions that trouble them.
- Challenge answers on the basis of an explicit concern for truth.
- If you provide a choice of ready-made answers, be sure students have a variety of likely responses to a question, so that they do not vary answers simply out of boredom.
- Follow answers with further questions to show interest in the content of student responses.[3]

Reflecting on these suggestions, I decided to be much more explicit with learners about what was going on in a given language activity. If, for instance, I asked them to write about their family, I now told them they could choose one of two genres. They could, if they wished, elect to do a piece of creative writing about a fictitious family and make up all the details, trying to use as wide a variety of language as possible. Or they could write about themselves, in which case I asked them to work at finding the vocabulary and expressions they needed to give an accurate, truthful picture. When an activity involved answering personal questions, I invited

3. Summarized from Myhren, 1991.

learners to <u>tell</u> me privately if there were areas they would have me avoid.[4] More importantly, I began to teach them strategies for politely deflecting unwelcome questions, a communicative skill that had not been dealt with in our language course before. In response, some students began using phrases such as "I'm afraid that's none of your business" with real enthusiasm!

More can no doubt be said and debated about the issues raised by this example.[5] However, what is most pertinent for the topic at hand is the process involved, and the way it exemplifies the complex interweaving of beliefs, values, experiences, and pedagogy. Experiences that provoked conscious reflection on the relationship between my Christian beliefs and my ways of teaching led me to make adjustments in my pedagogy. This did not mean that I simply stated my beliefs and deduced some Christian techniques from them by inevitable logical steps. It was much more an interactive process in which my values, my ongoing experience of a teaching situation, my understanding of communicative teaching methods, the advice and objections of colleagues, and the reflections of another Christian in the field were all brought into dialogue with each other. The interaction of these factors led to a series of modifications in the way I approached my teaching, and an ongoing sense that I needed to rethink what I was doing. My Christian beliefs did not provide me with teaching strategies in advance, but they did make a substantial contribution in staking out an area of concern within which my classroom practice could develop and change.

The Wide Diversity of Christian Views

The complexity of this process may help explain why, when it comes to teaching methods, Christian language teachers seem to have quite divergent views. At one end of the spectrum lies the experience of a friend who attended a seminar hosted by the publishers of Christian curricular materials.[6]

The speaker introducing the seminar began by assuring his audience

4. This, I soon realized, was a very limited strategy — being asked to tell the teacher which areas are sensitive may imply having to admit to the teacher that one has problems in those areas, an admission that could carry its own embarrassment.

5. For further discussion see Myhren, 1991; Smith, 1997a.

6. I owe this anecdote to Doug Blomberg.

that the teaching method on which the materials were based had been revealed by God himself to this generation of his church. The audience should therefore be very careful. If during any of the sessions they found themselves having critical thoughts about the materials, they should resist them as temptations from Satan. Nor should the matter be taken lightly. To reinforce his admonition, the speaker reminded the seminar participants that when the Israelites grumbled against Moses while crossing the desert, the ground opened up and swallowed some of them. In the same way, he insisted, if anyone should fail to heed the warning he had just given, God's judgment might well come into his or her life.

At the opposite extreme lies the view that faith and teaching methods have little to do with one another. An experienced Christian language teacher once asked me in a church in Toronto about my research. When I tried to explain that I was looking at the connection between Christian belief and teaching methods in foreign language education, I was met with blank incomprehension. Her response was succinct and to the point: "Is there a Christian way to boil water?"

The Christian educational community tends to be polarized on the relationship between faith and method. Some insist they can identify God's true way of teaching. Others express faint pity for anyone foolish enough to think the question has any meaning. Some are convinced that since all things in creation are claimed by Christ, there must be a single biblical teaching method. For others, such a notion conjures up a strange world where the Christian teacher holds the chalk differently, uses different visual aids, and asks questions differently — a world so hard to imagine in practice that they conclude with a shake of the head that the whole idea is nonsensical. After all, grammar is grammar, and teaching methods are teaching methods.

So, does our trail go cold when we get to methodology? Is the notion of a Christian foreign language pedagogy just a pious oddity or a sign of dogmatic extremism? Wouldn't we have stumbled onto it before now if there were such a thing? In the rest of this chapter we will take a more systematic look at this question, before considering in chapter 9 some specific examples where faith and pedagogy cross paths.

Faith in Method

Donald Schön pointed out long ago that when one seeks to solve a problem, it can be more fruitful to focus first on how the problem has been posed than to set one's sights immediately on solving it.[7]

With this advice in view, let's take a quick look at the ideas evoked in our minds when we label something an instance of "method." For example, reflect for a moment on how we would react if someone were to say "I have found a new *way* of practicing my golf swing" over against "I have found a new *method* for practicing my golf swing." What differences in connotation do we sense in these two statements?

When Descartes lamented the degree to which the beliefs of his contemporaries were based on mere custom and example, the solution he sought came in the form of a "true method of arriving at knowledge."[8] Since then, the concept of reliable method has remained a potent ideal, especially in the natural and social sciences. "Method" has become a favored term for anything that is to have an air of rigor, of being based on grounds more systematic and reliable than tradition and guesswork. To do something "methodically" is to do it with a level of self-discipline designed to ensure the desired results. Our culture's well-known faith in "the scientific method" is perhaps the most familiar example of our confidence in the ideal espoused by Descartes.

If "method" is to save us from the messiness of unexamined custom, haphazardness, and disagreements, and assure the achievement of our goals, it needs ideally to have certain characteristics:[9]

- It must be *self-sufficient*, in the sense that it must admit nothing into its workings that is clouded by custom, tradition, belief, or prejudice.
- It must be open to rigorous, thorough, and self-conscious *regulation*, so that no contamination creeps into the process and compromises its validity.
- It must be *repeatable* without variation, so that it can produce identical results at various times and in different places.
- It must be *comprehensive* in its grasp; it must take all the relevant fac-

---

7. Schön, 1979.
8. Descartes, 1968, 39-40.
9. Cf. Descartes, 1968; Dunne, 1993; Weinsheimer, 1985.

tors into account, so that the results will not be threatened by our having missed vital elements.

These ideals, which together make up a vision of a self-consciously controlled, self-enclosed, ahistorical, encompassing, certain, and repeatable method, have been common enough themes in the modern period. Although these rigorous standards are particularly associated with the scientific method, the enormous prestige of natural sciences in our culture has spread their influence well beyond the bounds of the sciences. It is therefore not surprising that attempts to ground teaching scientifically and to think of it in terms of method have often leaned toward the mind-set particularly dominant in the natural sciences.

These cultural developments are relevant to our theme in two ways. First, as applied linguists have labored to place foreign language pedagogy on a scientific footing, hoping thereby to achieve more reliable success,[10] the ideals of repeatability, assured results, and rigorous checking, along with the search for the one best comprehensive method, have been prominent. Until quite recently the quest was for the single correct teaching method that, being an appliance of science, would guarantee results.

Second, it is woven into the very fabric of the scientific concept of method as widely understood in modernity that it excludes factors like tradition, beliefs, personal commitment, variations in personal character, and the like. That is precisely what method is explicitly designed to do; it could not achieve the context-free, repeatable rigor to which it aspires if it allowed these factors to interfere. Thus they are excluded not just accidentally or temporarily, but *by definition*. If one accepts these terms, talk of a *Christian* method is a kind of nonsense, like talking about dry water or warm snow. Once we adopt a certain terminology, some things become very hard to say: a modern "method" simply is not the kind of concept that can have the adjective "Christian" defining it.

The two extreme positions held among Christians may now be somewhat more understandable, for they represent two different responses to what is implied when one talks about teaching in terms of "method."

One response, which advocates the quest for God's method, seems to sense that if a Christian teaching "method" is what our convictions require us to look for, then there will be a single best, self-sufficient, totally reliable

10. See Weideman, 1987.

candidate. The other position likened the notion of a Christian teaching method to the odd idea of a Christian way to boil water. This view may be grounded in an understanding that there is simply no logical space within the concept of "method" for particular beliefs and commitments. Both responses implicitly accept the modern scientific ideal of method as appropriate to teaching; they simply respond in different directions. Both face a puzzle handed down by our intellectual history that is simply insoluble as long as its terms of reference are accepted.

The Erosion of Faith in Method

If history had not moved on, our discussion of method could well end here. However, as time has passed, it has become increasingly clear that we don't need to accept the terms of reference described above. It actually may be quite unwise to do so.

Despite its previous position of dominance, method no longer enjoys the unquestioned authority it once had. In fact, some of this century's important thinkers have devoted considerable energy to dismantling the modern ideal of guaranteed success through the application of method. A general critique of its efficacy has been offered by figures such as Gadamer, Polanyi, and Feyerabend.[11] To their analyses can be added the wider postmodern suspicion of any claim that universal answers can be found anywhere. In fact, postmodern thinkers have contested every one of the modern ideals associated with method, offering in their place a view of knowledge as plural, historical, uncertain, shifting, partial, and influenced by a variety of forces. It is thus not surprising that literature on language teaching, too, has begun to echo criticism about the validity of method as traditionally conceived.

11. Feyerabend, 1975; Gadamer, 1989; Polanyi, 1958; cf. also Dunne, 1993; Plantinga, 1996; Weinsheimer, 1985. Polanyi, for instance, has argued that committed, personal knowledge rather than "the vain pursuit of a formalized scientific method" provides "the only relation in which we can believe something to be true" (311). On the side of the humanities, Gadamer has argued that the Enlightenment "prejudice against prejudice" (270) has obscured the positive enabling role prior assumptions can play. It is interesting to note Gadamer's comment that the "prejudice against prejudice itself, which denies prejudice its power," is "primarily directed against the religious tradition of Christianity — i.e. the Bible" (270, 272).

The main arguments against continued reliance on method in foreign language education deal with three concerns: the limitations of empirical research in determining the best method, the persistent role of commitments in shaping any method at all, and the failure of the ideal of method to do justice to good practice in the classroom.

The Limitations of Empirical Research

The very proliferation of different teaching methods has undermined confidence that we are on our way to a single scientifically based answer as to which of them is superior. Throughout the years, finding a scientifically validated "best method" has always remained the elusive rainbow's end, and a shifting pattern of rival designs — audio-lingual, communicative, humanistic, natural, proficiency-oriented, critical, cognitive, content-based — have all vied for a dominance that has usually proved to be local and short-lived. Little wonder that A. Davies describes applied linguistics as a loose federation, "often warring . . . more on the model of Yugoslavia than of Australia or the European Community." "[I]n no case," he continues, "is there a single monolithic, unitary view, nowhere is there complete agreement on what the discipline is about."[12] Given this reality, such observations as the following are not surprising: "Viewed historically, language teaching has always been subject to change, but the process of change has not resulted from the steady accumulation of knowledge about the most effective ways of teaching languages: it has been more the product of changing fashion."[13]

There has, of course, been an ongoing effort to compare methods empirically in order to establish which are the most effective. However, the results have been somewhat less conclusive than one might hope.

One of the problems emerging from this effort has to do with defining method as an experimental variable.[14] While past discussions of language teaching have characterized the field in terms of allegedly distinct rival methods, recent commentators have stressed not only the highly diverse characteristics of various methodologies, but also the considerable

12. A. Davies, 1993, 15.
13. Wilkins, 1972, 207.
14. Kinginger, 1997, 6.

overlapping one finds among those methods composing the standard list. Largely as a result of this lack of clarity, the term "method" has been used to describe anything from a specific bundle of techniques to a broad and general approach.[15] A closer inspection of various versions of the standard list even reveals considerable uncertainty as to how many methods one can distinguish within the field.[16]

In addition, one must take a huge number of variables into account when studying methods in a classroom setting, a difficulty that has led either to inconclusive investigations of entire methods or to more easily controllable small-scale studies of particular combinations of techniques that have only limited implications.[17] The result of this dilemma has been a growing consensus that methodologies are not readily susceptible to global comparison in empirical terms.[18] Thus, utilizing the standard list of methods for doing empirical studies has become a problematic way of differentiating among language teaching practices.[19] Likewise, many think that selecting one method and sticking to it offers little guarantee of any improvement in the quality of instruction.[20]

The Failure to Exclude Commitments

Why are there so many rival methods in the first place?

A variety of explanations have been offered, including the lack of effective communication between teachers and applied linguists, the effect of market forces, the personal preferences of teachers, and political or economic pressures.[21] The factors leading to this proliferation are no doubt many and complex, but one of them is particularly relevant to the present

15. Brumfit, 1991; Larsen-Freeman, 1991, 122.

16. Pennycook, 1989, 602.

17. See Larsen-Freeman, 1991.

18. Larsen-Freeman, 1991, 121-22. Larsen-Freeman points out the inverse problem, that the small-scale studies that have proliferated in reaction to the problem of global evaluation provide insufficient grounds for generalization (123). For a list of variables involved, see Brumfit, 1984. Brumfit goes so far as to state in connection with this survey of variables that "no-one is going to prove, even provisionally, that a particular language teaching procedure is better than another" (19-20).

19. Larsen-Freeman, 1991.

20. See, e.g., Byrnes, 1998, 273-74.

21. Kramsch, 1995a; O'Driscoll, 1993; Pennycook, 1989; Richards, 1984.

discussion. It involves the recognition that discussions of language teaching are embedded in broader cultural and philosophical commitments. Rather than being immune to broader discussions of how we should live, the shifting fate of teaching methods is itself bound up with them. Thus Davies comments that ·

> it may be that we shall always have to take account of changing fashion simply because we have no way of finally establishing "the best way" to learn or teach a language. Since there is no easy way of evaluating the internal logic of a theoretical model of language, the question of what constitutes the best language-learning theory may not be a matter for experimental research at all, but a matter for philosophical argument about what kinds of aims we are interested in at any one time.[22]

It is our conviction that discussions of teaching methods, especially the more heated ones, are inspired by a variety of commitments that go far beyond narrow considerations of technique. Such dispute involves not only experimental results but also various kinds of convictions — philosophical, ethical, social, political. We would argue that many of these convictions are related to the concerns of Christian faith.

This insight opens up new ways of examining the processes of language teaching. It mandates that we explore how a pedagogy is related to the particular visions, interests, and beliefs that have shaped its construc-

---

22. Davies, 1993, 14. Davies argues that the development of teaching methods is always bound up with "speculation," which he defines as "philosophy which constructs a system of knowledge from many fields (the sciences, the arts, religion, ethics, social sciences) and theorizes (reflects) about such things as its significance to humankind, and about what it indicates about reality as a whole" (16, citing Angeles). Cf. Molero, 1989: "ML teaching methods, like methods in other disciplines, have not created the 'fashion' of swinging from the positivist paradigm (step by step learning according to a pre-established plan . . .) to the subjective one (open to genuine convergence of individual and/or group value judgements by spontaneous decisions of learners). Both follow different traditions and are grounded in the history of human thought. What sounds amazing is that each time the pendulum swings from one tradition to the other we react as if we had discovered the ultimate truth. ML teaching methods, as some sources put it, have swung from wholesale self-decision to highly logically structured (prescriptive) models and back again, not bringing discoveries but causing heretical controversies and contradictions, for on each occasion heresy consisted of maintaining ideas which contradicted current dogma" (161).

tion. In other words, we should investigate not only concrete language teaching practices, but also the commitments and guiding metaphors that animate and sustain these practices.[23]

This, of course, is the kind of exploration in which this book is engaged. We join other critics in rejecting the Cartesian and positivist ideals of excluding and superseding such particular perspectives and commitments in the name of a pure method. Any investigation of different ways of teaching languages must of necessity be sensitive to diversity of perspective and belief, rather than moving toward the illusive goal of some single best method.

The Failure to Honor Classroom Reality

A further objection to the traditional concept of method has to do with the relationship of theory to practice. The ideal of method, Alastair Pennycook argues, has always imposed upon its practitioners a particular way of proceeding based on its alleged scientific authority.[24] Thus teachers are supposed to simply implement the methods designed by university-based theorists in accordance with the instructions they are given.

This expectation not only masks the commitments that have shaped the methods the experts recommend, hiding them behind a veil of presumed objectivity; it also pays little attention to the wisdom and good practice teachers themselves develop in the classroom.[25] Moreover, the picture that emerges at the level of actual practice may be much less neat and conceptually unified than the academic ideal. As Pennycook notes, "there is far less concordance than expected among what teachers claim to be doing, what researchers anticipate to be happening, and what actually appears to be occurring in classes."[26]

In sum, the ideal of a language teaching method characterized by unity, totality, certainty, and scientific control has come under sustained attack. One does not have to go far in the recent literature on the topic to discover criticism of the lack of clarity that has accompanied talk of teach-

23. Kramsch, 1995a.
24. Pennycook, 1989, 609.
25. For discussion of the weaknesses of "technical rationality" as applied in the professions, see Schön, 1983.
26. Pennycook, 1989, 606.

ing methods, skepticism regarding the possibility of discovering the single best method for all contexts, calls to acknowledge the ideological factors at play in the continuing diversity of methods, and attempts to move away from models that privilege theory over practice. Perhaps *method*, despite the familiarity of the term, is not the best word to describe what we actually do in the classroom.

The attack on method has resulted in a variety of suggestions for fresh ways forward in what B. Kumaravadivelu has termed the "post-method condition," proposals that attempt to move away from talk of "teaching methods."[27] The guards appointed to keep beliefs safely outside the classroom door are looking increasingly geriatric, and a picture of teaching processes is emerging in which there is much more room than before to discuss the difference specific beliefs about people and language might make in the processes of teaching and learning languages. Now that the obstacles to doing so look less forbidding, let's take a more positive look at how faith may relate to designing foreign language instruction.

How Do Beliefs Affect Teaching?

We begin by looking back to a short but classic article published in 1963 by Edward Anthony titled "Approach, Method and Technique."[28] Since the words "method" and "technique" have too many unhelpful connotations in the present context, in the paragraphs that follow we will adopt Richards and Rodgers's substitution of "approach," "design," and "procedure" for Anthony's original terms (see Figure 8.1, p. 163).[29]

In his article, Anthony envisaged three levels of description necessary for making sense of a teaching sequence.

Procedures are specific classroom actions applied to achieve specific objectives. They might include administering a quiz, projecting a picture on a screen, or asking a question. A casual visitor to a class sees mostly procedures.[30]

27. Kumaravadivelu, 1994.
28. Anthony, 1963.
29. Richards and Rodgers, 1982; Richards and Rodgers, 1986.
30. Anthony, 1963, 66.

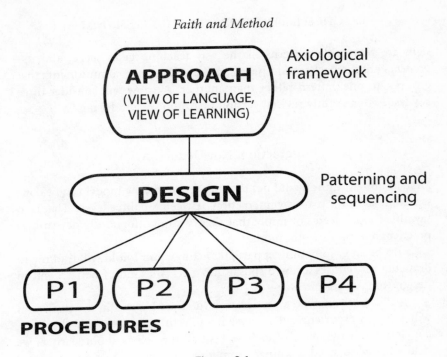

Figure 8.1

Procedures, however, do not occur randomly. They are organized and patterned so as to have overall consistency and direction. This overall constellation of procedures is what is meant by *design*.

A design is, in turn, dependent on a wider framework of assumptions and beliefs; it is a way of realizing or making concrete a certain vision of things. In Anthony's view, the overall coherence of a design, in spite of the variety of procedures it may include, derives from its consistency with a set of beliefs about the nature of language and of language learning.

This wider framework is what is meant by an *approach*. Examples would include the humanistic belief that the individual's emotions should be given priority, or the assumptions about the importance of habit formation that informed behavioristic approaches. To quote Anthony, an approach "states a point of view, a philosophy, an article of faith — something which one believes but cannot necessarily prove."[31]

In sum, then, *procedures* are individual actions in the classroom; *de-*

31. Anthony, 1963, 64.

signs are repeatable patterns in the way teaching takes place; and *approaches* are the background beliefs, orientations, and commitments that give rise to one pattern rather than another. We now will consider three key issues this slightly revised version of Anthony's model raises.

Interaction, Not Deduction

First, although Anthony did not develop the point, the model can be construed to allow for two-way interaction between the three levels. That is to say, this model need not imply that theory straightforwardly determines practice in a top-down fashion.

To be sure, sometimes a particular conviction I hold will lead me to draw the procedures at my disposal into a certain kind of pattern and to design things a certain way.

Conversely, however, on occasion the time I spend in the classroom will result in experiences that cause me to rethink some of my cherished convictions. (How many of us have kept all the beliefs about learners we held when we started teaching?) Sometimes I may discover a new procedure through happy improvisation — and only later work out where it fits in the design, and then develop theories to explain why it works. What is important, as the example at the beginning of this chapter illustrated, is that I be attentive not only to my designs, but to the perceptions and responses of the students I am teaching, if I want to understand the effect my pedagogy actually has.

That is to say, a design does not simply follow by fixed logical steps from a set of convictions; it involves fallible creativity and experimentation, developing procedures and then observing what they do. There might be several different designs that are equally consistent with the same approach. What we need is not a deductive but a dynamic model, one that takes seriously the loose flow of ongoing adjustment that takes place between the various levels the model identifies. If this is the case, perhaps we could represent Anthony's model like Figure 8.2 (p. 165).

But the creative process that underlies the design of an instructional sequence is much more complex than the figure illustrates. It also entails the teacher's particular skills, personality strengths, experiences, and tradition of schooling — as well as a variety of potential constraints such as the age and background of students, parental expectations, budgetary limita-

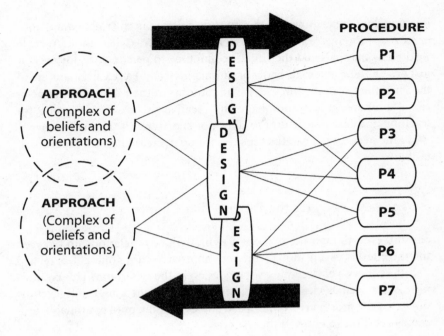

Figure 8.2

tions, educational policies, school regulations, classroom size, and many more.[32]

   The complex nature of the teaching process and the presence of all these variables does not, of course, mean that the convictions embedded in an approach are irrelevant. Consider a parallel: the teacher's influence is not rendered superfluous simply because he or she does not produce or control every event in the classroom.[33] The complexity of teaching and

   32. This points to the possibility of a given teacher believing in a particular approach but, whether consciously or unawares, using a constellation of techniques that is in tension with certain elements of that approach. The discussion of Curran's work in chap. 9 provides an example of this. In such a case, the approach that is operative is surely the one implied by the actual practices rather than the one simply assented to or verbalized.

   33. Again, this does not mean that such beliefs or orientations only have an effect at the level of approach, remaining insignificant for the procedures adopted, for it is the beliefs and orientations making up the approach that guide the coherence of the

learning does mean, however, that rooting a design in the right convictions is not a sure guarantee of its quality. Teachers with an admirable worldview may misread the situation, fall prey to personal weaknesses, or just design their materials badly or unimaginatively. Here Christians are in the same boat with everyone else. The contours of their faith and character can illuminate, guide, and shape the creative process of designing for teaching and learning, but faith does not short-circuit the process or remove the necessity of careful, sensitive thought, creativity, and experimentation.

It's the Pattern That Counts

Second, even though there is not a tight, deductive relationship between the three levels in our model, different approaches are nonetheless related to different ways of designing what goes on in the classroom. This connection is not seen as clearly in the individual procedures used (all teaching draws for the most part from a broad and expanding pool of available procedures) as in the *patterns* that emerge.

For example, taken on their own, procedures like seating learners in a circle or asking them to think of a topic for discussion could find a home within a wide variety of approaches.[34] If, however, the class is regularly seated in a circle and the teacher consistently remains outside it and refuses to take the initiative in terms of shaping the conversation, then we have something that quite clearly expresses the philosophy of Community Language Learning (see chapter 9).

Perhaps an allusion to music will help clarify the point. Much as a

---

design, a design that in turn structures the utilization of procedures. In a given episode of language teaching, approach, design, and procedure are simultaneously operative — they are not distributed between the university and the school classroom. The creativity and loose fit between approach, design, and procedure mean that beliefs and orientations do not correspond one-to-one with procedures; they do, however, have their impact on the choice, arrangement, and development of procedures.

34. A given approach or design may require, recommend, or exclude certain specific procedures (as a communicative approach generally requires an information gap, or Community Language Learning excludes error correction during beginner-level oral practice), and may permit a range of others in varying proportions. Cf. Allen, 1993. For a response to and expansion of Allen's account, see Smith, 1995.

composer combines the notes, rhythms, and instruments available to all musicians into a distinctive musical piece, a language teacher configures a range of procedures in the light of her convictions and beliefs and helps give shape to an educational experience with its own particular emphases and priorities.[35]

In short, we miss the point if we merely look at individual procedures to see whether Christians do them differently, and conclude from such observation that there can be no Christian perspective on teaching methods, since we all draw from the same pool of procedures. What matters is which procedures are chosen, when they are chosen, how they are arranged, and *why* they are patterned as they are.

Expanding the Idea of an Approach

Third, and here is the crucial point in terms of where our argument is leading, Anthony's understanding of an approach as containing beliefs about language and language learning is far too narrow. Equally limiting is the tendency in later discussions to equate such beliefs with *theories* from linguistics, psycholinguistics, sociolinguistics, or second-language acquisition research.[36] From our discussion thus far it should be clear that there are many more factors that give shape to an approach: our personality and character qualities, the spirit of the age, and our professional socialization, to name just a few. This expanded list of variables, we are convinced, can also include Christian convictions and Christian spirituality.

Anthony's characterization of an approach in terms of *beliefs* raises

35. Brumfit, 1991, 138; Swaffar, Arens, and Morgan, 1982. Even if the conscious criterion at work in a given classroom is a pragmatic one of what "works," only the most doggedly randomized (and therefore unprofessional) selection of activities is likely to avoid exhibiting some implicit pattern of emphasis. Some empirical support for this point is provided by the study of teacher responses to questionnaires designed to elicit methodological priorities in Swaffar, Arens, and Morgan, 1982. The authors of the study conclude: "Methodological labels assigned to teaching activities are, in themselves, not informative, because they refer to a pool of classroom practices which are universally used. The differences among major methodologies are to be found in the ordered hierarchy, the priorities assigned to tasks. Not *what* classroom activity is used, but *when* and *how* form the crux of the matter in distinguishing methodological practice" (31).

36. Richards, 1984, 7; Richards and Rodgers, 1986, 16-19.

the possibility that *Christian* beliefs may be relevant. Obviously, not all beliefs that inform an approach will be confessional in character; some may involve quite mundane matters, such as the belief that classes with thirty students are too large for fruitful instruction to take place. Furthermore, not all aspects of the Christian faith will necessarily be relevant to teaching strategies; a particular view of baptism, for example, doesn't seem to be an obvious candidate for influencing our foreign language pedagogy. On the other hand, Christian beliefs about society, culture, the nature and calling of human beings, the proper norms for communication between people, and the purpose of education, to name just a few, could be very relevant. Specifically Christian beliefs are only one component of the total body of convictions that might affect a teaching process, but they are, we maintain, a significant part.[37]

Also, our approach to teaching does not just involve our beliefs functioning somehow as disembodied principles. It also encompasses our lived spirituality, the way we are oriented toward God, others, and the world. Christian character, the teacher's spirituality, and the ethos fostered in the Christian classroom can all be seen as shaping aspects of an approach.[38]

An approach can also be shaped by particular metaphors through which we think about pedagogical matters.[39] As in the present study, a Christian orientation may be expressed not only in conceptually articulated beliefs, but also in a preference for particular metaphors for teaching and learning (see chapters 4 and 5). Looking at foreign language pedagogy in terms of hospitality to the stranger, for instance, can contribute to the shaping of our pedagogy.

In sum, although we should be wary of claiming that our teaching designs somehow flow purely from our stated beliefs, we should nevertheless see foreign language pedagogy as an area in which our faith, when lived out with integrity and imagination, can make a significant difference.

37. This is a brief statement of a complex issue. Distinguishing "specifically Christian beliefs" from other kinds is not intended to suggest that Christian faith is narrowly concerned with what Western culture tends to construe as the religious (as opposed to the secular) parts of life. The purpose of the present argument is to show that Christian commitment can affect an area as apparently nonreligious as foreign language pedagogy.

38. Palmer, 1983; Palmer, 1998; Schwehn, 1993; Tench, 1985.

39. Cf., e.g., Block, 1992; Huebner, 1985; Kramsch and von Hoehne, 1995; Ortony, 1979; W. Taylor, 1984; Thornbury, 1991.

Conclusion

Earlier in this chapter we encountered the claim that there is a single Christian method that will differ in every respect from its alternatives. We also heard a more skeptical voice insisting that methods have nothing at all to do with faith. These alternatives, as we have tried to show, are too simplistic. Both fail to do justice to the creative and dynamic patterning pertaining to teaching processes. The first seems to imply that pedagogical designs can leap fully formed from theological convictions and are valid for all times and places. The second fails to notice that differences in designs and procedures reflect varying worldviews.

Through a process that is both complex and creative, our faith and the outworking of that faith in a lived response to God can be factors in shaping the way we teach. The model we have suggested will not yield one single Christian design that would be the ideal for all times, all places, and all learners;[40] instead it offers a creative, dynamic way of bringing our faith to bear on our teaching. Our next chapter will apply this model to more concrete examples of pedagogical proposals.

40. Compare the variety of differing designs for classroom practice that are conventionally grouped together under the heading of humanistic approaches. These both differ from one another in the detail and show a common consistency with various convictions characteristic of the general approach (Stevick, 1990). A given design will have a good or a poor fit with a given approach, but an approach is by its very nature *not* a set of detailed specifications for constructing a design, or a blueprint that details the outcome in advance. Designing a pedagogical sequence is a process of translating an approach into a constellation of more detailed procedures at a particular place and time.

CHAPTER NINE

Two Case Studies: Curran's Community Language Learning and Kramsch's Critical Foreign Language Pedagogy

Neighborly love is not a choice. It is an inherent dimension of being human.

James Olthuis

A small group of students is seated in a circle in a language classroom. They have come to learn French, and are still working at a beginner's level. There is a cassette recorder in the center of the circle, and a facilitator stands behind the students. When they feel ready, the learners begin a conversation among themselves, discussing what they did over the weekend. When one of them wishes to talk, she indicates this to the facilitator, who comes and stands beside her. She states what she wants to say in her native language. In a warmly supporting tone the facilitator translates her words into French; the student then says the French phrases to the group. The facilitator does not comment on any errors she might make. Each contribution is taped. After a while the conversation comes to an end, and the learners listen to the recordings and discuss with the facilitator any new features of the French language that may have emerged during the exercise.

In another classroom students are working in pairs. They are telling stories to one another in German. More precisely, they are telling the same story to their partners over and over again, each time changing the context of the story or the manner in which they are narrating it. They imagine themselves to be at a party or a job interview and relate the story in a way that would fit those settings. They try getting through the story more quickly each time. They first speak to their partner seated face-to-face, then back-to-back. They share the story in whispers, they interrupt one another, or both of them tell it simultaneously and try to shout each other down, to impose their story on one another. The activity leads them to reflect with the teacher on how the changing personal and social contexts shaped the narrative they have told.

*   *   *

In chapter 8 we outlined a model of how Christian faith might relate to the ways teaching and learning are patterned in the classroom. We showed how particular visions of life can inform an approach, which then plays a guiding role when a teacher chooses procedures and organizes them into a design. We suggested that while beliefs of various kinds are involved in forming an approach to teaching, Christian beliefs also can play a significant role. We illustrated this through an example of how in one classroom David Smith's interest in the implications of a concern for truth led him to make a series of adjustments in his teaching.

In this chapter we offer two case studies that further illuminate how basic orientations to the world affect teaching and learning. While the example in the last chapter involved a process of adjustment in response to a specific incident in a foreign language classroom, this chapter will turn to more fully developed pedagogies discussed in literature on foreign language education and taught in teacher training courses. We will test whether Christian beliefs have any relevance to these pedagogies. As we emphasized at the outset, we do not intend in this book to offer a comprehensive survey of pedagogical approaches in our discipline. Our aim is rather to explore specifically whether the themes of blessing and hospitality to the stranger might enable us to ask critical questions of the pedagogical options available to our profession.

For the purposes of illustration, we will focus on the two approaches reflected in the cameos above. The first is from Charles Curran's Community Language Learning, a pedagogy that attained prominence in the 1970s and reflects the ethos of the affectively oriented connoisseur introduced in chapter 6. The second illustrates Claire Kramsch's critical foreign language pedagogy, an interesting, fresh development in foreign language education that we associated in chapter 6 with the figure of the revolutionary. Both examples thus illustrate quite clearly how the orientations described in chapter 6, and their underlying ideological assumptions, shape pedagogy. In addition, Curran's pedagogy is interesting not only because it gained a place in standard discussions of methodology, but also because he claimed it was founded on a Christian understanding of the person.[1] We have mentioned Kramsch's work more than once in this study simply because we consider her writings to be among the most insightful of contemporary contributions to foreign language pedagogy.

We will discuss each author's work in the light of the themes we have been developing. We intend not to offer a global critique or overall evaluation of each pedagogy, but rather to home in on any specific points of tension with a Christian framework. The point is not to use such a framework as a means of rejecting pedagogical designs wholesale, but rather to explore particular areas of compatibility or incompatibility.

Community Language Learning

The work of Charles A. Curran was part of a broader movement in the 1960s and 1970s away from an overemphasis on the cognitive, on what Carl Rogers called "education from the neck up,"[2] and toward a pedagogy that sought to integrate the emotions and personal experiences of the student into the learning process. This effort to renew education in the light of humanistic psychology emphasized a view of the learner as "essentially active, voluntary, responsible, relational, caring and free."[3] Curran, a student and colleague of Rogers, contributed to the movement a way of teaching based on Rogers's nondirective, client-centered approach to counseling, with its strong emphasis on the feelings and the autonomy of the client.

Curran's intent was clear: He wanted to overcome the split in traditional education between the cognitive, affective, and somatic aspects of the human being and to focus the attention of educators on the "whole

1. Curran, 1972, 49.
2. Rogers, 1969, 4.
3. Yoshikawa, 1982, 391. In this emphasis on emotional wholeness and individual freedom, humanistic psychology sought to chart a third path between behaviorism and Freudianism. Cf. May, 1969.

person." He wanted to encourage teachers to work toward learners' emotional well-being and self-awareness, so that their mind and body could be reconnected into an integrated whole.[4] To this end, he looked for a pedagogy that would minimize the student's feelings of insecurity and alienation. In doing so he hoped to create a warmly affirming sense of community in the classroom. His aim was to "incorporate teachers and learners together in a deep relationship of human belonging, worth and sharing."[5] The scenario sketched at the beginning of this chapter depicts one of his best-known suggestions for achieving this objective.

The classroom is laid out as it is because Community Language Learning requires the teacher to relinquish his or her godlike position, characterized by superior knowledge, power, and authority, and to take up instead an emotionally supportive but nondirective role. The teacher is to move out of the learner's space; she is not expected to teach, but rather to help create a warm and reassuring group context within which students can take charge of their learning. They choose what to say and when to say it; they, not their teacher, provide the content of the educational process. After all, the source of learning, Curran argues, lies within the learner. The teacher is there primarily to offer nonjudgmental affirmation and to give support when students call on her to do so.[6]

The class described above was made up of beginners still dependent on the teacher for the phrases they needed in order to communicate. In all, Curran proposed five stages through which learners would progress from total dependence to complete independence, in which they are at ease and fluent in the new language. As they become more confident and more emotionally secure in the new tongue and therefore less intimidated by outside help, the teacher can begin to correct their errors when appropriate.

---

4. Curran writes: "When we ask how man functions, we find that every moment of life is a total response. Every stimulus that comes to us from the world about us evokes response by the whole of our being. There is no such thing as a purely physical reaction, or a purely emotional, or a purely mental, or a purely spiritual . . . the lines of continuity reach off into all the rest of our being, and there is no part that is not to some degree involved" (Curran, 1968, 63). On the centrality of the emotional, see Curran, 1969, 11, 222; Curran, 1972, 3, 33.

5. Curran, 1972, 29.

6. Compare Rogers, who proposed abandoning the idea of teaching altogether, arguing that teaching causes the learner to distrust his or her own experience (1969, 152-55).

Curran's concern for the emotional well-being of students was highly attractive in the 1970s, when there was a flurry of interest in his ideas. A feature of his work likely to arouse the curiosity of the Christian language teacher in particular is his claim to be offering a view of education that was in tune with the Judeo-Christian tradition and a biblical view of knowledge.[7]

Drawing on his background as a Roman Catholic priest, Curran freely adopted terms such as "incarnation," "redemption," "dying to self," and "new birth" as metaphors to articulate various aspects of his educational theory.[8] Nevertheless, his theory is open to critique when examined in the light of the issues raised in this book. To see why, we must look in a little more detail at his view of the person and of community.

The Individual and the Other

Curran developed his view of the "whole person" under the influence of Jean-Paul Sartre and Carl Rogers. Thus he strongly emphasizes individual existential experience and the overcoming of existential anxiety. He argues that there are two wills in conflict within the individual, the will to power and the will to community.

The will to power, as he sees it, is a self-centered desire to control others, to be God, while the will to community expresses the longing to give oneself to another.[9] We begin as isolated individuals with the drive to transcend our limits by increasing our power. Soon, however, we encounter others, who represent a threat to our ambitions to be God because we cannot control them.[10] Only if we learn to restrain our will to power and submit to our limits and to the realities of a world shared with others can our will to community emerge.

Given his Christian orientation, one might expect Curran to en-

7. Curran, 1968, 41, 90; Curran, 1969, 5, 186; Curran, 1972, 49.

8. See the discussion in Stevick, 1990, 71-99. The theological dimension of Curran's thinking is most developed in his work on psychotherapy. If one pays attention only to his writings on education, one easily misses this foundational aspect of his work.

9. Curran, 1968, 114; Curran, 1969, 30, 157; Curran, 1972, 64-65; cf. Sartre, 1957, 63.

10. See Sartre, 1966, 342-44, 352-54.

courage the will to community and to reject the will to power. Instead, because of his existentialist emphasis on the autonomy of the individual, he argues that the will to power should be affirmed. Adults should approve of and encourage children's self-assertion, he maintains, so that they can develop self-esteem and not feel threatened by others.[11] According to Curran, as children grow in emotional security and experience unconditional affirmation, including affirmation of their will to power, their basic goodness will emerge and they will become constructive members of the community.

These ideas shape the structure of Curran's pedagogy. In order to place power in the hands of the learner, and to affirm the learner's self-assertion, the teacher must become as passive as possible.[12] This is not only true for younger learners, but also for adults. For both, the final result will be a balance between the will to power and the will to community. As Curran states: "An adult is then also encouraged to learn aggressively and assert his knowledge — supported by the community around him. At the same time, each individual experiences a committed awareness of, and concern for, the community he is engaged with. This provides a learning structure balanced between the forces of self-assertion and the need to belong."[13]

However, Curran and others found that, as learners move through the third of the five stages of learning described in his theory, they often begin to manifest aggression and anger if they feel that anyone else is standing in the way of their progress. They also develop hostility and resentment toward continued dependence on the teacher. This anger and animosity also shows itself in "direct hostility to other group members, especially if their behavior or manner seems to impede the person's progress in learning."[14]

Again, given Curran's claim that his is a Christian pedagogy, we might expect ideas such as sin, repentance, reconciliation, and humility to become pivotal at this point. Instead, in keeping with the existentialist basis of his theory, he insists that hostility should be freely expressed "without any feeling of guilt or of a need to apologize afterwards."[15] The

11. Curran, 1976, 7.
12. Curran, 1972, 91-93.
13. Curran, 1976, 7.
14. Curran, 1969, 217.
15. Curran, 1969, 219; Curran, 1972, 102.

self-esteem of the individual must not be threatened by subjecting his or her behavior to negative criticism by the teacher. If the person is accepted without judgment, Curran asserts, he or she will pass through this "adolescent" stage of learning and will grow into community with others.[16]

In other words, in Curran's design of the learning situation, he tries to resolve the conflict within the student between dependence and independence by making the teacher passive, while affirming the learner's power, no matter how negatively it is expressed. At the same time, however, he stresses the individual's need for a community that can provide him or her with affirmation and a sense of worth.

In our judgment, Curran never really reconciles these two poles, and, as a result, the learner is left, by his own admission, precariously "balanced between the forces of self-assertion and the need to belong."[17] Curran himself appears to be quite comfortable with this inherent conflict between a person's quest for autonomy and her social integration.

However, this key aspect of Curran's thought runs counter to the themes we have sought to develop in this book. Even if we leave aside for the moment the question of whether Curran's view of human nature is overly optimistic, his sanction of aggression and hostility appears to threaten the maintenance of edifying relationships between self and other. In this scheme of things, the self is understood as autonomous and needs to achieve power over others in order to grow, whereas others are understood as a threat and enemy to the self's drive for autonomy and freedom.

A Christian approach seems to us to point in a different direction. If being made in God's image means, among other things, being created for loving relationships with others, and if our selfhood, biblically understood, is not defined by our own aggressive self-assertion, then the basic, existential antagonism between self and other that Curran affirms is a distortion of God's good intention for our life and a symptom of human brokenness and sin. The good connections of creation have been broken by the fall, but the call that comes to us in our redemption is to restored

---

16. Curran's optimism on this point may be compared with Bolitho's report that "on occasion . . . I had to intervene and suspend a session when two students with a hearty contempt for each other used the freedom of the CLL situation to vent their aggression on each other" (Bolitho, 1982, 85).

17. Curran, 1976, 7.

connections.[18] This restoration does not happen through antisocial self-assertion, but rather through yielding our desire for control and opening ourselves to God and to others.

It is not a question here of pretending that hostility does not exist, that Curran's description of our self-assertion over against others is not all too often accurate, or even that we should not respond with concern and understanding when hostility is expressed. The key question is how we respond pedagogically to such hostility. Curran's basic assumptions lead him to respond with affirmation, and with a rejection of ideas of sin or reconciliation. This seems to be more than a passing aberration, since it is rooted in his wider theory of the "whole person." We suggest, in contrast, that affirmed hostility does not lead to embrace, and that Christian educators must part company with Curran at this point.

Limitations of Community

In the light of our themes of hospitality and being a blessing as a stranger, a further weakness in Curran's theory appears. Let us assume for a moment that a sense of community *does* follow from Curran's pedagogy. What kind of community will this be?

Community can have various definitions; we are, for instance, members of cultural, regional, national, religious, political, and intellectual communities. For Curran, however, the notion of community seems to refer only to the warm sense of togetherness to be experienced in the learning group.[19]

This understanding of a community obviously is extremely narrow. Cultural or ethical factors, for instance, do not play a role; all that matters and holds the group together is the affective experience of belonging. Curran's learning community is, moreover, focused inward — upon itself and its own shared experiences; it does not look outward toward a wider world, different cultural perspectives, or a broader purpose beyond the emotional well-being of the group members.

18. Olthuis, 1989, 316; cf. Olthuis, 1993, 160-61: "Community, mutuality, neighborliness, intersubjectivity are constitutive of the nature of each human person . . . [therefore] in distinction . . . from any form of individualism . . . neighborly love is not a choice. It is an inherent dimension of being human."

19. Cf., e.g., Curran, 1972, 32-33.

This inward focus is an integral part of Curran's approach to education. The cultural background and context out of which students come into the classroom are not, in his view, of any great significance for their identity; what they bring to the group is, according to Curran, a set of shared emotional needs that transcend all differences in background, gender, race, class, and the like.[20] Moreover, since the learners create the content of learning, the curriculum for language study is constructed from within their own internal frames of reference. Thus, the target language acquired supplies above all a new medium for *self*-exploration and *self*-expression.

Consequently, Curran's pedagogy provides little encouragement to focus on learning how to prepare for the roles of host or stranger, or how to make space for and listen to voices from abroad. Curran assumes that cultural differences play a minor role in second-language communication, as long as speakers come with an attitude of affective openness and with secure self-esteem. Community Language Learning, therefore, puts most of its energies into creating a secure, warm, comfortable environment for students. In doing so, it is in danger of building a home that is self-enclosed and that knows little of hospitality to the stranger.[21]

Critical Foreign Language Pedagogy

Claire Kramsch's contributions to foreign language pedagogy, formulated above all in her landmark study *Context and Culture in Language Teaching* (1993), contrast sharply with Curran's emphasis on the individual's emotional experience. Taking her cues from semiotics, sociolinguistics, and from the school of critical pedagogy, Kramsch advocates foreign language education that brings cultural difference to the fore. In contrast to the goals of Curran's self-enclosed affective community, Kramsch offers creative ways of sensitizing students to cultural difference and emphasizes the importance of being challenged and unsettled by the stranger. Language learning, in Kramsch's view, is to focus on conflict rather than consensus building.[22]

20. Curran, 1968, 40.
21. For a more detailed discussion of Curran in relation to Christian education, see Smith, 1997b.
22. Kramsch, 1995c.

In contrast to the ideal of the free, autonomous individual of humanistic education, critical pedagogy begins with an image of the learner as submerged in and dominated by a particular cultural situation. This situation seems normal because of its familiarity; students, just like the rest of us, are used to the culture in which they have grown up, and thus uncritically take much of it for granted. According to theorists of critical pedagogy, this sense of normality helps hide the evils in their cultural setting; it also tends to keep students subjugated and passive.

Critical pedagogy seeks to awaken the learners' consciousness of their own context, so that they become critically aware of it and begin developing their own voices. Through this process of attaining critical consciousness, learners are to participate in a struggle to redefine social reality in more liberating ways, as they raise their voices in conflict with the frameworks of meaning that have been imposed on them.[23] The central interest in this pedagogy is on "how teachers and students sustain, or resist, or accommodate those languages, ideologies, social processes, and myths that position them within existing relationships of power and dependency."[24]

Kramsch applies these insights to foreign language pedagogy. She considers the view of language and culture characteristic of current communicative theories inadequate, since it sees language only as a transparent vehicle for transmitting information that supposedly exists "out there," independent from language.[25] It fails, therefore, to take sufficient account of the ways our discourse is shaped by our culture, our context, and our worldview. It does not acknowledge that the words I must use when I speak are already inhabited by the assumptions, values, beliefs, traditions, expectations, and prior conversations of my discourse community.[26]

Given the formative and complex role culture has in shaping language, and language has in shaping culture, learning another language does not, according to Kramsch, mean simply learning a set of new cultural facts that are transmitted by means of new words. Instead, it involves discovering how the foreign language "expresses," "embodies," and "symbolizes" a "cultural reality"[27] unlike my own. In the process of learning the

23. See, e.g., Freire, 1996; Giroux, 1997; Giroux and McLaren, 1989.
24. Giroux, 1997, 134.
25. Kramsch and McConnell-Ginet, 1992.
26. Kramsch, 1991, 226; Kramsch, 1993, 43.
27. Kramsch, 1998a, 3.

new language, students should become aware of how the way they speak reflects the social environment that has shaped them and, at the same time, should become conscious that native speakers of the target language speak out of notably different cultural contexts. They should learn that contexts are socially constructed and reconstructed through the linguistic interaction of individuals.[28] What learners need as they seek to understand texts in another language is "not an ever greater amount of information, but an awareness of their own frame of reference."[29]

By way of illustration, Kramsch cites an incident in one of her German classes when a student produced the sentence: "Ich mag Herausforderungen, aber diese Klasse ist lächerlich!" (intended meaning: I like challenges, but this class is ridiculous!).[30]

In contrast to Curran, Kramsch homes in on the errors the student made in this sentence. The word *lächerlich*, she points out, suggests in German a ridiculously small task rather than a burdensome undertaking. More significantly, she notes, the noun *Herausforderungen* would not be a natural choice for a German speaker discussing education. Its use instead reflects an American's attempt to employ a German word to express a notion of challenge that is rooted in her own cultural assumptions. This American notion of challenge, Kramsch continues, is related to the entrepreneurial spirit, to obstacles to be overcome by effort and initiative. Far from being a value-free concept, it may even be used to mask responsibility, as when environmental catastrophes are described as "challenges" by their perpetrators.[31] The student's sentence thus embodies a tension between German and American meanings, but does not fully coincide with either. In this way, Kramsch argues, the student attempts to speak with her own voice, while at the same time revealing in a single sentence a clash of cultural voices or worldviews.

Kramsch urges teachers to seize these moments of breakdown, which reveal the imperfections and failures of attempts at communication, as educationally valuable. She professes to be "more interested in fault lines than in smooth landscapes."[32] As the learner struggles to express his personal meanings in a new language, the resulting clash of worldviews may

28. Kramsch, 1993, 46.
29. Kramsch, 1993, 124.
30. Kramsch, 1993, 16.
31. Kramsch, 1993, 32.
32. Kramsch, 1993, 2.

help him become conscious of the ways he has been formed by his own culture. Furthermore, learners are to realize that meanings are not simply given, but that they themselves have a role in shaping them; hence the design of activities such as the one described in the scenario at the start of this chapter, which highlights shifting contexts and conflicting voices.

In the light of the intimate interconnection of language and culture, Kramsch believes that the traditional emphasis on the ideal of becoming exactly like the native speaker is mistaken. The teacher's task is not to "have learners . . . parrot a society's conventional discourse but find a voice of their own in the foreign language."[33] Foreign language learning should not be about the impossible attempt to replace one's cultural identity with that of the other; it is rather "a place of struggle between the learners' meanings and those of the native speakers."[34]

Through the study and use of the new language, students are to be made less comfortable in their own cultural context. As their previously unquestioned sense of self is unsettled and destabilized, they can thereby be made critical of their own culture and then engage in the process of transforming it.

Kramsch's critical foreign language pedagogy seems, then, to be strong precisely where Curran's Community Language Learning is weak: in taking account of cultural difference. Indeed, we very much welcome this emphasis on otherness, and find Kramsch's account of cross-cultural communication interesting and insightful.

How, then, does Kramsch's pedagogy fare when considered in the light of our stated goals of foreign language teaching? Does it help students to be a blessing as strangers and to offer hospitality to strangers in their midst? As was the case in our treatment of Curran, here, too, answering this question requires a consideration of basic assumptions concerning personhood and community.

Subjugation and Empowerment

In Kramsch's view, learners do not start out as free, autonomous individuals. Our identities are woven into a complex social fabric, and our lan-

33. Kramsch and McConnell-Ginet, 1992, 12.
34. Kramsch, 1993, 24.

guage, the medium in which our identity is formed, is filled with words whose meanings have already been defined by others. Kramsch does not focus on the constructive role communal belonging plays in the formation of identity, or on the ways we are nurtured by this pervasive social and cultural context, but rather on its power over us. She presents the initial situation of the learner as one of subjugation and powerlessness.[35]

When the individual becomes a student in an educational setting, this subordination to the cultural power of others is intensified. Students, Kramsch argues, are subjected to norms of knowledge and interaction that reflect broader cultural ideologies and are actively imposed by a teacher within the culture of an institution. In the foreign language classroom, learners experience an additional level of subordination, because they are expected to conform to a new linguistic and cultural system they did not construct.

Pedagogy must therefore aim at empowerment. My voice is, Kramsch argues, "enmeshed with and regulated by the voice of the other."[36] To simply accept this, however, would be to yield to the subjugation of my voice. If I instead resist, then as a learner I can grow as I discover my power to assign new values to what seemed to be predetermined meanings, and thus take control over discourse.[37]

This brings my voice into conflict with the voices of others. Rather than just accepting meanings from others, I now am to gain satisfaction through imposing my own meanings: "There is little pleasure in accepting ready-made meanings, however pertinent. The pleasure derives both from the power and process of making meanings out of *their* resources and from the sense that these meanings are *ours* as opposed to *theirs*."[38]

Learners, in Kramsch's view, should therefore be encouraged to engage in power games with each other and with the teacher, for both pleasure and learning are, for Kramsch, associated with the assertion of power over language and therefore over others.[39] Communication becomes conflict as a multiplicity of voices struggle to define meaning. In the classroom this means tension between the learner's autonomy and the teacher's control. In a manner reminiscent of Curran's third stage, this power struggle is

35. Kramsch, 1993, 238; Kramsch and von Hoehne, 1995, 335.
36. Kramsch, 1993, 128, citing Sheldon.
37. Kramsch, 1993, 238-39.
38. Kramsch, 1993, 238, citing Fiske.
39. Kramsch, 1993, 30.

affirmed as the way things should be: "The struggle between the desire of students to appropriate the foreign language for their own purposes, and the responsibility of the teacher for socializing them into a linguistically and socioculturally appropriate behavior lie at the core of the educational enterprise. Both are necessary for pleasurable and effective language learning. The good teacher fosters both compliance and rebellion."[40] This struggle between the teacher's and the learner's meanings is not merely inevitable; it is to be positively fostered, for "[t]his struggle is the educational enterprise *per se*."[41]

Pedagogical suggestions such as those described in the second cameo at the beginning of this chapter reflect this conflict-oriented understanding of language and learning. Activities in which learners try out different voices or even try to shout each other down and impose their speech on one another resonate with an understanding of language and learning as rooted in a conflict of voices and a struggle for power.

In spite of all the differences in emphasis between Community Language Learning and critical foreign language pedagogy, Kramsch's pedagogy raises issues similar to those we noted in Curran's work. In the accounts offered by both Curran and Kramsch, becoming an authentic person seems to require exerting an autonomous will to power and asserting oneself over against others. Both, then, leave us with the puzzle of how this pedagogical goal relates to loving our neighbor.[42]

Kramsch does write compellingly of the need to "pause and muster the effort to speak, quite literally, in terms of the other"[43] and of moments of life-changing connection with others, but these are described as hap-

40. Kramsch, 1993, 256.

41. Kramsch, 1993, 239.

42. Kramsch does propose *politeness* as a goal for learning a foreign language (Kramsch, 1996). Politeness is for her "not a personal feeling of solidarity" like empathy, but a "social capacity" (1) or "an interactional ability" (3) that stresses "the social nature of interpersonal relationships and their cultural relativity" (1). For Kramsch, teaching a foreign language does not primarily focus on the development of students' ethical or moral attitudes toward the speakers of the target language. Speaking is a social activity and students have to develop cognitive, affective, and behavioral competencies to know and practice the social norms and rules in a given culture. The individual learner has always the option to "abide by the rules or to flout them" (2). We agree that empathy is not enough, but we nevertheless think it is possible to conceive the goals of our pedagogy in broader terms than polite social interaction.

43. Kramsch, 1995b, 90.

pening inexplicably, surprisingly, like miracles or epiphanies.[44] Nor should we wonder that this is the case. If speaking is defined in terms of an ongoing rivalry between voices that are "by nature in conflict with one another,"[45] the task of explaining why we experience such moments of edifying connection is a daunting one.

Here we see a sharp contrast between Curran and Kramsch. Whereas Curran reaffirmed the necessity of intimate community, emphasizing this point to such a degree that the community of learners seemed self-absorbed and closed to the stranger, Kramsch has no desire to submerge actual differences and conflicts in a false consensus. The clash and conflict of cultural voices is designed to jolt the student out of her cultural comfort, forcing an often disturbing encounter with irreducible difference. Kramsch's hope is that the learner will find a home in a "third place," which has developed out of the permanent clash and confrontation of incommensurable value systems and is located in neither the home culture nor the foreign culture. This relocation to a "third place" will question the status quo and will bring about transformation. "It is a process," Kramsch states, "which makes language teachers into agents of social change."[46]

The "third place" that is the goal of learning is, then, "between and beyond the social order of the native culture and that of the target culture."[47] It will be defined differently by each learner,[48] and is compared to the experience of cultural migrants, who have "feelings of being forever 'betwixt and between,' no longer at home in their original culture, nor really belonging to the host culture."[49]

While Curran rendered hospitality difficult because of a concern to cling to the emotional comforts of home, Kramsch seems to render it equally problematic by relinquishing a sense of the positive dimensions of belonging — and of even having a home. Nevertheless, the difficulties in Kramsch's pedagogy, viewed from a Christian perspective, need to be stated with some care.

Just as with Curran, we would not wish to advocate a naive assumption that we live in a rosy world where there is no conflict involved in our

44. Kramsch, 1993, 2; Kramsch, 1995d, x.
45. Kramsch, 1993, 27.
46. Kramsch, 1996, 9.
47. Kramsch, 1993, 238.
48. Kramsch, 1993, 257.
49. Kramsch, 1993, 234.

use of and learning of language. Reconciliation does not come about by ignoring conflict. Nor do we wish to dispute the claim that learners need to confront differences in order to realize that their cultural perspective is not simply normal. On both counts Kramsch offers a great deal of very helpful discussion in her writings, and there are eminently good Christian reasons for being interested in any ways that we can become more aware of how we are conformed to the patterns of the world and of how we use language sinfully to assert our dominance over others.

Reference to sin brings us closer to the heart of the problem. As in the case of Curran, the difficulty arises when conflict based on the will to power is presented as normal and affirmed as simply an essential ingredient of education, leading to a construal of all differences as conflicts. If we are created for loving relationships with one another and with God, and if separation, hostility, conflict, and the desire for autonomous power do not reflect the biblical vision of the way things are supposed to be, then we must subject affirmations of the struggle to seize power to careful scrutiny. Kramsch, in several of the comments cited above, seems to take the broken, fallen world as normative and normal and to build her pedagogy on that conviction. We accept much of her description of the way things are, but nevertheless hold that pedagogy should set its sights by other norms. Since in our fallen world conflict and hostility are all around, we can learn much from theorists such as Kramsch who focus their attention on strife and struggle. But in the biblical vision, conflict is not the way things ought to be. Peace was in the beginning and will reign once more; in the meantime we are to be peacemakers, and our relationships with others are to be channels of grace.[50]

Eclecticism: An Alternative?

These brief and partial outlines of Curran's and Kramsch's approaches to foreign language pedagogy further illustrate the central contentions of chapter 8: that pedagogy is patterned by beliefs and commitments, and that beliefs shape instructional materials and strategies. While the example of truth telling in the foreign language classroom described in chapter 8 il-

50. For a more detailed discussion of Kramsch in relation to Christian belief, see Smith, 1997b; Smith, 1997d.

lustrated how Christian convictions can be crucial as we continue to modify our own classroom practices, the present chapter has given examples of how more theoretically articulated pedagogical designs can be critiqued from the standpoint of Christian faith. There are, of course, many more approaches than those represented by Curran and Kramsch. Thus there is a considerable need for further research that gives careful attention both to the commitments that shape such approaches and to their degree of compatibility with Christian faith.

It should be reemphasized that we are not arguing that Christians do not have much to learn from either Curran or Kramsch, or that they should not glean instructional ideas from their writings. As we pointed out in chapter 8, commitments become visible in the *patterns* that emerge in teaching, not in individual techniques.[51] While Christians may well hesitate to accept the overall framework offered by Curran, Kramsch, or some other theorist, they can likely weave many of the specific pedagogical suggestions these authors offer into designs that conform more closely to their own Christian convictions.

This raises a further issue that must be addressed before we leave the topic of pedagogy. It is not only Christians who may be reluctant to accept an entire ideological package. The skepticism concerning a single right method that we discussed in chapter 8 has led to a more general preference for some form of eclecticism. Instead of taking a particular pedagogical design and following it faithfully, most language teachers today prefer to draw ideas from a variety of sources and use a mixture of procedures in a way they judge appropriate to a particular teaching context. Such a strategy may see the teacher taking a much less ideologically consistent tack. This need not stem from a sheer love for variety — the ideal may rather be artful responsiveness to the situation at hand, unconstrained by a set of prior conceptions. If grand designs have been so constricting, better to stay free of them and to respond as the context requires.

What about such an eclectic stance? If we Christian teachers and theorists are also suggesting drawing from a variety of pedagogical sources, are we not undermining the whole argument developed in the past two

---

51. Although the possibility that certain techniques may be strongly associated with particular beliefs about teaching and learning is by no means excluded. The point we are seeking to emphasize is that it is necessary to attend to broader patterns in order to gain a sense of what individual techniques mean.

chapters, with its central emphasis on the role of basic assumptions and convictions in shaping an approach to language teaching?

In fact, drawing from various sources runs with, not against, the grain of our argument as long as the procedures gathered from here and there are woven together into a consistent pattern. The weaknesses of an *unprincipled* eclecticism are not hard to find.[52] Eclecticism obviously involves choosing elements to adopt from the various available pedagogical designs. But eclecticism in and of itself offers no criteria for selection, and therefore no way of knowing whether we have chosen the better — or the less helpful — elements of a given alternative. We need some basic convictions concerning what is pedagogically sound in order to choose well.

In other words, reasons stand behind the choices made in a responsibly eclectic approach, and these reasons reflect certain convictions and beliefs. Eclecticism is no more value-free than any other approach.[53] As we argued in chapter 8, the process of combining various elements into a coherent whole always involves designing particular ways of teaching in the light of certain implicit or explicit beliefs and assumptions.

One might object that, in the eclectic approach, mere pragmatic responsiveness to the context in which we teach directs our decisions, and not anything more principled, such as values and commitments.

In response, it should be pointed out that as soon as we appeal to a particular context to guide us in our choices, we must of necessity make a variety of judgments about it. By its very nature, every educational situation is extremely complex. Our task is, then, to decide which aspects of a

---

52. Byrnes, for instance, argues that "without criteria to guide instruction it is but a small step from being liberated from methodological dictates to succumbing to methodological anarchy. Instead of motivated pedagogical decision making we find random eclecticism, a bag of tricks, on-location how-tos that make successful foreign language teaching neither an art nor a science as claimed by the big methodologies, but an amateurish practice that, for good measure, requires a pleasant personality" (1998, 274).

53. As Prabhu states (albeit in continued reliance on the language of "method"): "Any such blending of different methods is either done with a perception of what is true about each method, or it is done without any such discrimination. If there is a perception of which part of what method is a partial truth, then that perception constitutes a theory, which happens to have an overlap of understanding with various other theories. It therefore represents a method, which is like any other method, with an overlap of understanding with others. There is no reason to think, on the strength of its being a blend, that it has any more of the truth than any other method" (1990, 164, 166).

given educational context are significant for teaching. We will have to choose, for instance, from among factors such as age, gender, local culture, religious background of learners, economic factors, national guidelines, learners' emotions, and learning styles.

Once we make our selection, we have to decide what relative weight to give each of the factors we have chosen as we design our curriculum. We have to ask ourselves, for example, whether age is more significant than gender or learning styles, or whether economic factors are more important than national guidelines.

In other words, working fruitfully with our context involves interpreting and ordering its bewildering array of features and responding in a way that meets our educational objectives. No two teachers will respond to the same context in identical fashion. It must be stressed, however, that their educational choices, whatever they might be, will necessarily reflect implicit beliefs, convictions, and orientations.[54]

Once we determine which factors are relevant and how they are weighed, we still have to decide whether we will respond to them as *constraints* or as *challenges*. For instance, if learners come from a community hostile to French speakers, does this strengthen or weaken the case for offering French as part of compulsory education?[55] If the prior experiences of learners make certain kinds of activities (for instance, reading longer texts) difficult for them, should those kinds of learning be stressed more strongly because of their educative value — or replaced by activities closer to learners' existing habits? In short, should the content of materials reflect, extend, or subvert the existing experiences, attitudes, and interests of students?[56] Similarly, if government policy appears to favor a reductive kind of learning, should teachers follow it — or resist it?

Answering questions like these inevitably draws in our beliefs and

---

54. Cf. Prabhu: "[I]f we look for variation merely on the assumption that the teaching context matters for teaching methodology, we are sure to find indefinite variation on many dimensions, thus making it impossible to justify any instructional method for any single group of learners. . . . Pointing to a bewildering variety of contextual factors as a means of denying the possibility of a single theory can only be a contribution to bewilderment, not to understanding" (1990, 164, 166).

55. This has been a live issue for some parent-funded Christian schools in Canada.

56. For conflicting views on this issue, see Kramsch's discussion of Richardson and Scinicariello about whether foreign language television materials should fit in with or clash with students' existing views of life (Kramsch, 1993, 189).

values. As we design our teaching materials, we typically accept some aspects of the situation and resist others. In so doing we take an evaluative position with regard to the factors concerned. The judgments involved in making all these decisions will be woven into our assessment of whether a given pedagogy "works."

In sum, our basic convictions concerning language, persons, and the educational process will inform the choices we make in responding to the context of learning. There simply is no such thing as value-free response to any context, and any *principled* eclecticism must recognize this fact.

*   *   *

Chapters 4–6 proposed and developed basic aims of foreign language education, while chapter 7 considered the views of the world implied in the content of course materials. In chapters 8 and 9 we have examined what might be seen as the area where Christian beliefs are least likely to make any difference. We demonstrated that, although the idea of a single Christian teaching method different from all others is not particularly helpful, it is possible and appropriate that Christian convictions play a significant role in shaping foreign language pedagogy.

Before concluding this volume, in chapter 10 we will briefly review sample curriculum resources that were designed with Christian concerns in mind, but not for explicitly Christian schools. We intend these examples to serve as a concluding indication both that some work has already been done in this area, and also that rich possibilities await further exploration. We invite others to join in the task.

CHAPTER TEN

Samples from a Curriculum Project

In the preceding chapters we explored various aspects of language teaching in the light of our Christian faith. In this final chapter we will relate some of the themes discussed earlier to resources produced by a curriculum project in which one of us (David Smith) has been involved as a writer.

This undertaking, called the Charis Project, began at Stapleford House Education Centre (now renamed The Stapleford Centre) in Nottingham, England, in 1994.[1] Its context is informed by the increased attention given to the moral and spiritual dimensions of education in the United Kingdom in recent years. While promoting these aspects of education has long been a stated aim of legislation in England, a recent spate of government documents has insisted that moral and spiritual development be seen as whole-school, cross-curricular concerns rather than (as has traditionally been the case) largely the preserve of specific subject areas such as Personal and Social Education and Religious Education.

It is in this context that the Charis Project has been developing Christian resources across the curriculum, seeking ways of integrating and highlighting moral and spiritual aspects of subject areas outside the province of religious education. The materials developed thus far have the following aims:

1. The examples used in this chapter are taken from the Charis Project materials and are reproduced here by permission of The Stapleford Centre. Further information about the Charis Project can be obtained from The Stapleford Centre, The Old Lace Mill, Frederick Road, Stapleford, Nottingham, UK (or visit http://www.stapleford-centre.org).

- to enable teachers to respond to the challenge of educating the whole person;
- to help teachers focus on the spiritual and moral dimensions inherent in their subject;
- to encourage pupils toward a clearer understanding of Christian perspectives on the fundamental questions that arise in all areas of knowledge; and
- to contribute to the breadth, balance, and harmony of pupils' knowledge and understanding.[2]

The first phase of the project developed materials for fourteen-to-sixteen-year-olds for English literature, French, German, mathematics, and science. These materials are used in both Christian schools and non-Christian state-maintained schools. It is, of course, the foreign language resources that interest us here.[3]

These materials were developed before the writing of this book, and not as a fully conscious application of the ideas we have discussed in preceding chapters. They do, however, represent a substantial attempt to develop curriculum resources for foreign languages in the light of Christian concerns, and the involvement of David Smith as a writer means there is some connection between the Charis foreign language materials and the thinking that characterizes the present volume.

In what follows we will describe examples of learning activities from the Charis French and German materials (Spanish materials are not yet available) that in some way illustrate issues we explored in earlier chapters. We do not present these examples as in any way definitive or as the best way of applying the perspective we have advocated. They serve rather as fallible pointers to the kind of work that could be done, and as samples of what has been attempted thus far.

We will look at examples from the Charis French and German materials in the light of four questions:

- What images of strangers do we present through our course materials?
- What aspects of the stranger's experience are considered to be of interest?

2. Baker et al., 1996b, vi.
3. Baker et al., 1996a; Baker et al., 1998a; Baker et al., 1996b; Baker et al., 1998b.

- For what kinds of interaction with the stranger do we prepare learners?
- How do these broader concerns relate to linguistic goals?

The Image of the Stranger

First, what kinds of images of the stranger do our course materials project? How do we present strangers who are not reduced to their consumption or leisure habits, but who more fully demonstrate their humanity as images of God?

One unit in the first Charis German book takes up the history of the White Rose movement. This movement was initiated by a group of students at Munich University who, in the early 1940s, motivated in part by the Christian faith, secretly resisted Hitler. After they had for some time been publishing and distributing tracts calling for Germans to stop supporting the war, they were caught by the Gestapo. The group's ringleaders were tried for high treason and summarily executed.

The topic of the White Rose is quite frequently included in German courses, but usually with more advanced learners and without reference to the faith dimension of its participants' motivation and attitudes.

The Charis unit begins with a photograph of Sophie and Hans Scholl and Christoph Probst, as the latter two were about to travel to the war front for active service. All three look very serious and somewhat anxious.

Learners are shown the photo without any captions and are asked what they see. By progressive questioning the teacher can move the conversation through the basic content of the picture (number of people, gender, age), appearances (clothes, facial expression), setting (How long ago? Where?), and mood (How are they feeling?), toward initial speculation as to what is going on (Why might they be feeling that way? What might be happening/or about to happen?).

The teacher then reveals, one by one, a series of further images that accompany the photo (see Figure 10.1, p. 194); discussion follows the presentation of each new image. Taken together, the series prompts an exploration of Sophie's family, her leisure interests, and her studies. Gradually the basic outline of the story of the White Rose emerges.

This activity allows students to utilize basic vocabulary: words having to do with, for example, age, gender, appearance, clothes, feelings, and family. Instead of practicing these words and concepts in conjunction with

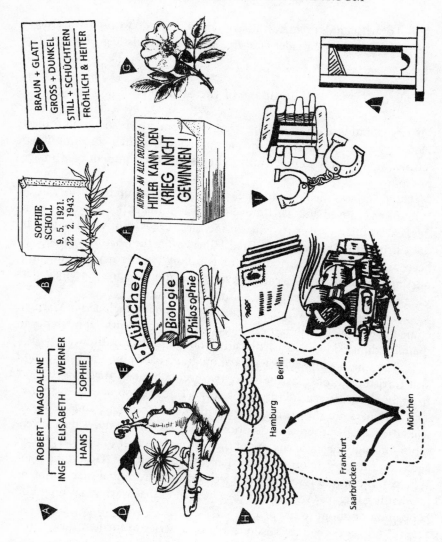

Figure 10.1

a cartoon image or an arbitrarily chosen picture, however, using this photo allows such practice to be grounded in a concrete historical setting. Learners can move beyond surface appearances and gradually get to know other aspects of the lives of the people whose image they are examining. As they do, they meet Germans who do not live just to work, shop, or play, but who believe in something strongly enough to be willing to lay down their lives for it.

Following this procedure need not mean that the teacher shift immediately into much more difficult levels of language use. It is possible to deal with depth dimensions of the life of the stranger before reaching advanced proficiency in the target language.

For example, a subsequent activity in this unit presents an account of a dream Sophie Scholl had in prison the night before her execution. In this dream she was climbing a steep path up a mountain toward a church. It was a sunny day, and she was carrying an infant in a white christening robe. Suddenly a crevasse opened up at her feet and she plunged in, but before she fell, she was able to place the infant safely on the other side. On waking, Sophie took the dream to mean that the cause for which she had fought would live on beyond her death, that justice would prevail.

A text such as this presents profound spiritual issues in language that is concrete and simple. Dreams, allegories, proverbs, fairy tales, and poems can all provide this combination of simple language with depth of meaning.

Learners can also respond without having mastered abstract language. Later in the same unit pupils are presented with a collection of statements made by various people at the time the White Rose was active. Sophie's sister, Inge, asks why they are the ones who must act against Hitler; couldn't someone else do it? Sophie replies that so many people have fallen for Hitler's regime that it is time for someone to fall in opposition to it.

One of the questions following these statements asks learners whether they identify more with Inge or with Sophie. The response can be brief and simple: "I am like Inge." However, before giving that answer, students must reflect on how the lives of these two strangers relate to and perhaps challenge or illuminate their own.

What this unit illustrates is how biographically based instructional segments can be used to explore different dimensions of the life of a member of the target culture. A similar approach can be taken for Spanish learners with figures such as Bartholomé de Las Casas from the colonial period, or Cardinal Romero from recent Latin American history; for

French students, public figures can be introduced such as Charles Péan, who campaigned for the closure of the Devil's Island penal colony in French Guiana. But also ordinary, uncelebrated inhabitants of the target countries whose experience of life is equally rich and appealing can get a voice.[4] Exploring the lives of these individuals not only gives more depth to the image of the stranger presented in our course materials; it also helps prepare learners to ask good, insightful questions of the foreigners they later meet and get to know. We will return to this point below.

Dimensions of Experience

A second question is implicit in the above discussion of biographical material: What aspects of the stranger's experience are of interest to us? Are we interested only in the material, practical dimension of that experience, or does it have other aspects we could explore?

Many foreign language course materials are organized around various topics or themes, such as food and drink, accommodations, or school life. Many of these topics can be approached in a way that pays attention to more dimensions of experience than they now commonly do.

Consider, for instance, food and drink. In most existing materials the word "bread" is dealt with as an item of consumption, in the context of either family meals or shopping transactions. But is this the only or even the most educationally interesting way to deal with this common vocabulary item?

Jacques Ellul's reflections on this very ordinary word are telling:

> Even the simplest word — *bread,* for instance — involves all sorts of connotations. When the word *bread* is pronounced, I cannot help but think of the millions of people who have none. . . . The communion service comes to me: the breaking of bread at the Last Supper. . . . I pass quickly to the moral lessons I learned as a child: that it is a crime to throw away a piece of bread, since it is a sacred substance. And from

4. A unit of work in Charis Deutsch, Einheiten 1-6, relates the life story of Frau Adeline Kelbert, an elderly German lady who had experienced life as a refugee through the Russian Revolution and the world wars and whose reminiscences provided fascinating material. This led to work in which learners prepare to interview older persons about their life story.

there, of course, I arrive at the enormous, incredible amount of waste-fulness in our society. . . . Memories come back to me: the warm, crusty bread of my childhood. The promised bread of life that will satisfy all hunger. And not living by bread alone. . . . Not all of these memories are conjured up every time I hear the word, and they do not all come at once, but it is a rarity when none of them follows the oft-repeated request: "pass the bread."[5]

This does not mean that every vocabulary item should be subjected to large-scale word-association exercises. Ellul's comment might, however, provide a reminder that the consumer context is not the only possible framework within which students can encounter commonplace words as meaningful. Ask a Muslim or a Christian like Ellul what significance bread has for them, and we enter a new multicultural and spiritual dimension. This expanded awareness can in turn broaden the context within which learners also think about the meanings of the word "bread" for them. It is along lines such as these that the theme of "bread" is developed in a Charis French unit.

Charis Deutsch, Einheiten 6-10, deals with the theme of light in a similar way. The word itself can be associated at one end of the spectrum with regular household items such as lamps, candles, or matches — or, at the other end, with the symbolism of good and evil. Moreover, to capital-ize on such associations brings to the fore practices rooted in the unique-ness of German culture. For example, pondering the role of candlelight vigils in the former GDR before the fall of the Berlin Wall and in more re-cent protests against racism and hostility toward foreigners, as well as the significance of light in the meaning and history of the advent crown — that is, thinking about the symbolic aspect of light and darkness in these ways — opens up German cultural themes.

Preparation for Meeting the Stranger

The content of our language courses is informed by an implicit vision of our students' future. If the words, phrases, functions, and situations we re-hearse in the classroom are focused on the linguistic needs of the tourist,

5. Ellul, 1985, 17-18.

then that is the role in which we cast learners in their future interactions with strangers. If the questions we practice asking in the classroom are all requests for information and services, then our learners' capacity for asking other kinds of questions when they visit the foreign culture will be limited. In short, the range of language and experience found in our courses represents a particular kind of preparation for encountering the stranger.

If we want that encounter to go beyond practical transactions in the ways outlined in earlier chapters of this book, at least two requirements for the content of our courses must be met. First, the syllabus must include the language needed to ask about and talk about personal and spiritually meaningful issues. Second, learners must have the opportunity to express themselves in the target language on these kinds of issues. As we noted above, such goals need not be restricted to advanced students.

For the second Charis German volume we developed a unit based on Dietrich Bonhoeffer. It begins with the story of his life, in particular his imprisonment and execution, using pictures and a simple German text. Learners are then presented with one of the poems he wrote while in prison, "Wer bin ich?" (Who am I?).

In this poem, Bonhoeffer reflects on the discrepancy between how other people see him and the way he feels about himself. Others compliment him for his calm courage, but inside he feels weary and lonely. Does this, the poem asks, make him a hypocrite? Or does he change from day to day? Bonhoeffer does not resolve this tension, but places the question of his identity in God's hand.

An immediate problem we faced was that the poem was too difficult in German for the language level of the students for whom we were devising the materials. To overcome this, we adapted the basic ideas of the poem for use as follows.

First, the unit presents learners with a collection of German adjectives they could use to describe someone's character: words like "shy," "brave," "friendly," "serious," "honest," or "lazy." After familiarizing themselves with this vocabulary, they are asked to draw a triangle around any words they have heard others use to describe them, a circle around any words they would use to describe themselves, and a square around any words that represent qualities to which they aspire.

They are then presented with a simplified outline of Bonhoeffer's poem (see Figure 10.2, p. 199). The exercise provides them with spaces to fill in the words with the triangles, circles, and squares around them, in or-

Ein Gedicht

Sieh dir Arbeitsblatt 4 noch einmal an. Wie hast du dich beschrieben? Schreib die Wörter im Gedicht auf.

Wer bin ich?

Wer bin ich? Sie sagen mir oft:

‚Du bist _____‘

_____

_____

_____

und _____.

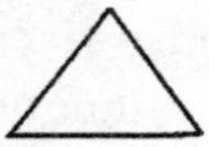

Bin ich das wirklich, was andere von mir sagen?
Oder bin ich nur das, was ich selbst von mir sage?

Ich glaube, ich bin _____‘

_____

_____

_____

und _____

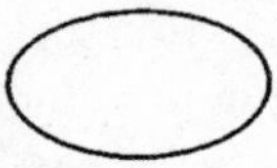

Wer bin ich? Bin ich beides zugleich?

Ich möchte aber so werden:

_____

_____

_____

_____

und _____

Wer kennt mich? Wer bin ich? Wer werde ich sein?

Figure 10.2

der to compose a simple poem about how others see them, how they see themselves, and how they would like to be. In this way, by loosely following Bonhoeffer's pattern, even learners of limited ability, without access to complex language, can compose a poem in German.

Relating the activity to Bonhoeffer's life and experience of imprisonment makes this more than an exercise in self-exploration; a stranger's questions to himself in a particular historical situation provide an opportunity for learners to be challenged and enriched, and to have their sense of the humanity of the stranger reinforced.

Another example of using a German poem to provide for open-ended reflection on personally meaningful issues involves the use of lines written by a German teenager (see Figure 10.3, p. 201). The poem is presented with the main verbs removed, but includes an explanatory phrase following each open blank. Translated, the exercise would read as follows:

Take time to _____; it is the source of strength.
Take time to _____; it is the secret of eternal youth.
Take time to _____; it is the source of wisdom.
Take time to _____; the day is too short to be selfish.
Take time to _____; it is the music of the soul.
Take time to _____; it is the greatest power in the world.

A list of the missing verbs ("pray," "think," "give," "laugh," "read," "play") is provided, and pupils are asked to reconstruct the poem. The point here is not that they correctly replicate the original, but that they think about how well the different verbs would fit in different places, and then produce a personal version of the poem.

One more example. As part of the process of developing a French unit with an ethical focus, questionnaires were sent out to a group of French teenagers, asking them how often they told lies, whether it was ever justified to do so, why honesty was important, to whom they would be most likely to lie, and how they would feel and react if they found out that a friend had lied to them.

Their richly varied responses provided the basis for a range of activities in which learners can respond to the ethical views expressed by their French counterparts. For instance, they are presented with ten reasons offered by the French students for considering honesty important, and asked to place them in what they consider to be their order of importance (see

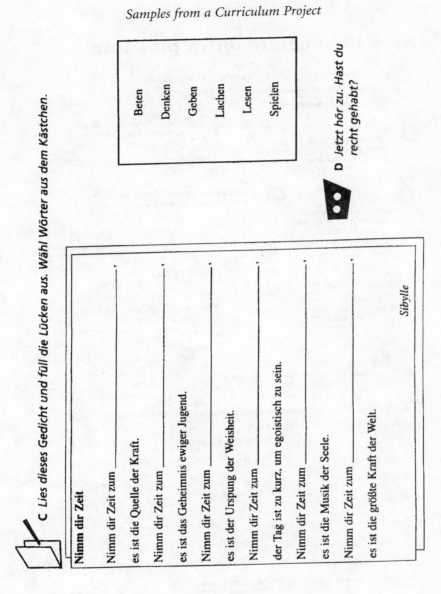

C *Lies dieses Gedicht und füll die Lücken aus. Wähl Wörter aus dem Kästchen.*

Beten

Denken

Geben

Lachen

Lesen

Spielen

Nimm dir Zeit

Nimm dir Zeit zum _____,
es ist die Quelle der Kraft.

Nimm dir Zeit zum _____,
es ist das Geheimnis ewiger Jugend.

Nimm dir Zeit zum _____,
es ist der Ursprung der Weisheit.

Nimm dir Zeit zum _____,
der Tag ist zu kurz, um egoistisch zu sein.

Nimm dir Zeit zum _____,
es ist die Musik der Seele.

Nimm dir Zeit zum _____,
es ist die größte Kraft der Welt.

Sibylle

D *Jetzt hör zu. Hast du recht gehabt?*

Figure 10.3

Avec l'honnêteté on va plus loin

Dans le sondage sur la Feuille de travail 1, on a demandé:
<<Est-ce que c'est important d'être honnête? Pourquoi?>>

A Lis les réponses de quelques élèves.

A Oui, c'est important, je ne voudrais pas devenir escroc, voleur, je préfère être honnête.

B Oui, parce-que si on est honnête on ne fait de mal à personne.

C Oui, car même si on regrette d'avoir menti, une fois que c'est fait, c'est fait.

D Oui, pour qu'on puisse avoir confiance en tout le monde – surtout aux hommes politiques.

E Oui, car ne pas l'être, c'est un péché.

F Oui, pour gagner la confiance des autres.

G Oui, c'est important pour se sentir bien dans sa peau! Lorsqu'on ment, on se sent mal!

H Oui, pour réussir dans nos études il faut être honnête (ne pas tricher ni copier lors des examens).

I Oui, parce-que tu as plus de chance d'être aimé des autres.

J Oui, sinon la vie serait injuste.

B A ton avis, quelle est la raison la plus importante pour être honnête?
Et la moins importante? Fais une liste.

Pourquoi être honnête?

1 _____ 6 _____

2 _____ 7 _____

3 _____ 8 _____

4 _____ 9 _____

5 _____ 10 _____

C A considérer

Peux-tu trouver d'autres raisons pour être honnête?

Figure 10.4

Figure 10.4, p. 202). This exercise not only engages the learners in ethical reflection, but also prepares them for talking to the stranger about moral questions. All of these activities are intended to make the target language a medium in which a broader range of experience, including its spiritual and moral dimensions, can be encountered even by learners who have not yet reached advanced levels.

Relating Broader Concerns to Linguistic Goals

When encountering the Charis Project materials, some teachers are intrigued by the human interest of the content but skeptical about the practicality of spending classroom time on such matters. After all, they have to cover enough linguistic material to get through the examination syllabus. Will it not be a distraction to wander off into all these other topics?

In response, linguistic goals need not be seen as necessarily in tension with broader educational concerns. For one thing, communicative approaches to language teaching have long maintained that using language more personally meaningful to the learner is likely to lead to more effective language learning and better retention. For another, broader concerns can be dealt with in a way that retains a clear linguistic focus. Two examples will illustrate this point with reference to grammar and vocabulary.

In an activity from the unit based on the theme of bread, mentioned above, students are asked to place words representing basic aspects of their lives — "bread," "family," "education," "money," "friendship," "television," "water," "faith," "love" — on a grid in descending order of importance. (See Figure 10.5, p. 204.) They are to do this by negotiating in pairs: "I think water is more important than money" or "I think television is less important than friendship."

In a follow-up activity pupils are asked to role-play as members of two families with very different levels of affluence, and renegotiate the scale of values from those perspectives. Different levels of support are given to learners of differing ability.

What are students doing here? In terms of language skills, they are completing a grammar exercise: by the end of the activity they will have repeatedly practiced sentences containing a comparative. In terms of meaning, they are holding a discussion in the target language about their basic values. The two dimensions of learning go hand in hand, reflecting the fact

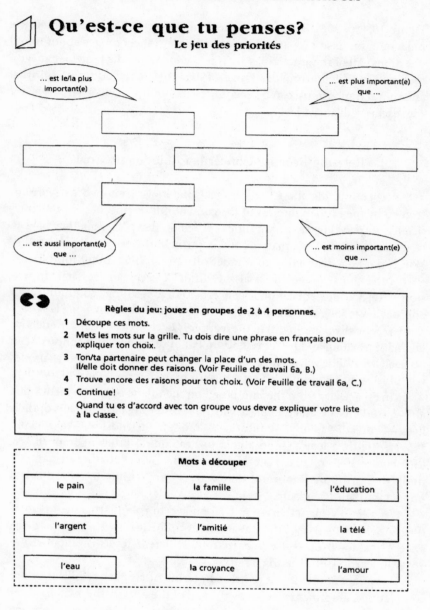

Figure 10.5

that the various kinds of responses to life that characterize us as human beings do not typically occur in isolation from one another, but as part of an integral whole.

A second example relates to covering required areas of vocabulary. The examination syllabi in the United Kingdom for the age range covered by the Charis materials typically include words for jobs, personal characteristics, and the various buildings in a town. These were all included in a Charis French unit based on the history of Montreal.

Montreal was founded in 1642 as a utopian Roman Catholic colony, with the purpose of spreading the Christian faith among the inhabitants of New France. Students are asked to imagine themselves founding a new colony in similar circumstances and to reflect on questions such as the following: Whom will you take with you? What character qualities, trades, and skills will be important? Which buildings will you construct first, and what will the priorities for further development be? Where will you locate the buildings? What will the rules for your new colony be?

After working with these questions, students have the opportunity to compare their responses with the choices made by the original settlers. In this way they can reflect personally and historically on the shape of social life in the situation outlined while covering familiar areas of vocabulary.

As we emphasized at the start of this chapter, we do not intend these illustrations to represent definitive prescriptions; they are merely examples taken from a particular curriculum project to illustrate the themes explored in this book. They are rooted in an attempt to integrate into the design of foreign language materials a Christian concern for the interconnection of the spiritual and ethical dimensions of being human with all of the other aspects of life.

As students are enabled to engage with spiritual and moral themes in their own lives in the new medium of the target language and to encounter the significance of such themes in the lives of speakers of that language, we hope they will begin to develop fresh capacities for carrying out their calling as good strangers and hosts. Perhaps in ways such as these we can move students just a little closer to embracing the stranger.

Epilogue

Some books offer teaching suggestions from a position of mastery, of having been successful in educational endeavors. This book has been more an attempt to reflect on what our faith requires of us language teachers, and it is written from the standpoint of still being very much on a journey rather than from one of having already arrived. This leaves us wanting to express two hopes in closing.

First, we hope others will reflect further on the issues we have raised and will take the discussion of what faith has to do with language teaching a few steps further. This book is an exploratory foray, not a definitive overview.

Second, we hope those who read these pages will be left with a sense of inspiration, vision, challenge, and hope. Jesus spoke critically of those who load burdens onto other people's backs, and we are aware of the danger that the already overworked Christian language teacher will be left with a sense of increased burdens and personal inadequacy. In order to resist this at least in some small way, we want to close with a reminder that the Christian faith centers on grace.

Seeking to relate our faith to our teaching should not mean looking for immediate perfection, but rather for ways of inviting God's grace into the imperfection of what we do. Our attitude as we reflect on all that we discussed in the preceding pages should be that of the children described by John Calvin:

Those bound by the yoke of the law are like servants assigned certain tasks for each day by their masters. These servants think they have accomplished nothing, and dare not appear before their masters unless they have fulfilled the exact measure of their tasks. But sons, who are more generously and candidly treated by their fathers, do not hesitate to offer them incomplete and half-done and even defective works, trusting that their obedience and readiness of mind will be accepted by their fathers, even though they have not quite achieved what their fathers intended. Such children ought we to be, firmly trusting that our services will be approved by our most merciful Father, however small, rude and imperfect these may be.[1]

1. Calvin, 1977, 3.19.5; p. 837.

Interpreting Babel

In chapter 1 we suggested that it is a mistake to read the Babel story in Genesis 11 as teaching that differences in language and culture are a result of a judgment that destroyed a golden age of uniformity. Since this reading runs somewhat against the grain of most popular interpretations of Genesis 11 (and not a few more scholarly ones), we would like to append here in more detail the grounds for our interpretation. A more extensive account can be found in Smith, 1996b.

We noted in chapter 1 that Genesis 11:1-9 should be read in the context of the wider narrative that precedes it, and that this wider narrative both affirms diversity and emphasizes repeatedly God's call to spread out over the earth. This background should inform our expectations as we approach the Babel story.

The issues involved in interpreting this story can be summarized briefly by three questions: Is the story concerned with the loss of a single original language? What kind of sin was involved in the Babel project? And is this simply a tale of judgment?

1. Was There a Single Language?

Many are surprised to learn that the interpretation of Genesis 11 as a story focused on the tragic loss of a common language is relatively recent. Early church interpreters were more preoccupied with the theme of pride, reading the Babel story in the light of classical tales of hubris. Emphasis on the loss of an original language arose in the late Middle Ages, against a background of the rise of the vernacular languages in Europe and the decline of Latin as the common European language.[1]

This period saw a dramatic increase in the number of artistic representations of the Tower of Babel, as it became a potent symbol for a unity that seemed to be slipping away. Umberto Eco records that

> There are no known representations of the Tower of Babel before the cotton Bible (fifth or sixth century). It next appears in a manuscript perhaps from the end of the tenth century, and then on a relief from the cathedral of Salerno from the eleventh century. After this, however, there are a flood of towers. It is a flood, moreover, that has its counterpart in the vast deluge of theoretical speculations originating in precisely this period as well.[2]

Interestingly, Genesis 11:1 translates literally as "the whole earth had one lip and common words." The word translated "lip" is not normally used elsewhere to refer to a particular language or dialect. It seems to refer more to a manner of speaking (cf., e.g., Isa. 6:5), suggesting that the "one lip and common words" may refer more to agreement or a shared project than a common dialect. Alternatively, some have argued that the "one lip" represents a *lingua franca*, a trade language.[3]

A recent study by Christoph Uehlinger has added some thought-provoking ideas to the discussion.[4] Examining various Assyrian royal inscriptions, Uehlinger finds a recurring pattern of the motifs of *one speech, building, naming,* and *world empire.* The first three are clearly present in the opening lines of the Babel narrative — the world had one speech, a city was being built, and the motive was to achieve a name. If the traditional association of Babel with Nimrod has merit, then the fourth motif may be present too in Genesis 10:11-12, verses that describe the rise of an empire with Babylon as one of its centers.

What, then, does the "one speech" motif mean? Uehlinger goes on to show that in the inscriptions studied, the one-speech motif serves as a

1. Bost, 1981; Eco, 1995, 8-10.
2. Eco, 1995, 17.
3. Hamilton, 1990, 350 n. 7.
4. Uehlinger, 1990.

metaphor for the subjugation and assimilation of conquered peoples, an image for the imposition of a single imperial rule. Thus, for example, Ashurbanipal II is referred to in royal inscriptions as one who "made the totality of all peoples/people speak one speech" and who "through his sovereign approach made the unruly and ruthless kings speak one speech from the rising of the sun to its setting."[5] The "one speech" is the subdued voice of submission to the new ruler, undisrupted by challenges to that rule. The "common words" of Genesis 11:1 are taken by Uehlinger to refer to the speech reported in verses 3-4, reflecting the common plans of the builders. In view of the biblical affirmation of the creativity of language before Babel discussed in chapter 1, it is highly interesting to find the one-speech motif itself identified with oppressively imposed conformity. In the light of such findings, it is by no means clear that Genesis 11:1 reports the kind of golden age that many in the modern era have glimpsed in it.

2. What Kind of Sin Was Involved?

The sin of the Babel builders is commonly identified as pride, and there are good grounds for such an identification. Genesis 1:26-27 is echoed in the repeated "Come, let us . . ." of 11:3-4, and the statement in verse 6 that if things continue then no plan of theirs will be cut off is echoed in Job 42:2:

> I know that you can do all things;
> no plan of yours can be thwarted.

Both allusions suggest an attempt to usurp God's role.

However, identifying pride does not in itself tell us very much about what the builders were actually doing, and it certainly does not automatically support the idea that they were trying to build a tower up to the sky.

The reference to a tower with its head in the heavens can be interpreted in two ways. Many commentators see a reference to a Babylonian *ziggurat*, pointing out that such a structure was topped by a shrine where

5. "der die Gesamtheit aller Völker/Menschen eine Rede führen liess" . . . "der durch sein herrscherliches Nahekommen die wilden und schonungslosen Könige von Sonnenaufgang bis Sonnenuntergang eine Rede führen liess."

heaven and earth were believed to connect. The main temple in Babylon was known as the house with the raised head *(Esagil)*.[6] The reference to the tower is thus commonly interpreted as a critique of Babylonian theology.[7] There is, however, another possible reading. Deuteronomy 1:28 ("The people are stronger and taller than we are; the cities are large, with walls *up to the sky*") and 9:1 ("You are now about to cross the Jordan to go in and dispossess nations greater and stronger than you, with large cities that have walls *up to the sky*") both refer to cities with walls up to the sky. Is the reference in Genesis 11 to the tower with its head in the heavens to be read any more literally? Might it not be largely a question of poetic hyperbole, much like the English word "skyscraper"? In support of this reading, Uehlinger points out that the building style described was used mainly for civil structures, and argues that the most plausible translation of the Hebrew word in question is "citadel" or "acropolis" rather than "tower."[8] Moreover, the narrative seems more interested in the city than the "tower," which disappears in verse 8, suggesting that it was "the building of the city, and not the tower per se, that provoked the divine displeasure."[9]

What the narrative places clearly before us are the motives mentioned in chapter 1 — the builders want to make a name for themselves and want to avoid obeying the command to spread. Here there is direct disobedience, the pride of rejecting God's design. In light of Uehlinger's suggestion that the text is concerned with empire building, it is interesting that making a name for oneself is associated in ancient Near Eastern kingship ideology with military gain and dominion, heroic feats and guaranteed dynasty.[10] The fact that naming is closely related to military conquest in the archeological parallels also fits well with the only other Old Testament reference to someone making a name for himself: "David [made a name for himself] after he returned from striking down eighteen thousand

6. Wenham, 1987, 237-39.

7. It is interesting to note that there may be a more direct polemic against Mesopotamian religion in Genesis 10:8-10 if (as Van der Toorn and Van der Horst argue) Nimrod is to be associated with the deity Ninurta. Ninurta's acts of heroism as a warrior and hunter were portrayed in Mesopotamian mythology as preceding his founding of Mesopotamian civilization, and he was regarded as king of the universe; in Genesis 10 he is firmly "before the LORD" (Van der Toorn and Van der Horst, 1990).

8. Uehlinger, 1990, 372-78.

9. Hamilton, 1990, 356.

10. Uehlinger, 1990, 383.

Edomites in the Valley of Salt. He put garrisons throughout Edom, and all the Edomites became subject to David" (2 Sam. 8:13-14).

A contrast is provided in the call to Abram, which closely follows the Babel story in Genesis 12: ". . . go to the land I will show you. . . . *I will make your name great*, and you will be a blessing" (Gen. 12:2). The building of the imperial city, which halts the eastward migration, is juxtaposed with the call of one man to vulnerable wandering, in faith that the one who called (as opposed to his own might and assertion) will make him into a "great nation." Here we have an ample contrast between pride and humility. In Walter Brueggemann's words, Babel

> attempts to establish a cultural, human oneness without reference to the threats, promises or mandates of God. This is a self-made unity in which humanity has a "fortress mentality." It seeks to survive by its own resources. It seeks to construct a world free of the danger of the holy and immune from the terrors of God in history. It is a unity grounded in fear and characterized by coercion. A human unity without the vision of God's will is likely to be ordered in oppressive conformity. And it will finally be "in vain."[11]

3. Was There a Judgment?

When it comes to judgment, one can observe a tendency to overenthusiasm among commentators. In rabbinic exegesis the judgment reached truly theatrical proportions, with the builders being transformed into monkeys, demons, or other monsters as a punishment for their pretensions.[12] When patristic interpretation laid the groundwork for the Christian interpretive tradition with its focus on hubris, the emphasis on punishment remained, and the story is still today presented as "the last of the great tales of universal judgment that punctuate the primeval history," ending on a "note of fierce condemnation of mankind's sinful folly."[13] There are, however, some clear indicators within the narrative that more may be going on than "fierce condemnation."

11. Brueggemann, 1982, 99.
12. Bost, 1981, 419.
13. Wenham, 1987, 244-45.

The central puzzle is the statement in verse 6 that tells us literally that "this is but the beginning of their doing" and that if this is what flows from their unity, then "nothing they plan to do will be beyond them." The traditional reading of these words suggests that omnipotence was only just beyond reach, so that soon people would be superhuman and nothing, not even usurpation of God's throne, would be "impossible" (NIV). But such a reading simply does not cohere with the biblical narrative in which the Babel story is situated. Just a few chapters earlier God judged humanity cataclysmically without recorded perspiration. In Genesis 1–10 God is simply not that small and humans are vulnerable creatures of dust.

The English expression "nothing will be beyond them" preserves the ambiguity of the verse, which could be more literally translated "no plan of theirs will be cut off." As with the question of sin, it pays to cast an eye back at the shape of the preceding narrative. The flood that resulted from comprehensive human degeneracy was followed by a promise that no further flood would occur (Gen. 9:15) and by a covenant with all living creatures (9:8-11). In light of this, the renewed descent into disobedience of Genesis 11:1-5 is a problematic development, to say the least. For if this sin is allowed to continue, it can only get worse — nothing will be beyond them! (A similar thought is expressed in Luke 23:31.) It is not that they will acquire new God-threatening powers, but that they will stop at nothing; the depth and measure of their sin will increase until only judgment is left as a response. This is what makes intervention so urgent: *we know from the preceding narrative that a further cataclysm must not occur, and we see precisely the conditions developing that might make one necessary.*

And so the LORD comes down, stooping to see the pathetic, puny efforts of the city builders (skyscraper indeed!), and, in mocking imitation of the builders' exhortations (no scared deity this), declares, "Come, let us go down and confuse their language so they will not understand each other." The biting ironies continue. Those who attempted to name themselves are, despite their best efforts, named, and not with a name they would have chosen (their own choice is not recorded for posterity). Their sinful solidarity, the "Come let us" of disobedience, is disrupted as exhortation begins to fall on deaf, or at least uncomprehending, ears. The plot to avoid spreading "lest we be scattered" proves to be a sure route to being scattered "over the face of the whole earth." The "one speech" of empire gives way to the many speeches of peoples on the face of God's earth.

And so, it seems, we are back to judgment. Or are we? That the pretensions of the city builders are mocked and undone is clear. That their project is judged and thwarted is equally clear. But to stop there is to miss the forward-looking dimension of this turn of events. It is at least as important to note that the danger has been averted — they have "stopped" (v. 8); their plans have been cut off, and things cannot develop any further in this direction.[14] There is no need now to begin scripting *The Flood II* and looking for a candidate for the Noah character. In fact, the outcome (stressed twice in the last two verses of the story, in case we missed the point) is not destruction but an enforced return to the path of blessing announced in Genesis 9:1: the LORD "scattered them . . . over all the earth" (vv. 8, 9).

Of course, things are not as simple as if sin had not occurred — active, cooperative "spreading" has become disciplinary "scattering" — but even the discomfort of discipline can have a positive purpose. As the empire is dismantled, maybe it will be possible to build human community again. Thankfully, in verse 10 we are still "after the flood," we can still go back to the sons of Noah to continue the narrative; the flood has not been superseded by a further cataclysm, necessitating a beginning over. The genealogy breathes a sigh of relief after the potentially catastrophic interruption of Genesis 11:1-9 and strides forward once more, moving us on to Abram (whose migration is likewise obedient and redemptive) and a more focused hope for the future of the post-Babel world.

Babel and Other Biblical Texts

This way of reading the Babel story not only does more justice to the detail of Genesis 11:1-9 than at least some of the alternatives, it also fits well with the way other parts of the Bible allude to Babel. Luke's allusions to Babel in Acts 2, where, instead of a return to uniformity, we find once more that blessing is associated with diversity and spreading, has already been discussed in chapter 1. Here we will add only a few brief comments on another relevant passage, Exodus 1–3.

14. Cf. Gerhard von Rad's comment: "A humanity that can think only of its own confederation is at liberty for anything, i.e. for every extravagance. Therefore God resolves on a punitive, but at the same time preventive, act, so that he will not have to punish man more severely as his degeneration surely progresses" (1960, 145). Gowan also notes that the threat was not to God, but to humanity (Gowan, 1988, 119).

The opening paragraphs of Exodus do not make much direct reference to God. Instead a series of allusions to the early chapters of Genesis signal to the alert reader what is going on. Thus in Exodus 1:7 the allusion to the fruitfulness and multiplication of Genesis 1:28 communicates to us that God's blessing rests upon the children of Israel. Similarly, in Exodus 2:3, when we read of a child being placed in an ark (the same term here as in Genesis 6), which is coated with pitch and set upon the waters, we are being told through the allusions to Noah that this child is special and connected in some way with God's plans for salvation.

What is interesting for present purposes is that these chapters also allude to Genesis 11.[15] Pharaoh's opening words are a direct echo of Genesis 11:3-4: "Come, let us . . ." Like the words of the builders, these words are spoken in opposition to the process of multiplying and spreading blessed by God. Pharaoh, in his opposition to God's intentions, employs the Israelites as slave labor. He uses them to build cities, one of which is named after a pharaoh. We are even told that the building materials are brick and mortar (cf. Gen. 11:3). What these allusions suggest is that Pharaoh is engaging in rebellion like that of the builders of Babel, and knowing this, we begin to look for God's response. Finally, in Exodus 3:8 we read: "I have *come down* to rescue them from the hand of the Egyptians" (cf. Gen. 11:7).

The opening chapters of Exodus portray a tyrannical rule that sets itself up against God's intentions, uses slave labor to make a name for itself through building projects, and refuses to allow the migration of a people whom God would have elsewhere. These themes echo closely what we found in Genesis 11, and indeed, the allusions to the Babel story seem to suggest that what Pharaoh is doing is like what the builders of Babel were doing. Exodus 1–3 thus offers further support from within Scripture for our understanding of Genesis 11.

15. Cf. Kikawada and Quinn, 1985, 116-17.

Select Bibliography

Allen, R. T. 1993. Christian thinking about education. *Spectrum* 25, no. 1, 17-24.

Anthony, E. M. 1963. Approach, method and technique. *English Language Teaching* 17, no. 2, 63-67.

Baker, D., H. Brammer, C. Chapman, S. Dobson, K. Heywood, and D. Smith. 1996a. *Charis Français: Unités 1-5*. St. Albans: ACT.

————. 1996b. *Charis Deutsch: Einheiten 1-5*. St. Albans: ACT.

Baker, D., S. Dobson, H. Gillingham, K. Heywood, D. Smith, and C. Worth. 1998a. *Charis Français: Unités 6-10*. Nottingham: Stapleford Centre.

————. 1998b. *Charis Deutsch: Einheiten 6-10*. Nottingham: Stapleford Centre.

Bakhtin, M. 1986. Response to a question from the Novy Mir editorial staff. In *Speech genres and other late essays,* translated by V. W. McGee, 1-9. Austin: University of Texas Press.

Bammer, A. 1995. Xenophobia, xenophilia, and no place to rest. In *Encountering the other(s),* edited by G. Brinker-Gabler, 45-62. Albany: State University of New York Press.

Banovitch, A. 1971. Le travail de J. A. Comenius à la réforme de l'enseignement des langues. *Acta Comeniana* 2:109-33.

Barrick, E. 1993. Poetry-writing as a means of spiritual self-expression in the intermediate French classroom. *Proceedings Journal of the North American Association of Christian Foreign Language and Literature Faculty* 3:23-41.

Bauman, Z. 1995. *Life in fragments: Essays in postmodern morality*. Oxford and Cambridge: Blackwell.

Beavis, A. K., and A. R. Thomas. 1996. Metaphors as storehouses of expectation: Stabilizing the structures of organizational life in independent schools. *Educational Management and Administration* 24, no. 1, 93-106.

Blake, R. J. 1998. The role of technology in second language learning. In *Learning foreign and second languages: Perspectives in research and scholarship,* edited by H. Byrnes, 209-37. New York: Modern Language Association of America.

Block, D. 1992. Metaphors we teach by. *Prospect* 7, no. 3, 42-55.

Bolinger, D. 1980. *Language: The loaded weapon.* London: Longman.

Bolitho, R. 1982. CLL: A way forward? In *Humanistic approaches: An empirical view,* edited by P. Early, 80-86. London: British Council.

Bonet-Maury, G. 1959. Hospitality. In *Encyclopedia of religion and ethics,* edited by J. Hastings, 6:797-825. New York: Charles Scribner's Son.

Bost, H. 1981. A propos de Babel comme symbole. *Etudes théologiques et religieuses* 56, no. 3, 419-29.

Brislin, R. 1986. *Intercultural interactions: A practical guide.* Beverly Hills, Calif.: SAGE Publications.

Bruce, F. F. 1988. *The book of Acts.* Rev. ed. Grand Rapids: Eerdmans.

Brueggemann, W. 1982. *Genesis.* Atlanta: John Knox.

————. 1988. *To pluck up, to tear down: Jeremiah 1–25.* Grand Rapids: Eerdmans.

Brumfit, C. 1984. *Communicative methodology in language teaching — the roles of fluency and accuracy.* Cambridge: Cambridge University Press.

————. 1985. *Language and literature teaching: From practice to principle.* Oxford: Pergamon.

————. 1991. Problems in defining instructional methodologies. In *Foreign language research in cross-cultural perspective,* edited by K. de Bot, R. P. Ginsberg, and C. Kramsch, 133-44. Amsterdam and Philadelphia: John Benjamins.

Burke, R. B. 1962. *The "Opus majus" of Roger Bacon: A translation by Robert Belle Burke.* New York: Russell & Russell.

Byram, M. 1989. *Cultural studies in foreign language education.* Clevedon, U.K.: Multilingual Matters.

————. 1997. *Teaching and assessing intercultural communicative competence.* Clevedon, U.K.: Multilingual Matters.

Byram, M., and M. Fleming, eds. 1998. *Language learning in intercultural perspective: Approaches through drama and ethnography.* Cambridge: Cambridge University Press.

Byrnes, H. 1998. Constructing curricula in collegiate foreign language departments. In *Learning foreign and second languages: Perspectives in research and scholarship,* edited by H. Byrnes, 262-95. New York: Modern Language Association of America.

Calvin, J. 1977. *Institutes of the Christian religion.* Vol. 1. Philadelphia: Westminster Press.

————. 1979. *Genesis.* Edinburgh: Banner of Truth.

Čapková, D., J. Cervenka, P. Floss, and R. Kalivoda. 1989. The philosophical significance of the work of Comenius. *Acta Comeniana* 8:5-17.

Caputo, J. D. 1997. *Deconstruction in a nutshell: A conversation with Jacques Derrida.* New York: Fordham University Press.

Caravolas, J.-A. 1993. Comenius (Komensky) and the theory of language teaching. *Acta Comeniana* 10:141-70.

Caroll, R. 1990. *Cultural misunderstandings: The French-American experience.* Chicago: University of Chicago Press.

Carvill, B. 1991a. Foreign language education: A Christian calling. *Christian Educators Journal* 30, no. 3, 29-30.

————. 1991b. Teaching culture from a Christian perspective: Is it any different? *Proceedings Journal of the North American Association of Christian Foreign Language and Literature Faculty* 1:13-18.

Carvill, B., and H. Westra. 1999. Listen and speak: Methodology. In *English Language Institute/China: Student Handbook: Summer Training Program for Middle School Teachers,* 3rd ed., 1-90. Changchun, China: North East Normal University Press.

Chastain, K. 1991. Light, salt, culture shock, and when in Rome. *Proceedings Journal of the North American Association of Christian Foreign Language and Literature Faculty* 1:1-10.

Clayden, E., C. Desforges, C. Mills, and W. Rawson. 1994. Authentic activity and learning. *British Journal of Educational Studies* 42, no. 2, 163-73.

Comenius, J. A. 1993. *Panorthosia or universal reform, chapters 19-26.* Translated by A. M. O. Dobbie. Sheffield: Sheffield Academic Press.

Cooling, T. 1994. *A Christian vision for state education.* London: SPCK.

Cooper, M. E. 1996. I was a stranger and you welcomed me: Exploring godly hospitality and its implications for Christian education. *Lutheran Theological Journal* 30:120-30.

Copeland, R. 1991. *Rhetoric, hermeneutics, and translation in the Middle Ages: Academic traditions and vernacular texts.* Cambridge: Cambridge University Press.

Curran, C. A. 1968. *Counseling and psychotherapy: The pursuit of values.* New York: Sheed & Ward.

————. 1969. *Religious values in counseling and psychotherapy.* New York: Sheed & Ward.

————. 1972. *Counseling-learning: A whole person model for education.* New York: Grune & Stratton.

————. 1976. *Counseling-learning in second languages.* Apple River, Ill.: Apple River Press.

————. 1982a. Community Language Learning. In *Innovative approaches to language teaching,* edited by R. W. Blair, 118-33. Rowley, Mass.: Newbury House.

————. 1982b. A linguistic model for learning and living in the new age of the person. In *Innovative approaches to language teaching,* edited by R. W. Blair, 134-45. Rowley, Mass.: Newbury House.

Davies, A. 1993. Speculation and empiricism in applied linguistics. *Edinburgh Working Papers in Applied Linguistics* 4:14-25.

Davies, J. G. 1952. Pentecost and glossolalia. *Journal of Theological Studies,* n.s., 3:228-31.

DES/WO/HMSO [Department of Education and Science/Welsh Office/Her Majesty's Stationery Office]. 1990. *Modern foreign languages for ages 11-16: Proposals of the Secretary of State for Education and Science and the Secretary of State for Wales.* London: HMSO.

Descartes, R. 1968. *Discourse on method and the meditations.* Harmondsworth: Penguin.

Dobbie, A. M. O. 1986. *Comenius' "Pampaedia" or universal education.* Dover, Kent: Buckland.

Draper, J. B., and J. H. Hicks. 1996. Foreign language enrollments in public secondary schools, fall 1994. *Foreign Language Annals* 29, no. 3, 303-6.

Dunne, J. 1993. *Back to the rough ground: Practical judgement and the lure of technique.* Notre Dame: University of Notre Dame Press.

Eco, U. 1995. *The search for the perfect language.* Oxford: Blackwell.

Ellul, J. 1985. *The humiliation of the word.* Grand Rapids: Eerdmans.

Feldmeier, R. 1992. *Die Christen als Fremde: Die Metapher der Fremde in der Antiken Welt, im Urchristentum und im 1. Paulusbrief.* Tübingen: J. C. B. Mohr.

Feyerabend, P. 1975. *Against method: Outline of an anarchistic theory of knowledge.* London: NLB.

Fowler, S., H. Van Brummelen, and J. Van Dyk. 1990. *Christian schooling: Education for freedom.* Potchefstroom, South Africa: Potchefstroom University for Christian Higher Education.

Freire, P. 1996. *Pedagogy of the oppressed.* Rev. ed. New York: Continuum.

Frisch, M. 1958. *Biedermann und die Brandstifter.* Frankfurt am Main: Suhrkamp.

Fromm, E. 1974. *The anatomy of human destructiveness.* London: Jonathan Cape.

Fuchs, O. 1988. Die Entgrenzung zum Fremden als Bedingung christlichen Glaubens und Handelns. In *Die Fremden,* edited by Ottmar Fuchs, 240-301. Düsseldorf: Patmos Verlag.

Gadamer, H.-G. 1989. *Truth and method.* 2nd ed. London: Sheed & Ward.

Geertz, C. 1973. *The interpretation of cultures.* New York: Basic Books.

Geissler, H. 1959. *Comenius und die Sprache.* Heidelberg: Quelle & Meyer.

Giroux, H. A. 1997. *Pedagogy and the politics of hope: Theory, culture, and schooling.* Boulder, Colo.: Westview.

Giroux, H. A., and P. McLaren, eds. 1989. *Critical pedagogy, the state, and cultural struggle.* Albany: SUNY Press.

Gittins, A. J. 1989. *Gifts and strangers: Meeting the challenge of inculturation.* New York: Paulist Press.

———. 1994a. Beyond hospitality? The missionary status and role revisited. *International Review of Missions* 83:397-416.

———. 1994b. The Christian as stranger: Responding to xenophobia. *Month,* 185-190.

González, J. L. 1998. For the healing of the nations: The book of Revelation and our multicultural calling. In *The one in the many: Christian identity in a multicultural world,* edited by T. R. Thompson, 1-7. Lanham, Md.: University Press of America.

Gowan, D. E. 1988. *From Eden to Babel: Genesis 1–11.* Grand Rapids: Eerdmans.

Greenway, E. 1994. College language departments and off-campus cross-cultural service experiences. *Proceedings Journal of the North American Association of Christian Foreign Language and Literature Faculty* 4:200-214.

Groome, T. H. 1988. The spirituality of the religious educator. *Religious Education* 83:9-20.

Gundry-Volf, J. M., and M. Volf. 1997. *A spacious heart: Essays on identity and belonging.* Leominster: Gracewing.

Gurevitch, Z. D. 1989. The power of not understanding: The meeting of conflicting identities. *Journal of Applied Behavioral Sciences* 25, no. 2, 161-73.

Hallie, P. P. 1979. *Lest innocent blood be shed.* New York: Harper & Row.

Hamilton, V. P. 1990. *The book of Genesis, chapters 1–17.* Grand Rapids: Eerdmans.

Hawkins, E. W. 1989. *Modern languages in the curriculum.* Rev. ed. Cambridge: Cambridge University Press.

Henning, W. A. 1993. On making value judgements about cultures. *Proceedings Journal of the North American Association of Christian Foreign Language and Literature Faculty* 3:65-82.

Hill, P. 1996. Comment. *Themelios* 21, no. 3, 15-16.

Hiltbrunner, O. 1972. Gastfreundschaft. In *Reallexikon für Antike und Christentum,* edited by T. Klauser, 8:1062-1123. Stuttgart: Anton Hiersemann.

Hirsch, S. A. 1914. Roger Bacon and philology. In *Roger Bacon: Essays,* edited by A. G. Little, 101-51. Oxford: Oxford University Press.

Hovdhaugen, E. 1982. *Foundations of Western linguistics: From the beginning to the end of the first millennium.* Oslo: Universitetsforlaget.

Huebner, D. 1985. Religious metaphors in the language of education. *Religious Education* 80, no. 3, 460-72.

Hüllen, W. 1979. *Didaktik des Englischunterrichts.* Darmstadt: Wissenschaftliche Buchgesellschaft.

Jelinek, V. 1953. *The analytical didactic of John Amos Comenius.* Chicago: University of Chicago Press.

Johnson, S. 1993. Reshaping religious and theological education in the 90's: Toward a critical pluralism. *Religious Education* 88, no. 3, 335-49.

Joldersma, C. 1999. What's so good about being different? Examining uniqueness through the lens of Emmanuel Levinas. In *Nurturing reflective teachers: A Christian approach for the twenty-first century,* edited by D. C. Elliott and S. Holtrop. Claremont, Calif.: Coalition for Christian Teacher-Educators.

Jury, E. C., and A. J. Peck. 1987. *Orientierung: Reading activities for GCSE German.* London: Mary Glasgow.

Kamperidis, L. 1990. Philoxenia and hospitality. *Parabola* 15:4-13.

Keatinge, M. W. 1967. *The "Great didactic" of John Amos Comenius.* 2nd ed. New York: Russell & Russell.

Kelly, L. G. 1969. *Twenty-five centuries of language teaching, 500 BC–1969.* Rowley, Mass.: Newbury House.

Kikawada, I. M., and A. Quinn. 1985. *Before Abraham was: The unity of Genesis 1–11.* San Francisco: Ignatius Press.

Kinginger, C. 1997. A discourse approach to the study of language educators' coherence systems. *Modern Language Journal* 18, no. 1, 6-14.

Kohák, E. 1996. Of dwelling and wayfaring: A quest for metaphors. In *The longing for home,* edited by L. S. Rouner, 30-46. Notre Dame:: University of Notre Dame Press.

Koyama, K. 1993. "Extend hospitality to strangers" — a missiology of theologia crucis. *Currents in Theology and Mission* 20, no. 3, 165-76.

Kramsch, C. 1986. From language proficiency to interactional competence. *Modern Language Journal* 70, no. 4, 366-72.

————. 1991. Culture in language learning: A view from the United States. In *Foreign language research in cross-cultural perspective,* edited by K. De Bot, R. P. Ginsberg, and C. Kramsch, 217-40. Amsterdam and Philadelphia: John Benjamins.

————. 1993. *Context and culture in language teaching.* Oxford: Oxford University Press.

————. 1995a. The applied linguist and the foreign language teacher: Can they talk to each other? *Australian Review of Applied Linguistics* 18, no. 1, 1-16.

————. 1995b. The cultural component of language teaching. *Language, Culture and Curriculum* 8, no. 2, 83-92.

————. 1995c. Embracing conflict versus achieving consensus in foreign language education. *ADFL Bulletin* 26, no. 3, 6-12.

————, ed. 1995d. *Redefining the boundaries of language study.* Boston: Heinle & Heinle.

————. 1996. *Proficiency plus: The next step* (EDO-FL-97-05). Washington: ERIC Clearinghouse on Languages and Linguistics.

————. 1998a. *Language and culture.* Oxford: Oxford University Press.

————. 1998b. The privilege of the intercultural speaker. In *Language learning in intercultural perspective,* edited by M. Byram and M. Fleming, 16-31. Cambridge: Cambridge University Press.

Kramsch, C., and S. McConnell-Ginet. 1992. (Con)textual knowledge in language education. In *Text and context: Cross-disciplinary perspectives on language study,* edited by C. Kramsch and S. McConnell-Ginet, 3-25. Lexington, Mass.: D. C. Heath & Co.

Kramsch, C., and L. von Hoehne. 1995. The dialogic emergence of difference: Feminist explorations in foreign language learning and teaching. In *Feminisms in the academy,* edited by D. C. Stanton and A. J. Stewart, 330-57. Ann Arbor: University of Michigan Press.

Kristeva, J. 1991. *Strangers to ourselves.* Translated by Leon S. Roudiez. New York: Columbia University Press.

Krumm, H.-J. 1995. Interkulturelles Lernen und Interkulturelle Information. In *Handbuch Fremdsprachenunterricht,* edited by K.-R. Bausch, H. Christ, and H.-J. Krumm, 156-61. Tübingen und Basel: A. Francke Verlag.

Kumaravadivelu, B. 1994. The postmethod condition: (E)merging strategies for second/foreign language teaching. *TESOL Quarterly* 28, no. 1, 27-48.

Lakoff, G., and M. Johnson. 1980. *Metaphors we live by.* Chicago: University of Chicago Press.

Landis, D. B., and W. Richard. 1983. *Handbook of intercultural training.* New York: Pergamon.

Larsen-Freeman, D. 1991. Research on language teaching methodologies: A review of the past and an agenda for the future. In *Foreign language research in cross-cultural perspective,* edited by K. de Bot, R. P. Ginsberg, and C. Kramsch, 119-32. Amsterdam and Philadelphia: John Benjamins.

Latourette, K. S. 1939. *A history of the expansion of Christianity.* Vol. 2, *The thousand years of uncertainty.* London: Eyre & Spottiswoode.

Lehberger, R. 1986. *Englischunterricht im Nationalsozialismus.* Tübingen: Stauffenberg Verlag.

Little, A. G. 1914. On Roger Bacon's life and works. In *Roger Bacon: Essays,* edited by A. G. Little, 1-31. Oxford: Oxford University Press.

Luther, M. 1962. To the councilmen of all cities in Germany that they establish and maintain Christian schools. In *Luther's Works,* edited by H. T. Lehmann and W. I. Brandt, vol. 45: *The Christian in society II,* 347-78. Philadelphia: Muhlenberg Press.

Macintyre, P. D., et al. 1998. Conceptualizing willingness to communicate in a L2. *Modern Language Journal* 82:545-62.

Manschreck, C. L. 1958. *Melanchthon: The quiet reformer.* New York: Abingdon Press.

Marshall, P. 1988. Calling, work and rest. In *Christian faith and practice in the mod-*

ern world: Theology from an evangelical point of view, edited by M. A. Noll and D. F. Wells, 199-217. Grand Rapids: Eerdmans.

Martin, J. 1995. Rwanda: Why? *Transformation* 12, no. 2, 1-3.

Matter, J. F., ed. 1992. *Language teaching in the twenty-first century: Problems and prospects.* AILA Review 9.

May, R., ed. 1969. *Existential psychology.* New York: Random House.

Meyer, M. A. 1995. Erziehungswissenschaft. In *Handbuch Fremdsprachenunterricht,* edited by K.-R. Bausch, 45-52. Tübingen und Basel: A. Francke Verlag.

Molero, F. M. 1989. A current assessment of modern language teaching methods. In *Foreign language learning and teaching in Europe,* edited by G. M. Willems and P. Riley, 159-71. Amsterdam: Bureau Lerarenopleiding and Free University Press.

Moskowitz, G. 1982. Self-confidence through self-disclosure: The pursuit of meaningful communication. In *ELT Documents 113 — humanistic approaches: An empirical view,* edited by P. Early. London: British Council.

Mouw, R., and S. Griffioen. 1993. *Pluralisms and horizons.* Grand Rapids: Eerdmans.

Munby, H. 1986. Metaphor in the thinking of teachers: An exploratory study. *Journal of Curriculum Studies* 18, no. 2, 197-209.

Murphy, D. 1995. *Comenius: A critical reassessment of his life and work.* Dublin: Irish Academic Press.

Murray, H. 1990. *Do not neglect hospitality: The Catholic worker and the homeless.* Philadelphia: Temple University Press.

Myhren, P. 1991. The nature and role of personalized questions in the foreign language classroom. *Proceedings Journal of the North American Association of Christian Foreign Language and Literature Faculty* 1:132-44.

Neill, S. 1986. *A history of Christian missions.* Harmondsworth: Penguin.

Neuner, G., and H. Hunfeld. 1993. *Methoden des fremdsprachlichen Deutschunterrichts: eine Einführung.* Berlin: Langenscheidt.

Nichols, F. W. 1995. *Christianity and the stranger: Historical essays.* Atlanta: Scholars Press.

Noblitt, J. S. 1995. The electronic language learning environment. In *Redefining the boundaries of language study,* edited by C. Kramsch. Boston: Heinle & Heinle.

Nouwen, H. J. M. 1972. Education to the ministry. *Theological Education* 9:48-57.

————. 1974. Hospitality. *Monastic Studies* 10:1-28.

————. 1986. *Reaching out: The three movements of the spiritual life.* New York: Doubleday.

O'Driscoll, J. 1993. A relationship on the rocks: The applied linguist and the language teacher. *ITL: A Review of Applied Linguistics* 101, no. 2, 107-31.

Ogletree, T. 1985. *Hospitality to the stranger.* Philadelphia: Fortress Press.

Olthuis, J. H. 1989. The covenanting metaphor of the Christian faith and the self-psychology of Heinz Kohut. *Studies in Religion* 18, no. 3, 313-24.

————. 1993. Be(com)ing human as gift and call. *Philosophia Reformata* 58, no. 2, 153-72.

Omaggio Hadley, A. 1993. *Teaching language in context.* 2nd edition. Boston: Heinle & Heinle.

Ortony, A. 1979. *Metaphor and thought.* Cambridge: Cambridge University Press.

Palmer, P. J. 1983. *To know as we are known: A spirituality of education.* San Francisco: Harper & Row.

————. 1998. *The courage to teach: Exploring the inner landscape of a teacher's life.* San Francisco: Jossey-Bass.

Pedersen, H. 1962. *The discovery of language: Linguistic science in the nineteenth century.* Translated by J. W. Spargo. Bloomington: Indiana University Press.

Pederson, K. M. 1992. The discipler's feedback in the disciple's pilgrimage toward perfection: A model for feedback in the Christian foreign language classroom. *Proceedings Journal of the North American Association of Christian Foreign Language and Literature Faculty* 2:1-93.

Peers, E. A. 1927. *A life of Ramon Lull, written by an unknown hand about 1311 and now first translated from the Catalan.* London: Burns, Oates & Washbourne.

————. 1929. *Ramon Lull: A biography.* London: SPCK.

Pennycook, A. 1989. The concept of method, interested knowledge, and the politics of language teaching. *TESOL Quarterly* 23, no. 4, 589-618.

————. 1990. Towards a critical applied linguistics for the 1990s. *Issues in Applied Linguistics* 1, no. 1, 8-28.

Perkins, J. 1980. Strength through wisdom: A critique of U.S. capability. *Modern Language Journal* 64, no. 1, 9-57.

Plantinga, A. 1996. Methodological naturalism? In *Facets of faith and science,* edited by J. M. van der Meer, vol. 1: *Historiography and modes of interaction,* 177-221. Lanham, Md.: University Press of America/Pascal Centre for Advanced Studies in Faith and Science.

Pohl, C. 1999. *Making room: Recovering hospitality as a Christian tradition.* Grand Rapids: Eerdmans.

Polák, V. 1972. Les idées de J. A. Comenius et la linguistique moderne. *Acta Comeniana* 3:377-82.

Polanyi, M. 1958. *Personal knowledge: Towards a post-critical philosophy.* London: Routledge & Kegan Paul.

Postman, N. 1995. *The end of education: Redefining the value of school.* New York: Knopf.

Prabhu, N. S. 1990. There is no best method — why? *TESOL Quarterly* 24, no. 2, 161-76.

Přivratská, J. 1983. Panglottia — the universal reform of language. *Acta Comeniana* 5:133-42.

Reents, C. 1992. Comenius' Impulse zur Mädchenbildung? Oder: Die Gleichheit von Mann und Frau als Ausdruck ihrer Gottebenbildlichkeit. In *Jan Amos Comenius 1592-1992: Theologische und pädagogische Deutungen,* edited by K. Goßmann and C. T. Scheilke, 49-69. Gütersloh: Gerd Mohn.

Richards, J. C. 1984. The secret life of methods. *TESOL Quarterly* 18, no. 1, 7-23.

————. 1993. Beyond the text book: The role of commercial materials in language teaching. *RELC Journal* 24, no. 1, 1-14.

Richards, J. C., and T. S. Rodgers. 1982. Method: Approach, design and procedure. *TESOL Quarterly* 16, no. 2, 153-68.

————. 1986. *Approaches and methods in language teaching: A description and analysis.* Cambridge: Cambridge University Press.

Rifkin, B. 1998. Gender representation in foreign language textbooks: A case study of textbooks of Russian. *Modern Language Journal* 82, no. 2, 217-36.

Rivers, W. M. 1983. *Communicating naturally in a second language: Theory and practice in language teaching.* Cambridge: Cambridge University Press.

————. 1993. Cultures, languages and the international smorgasbord: Musings for a new millennium. *Canadian Modern Language Review* 50, no. 1, 150-57.

Robins, R. H. 1979. *A short history of linguistics.* London: Longman.

Rogers, C. R. 1969. *Freedom to learn.* Columbus, Ohio: Charles E. Merrill.

Ruff, P. Y. 1999. *Au-Delà de l'Identité.* Paris: Les Éditions Fischbacher.

Russell, L. M. 1996. Practicing hospitality in a time of backlash. *Theology Today* 52:476-84.

Sacks, S., ed. 1979. *On metaphor.* Chicago: University of Chicago Press.

Sadler, J. E. 1966. *Comenius and the ideal of universal education.* London: George Allen & Unwin.

Sartre, J.-P. 1957. *Existentialism and human emotions.* New York: Philosophical Library.

————. 1966. *Being and nothingness.* New York: Washington Square Press.

Schaffer, C. S. 1998. Exclusive inclusiveness: A critique of the first-year German textbook *Kontakte. Language in God's World* 18, 25-31.

Schaller, K. 1992. Erziehung zur Menschlichkeit, Komenskys kritischer Beitrag zu Gegenwartsproblemen der Erziehung. In *Jan Amos Comenius 1592-1992: Theologische und pädagogische Deutungen,* edited by K. Goßmann and C. T. Scheilke, 17-30. Gütersloh: Gerd Mohn.

Schön, D. A. 1979. Generative metaphor: A perspective on problem-setting in social policy. In *Metaphor and thought,* edited by A. Ortony, 137-63. Cambridge: Cambridge University Press.

————. 1983. *The reflective practitioner: How professionals think in action.* New York: Basic Books.

Schwarz, H. 1990. *Evangelical perspectives on education: A bibliography.* Nottingham: Stapleford House Education Centre.

Schwehn, M. R. 1993. *Exiles from Eden: Religion and the academic vocation in America.* Oxford: Oxford University Press.

Seelye, N. H. 1993. *Teaching culture: Strategies for intercultural communication.* Lincolnwood, Ill.: National Textbook Company.

Seelye, N., and A. Seeley-James. 1995. *Culture clash: Managing in a multicultural world.* Lincolnwood, Ill.: National Textbook Company.

Seerveld, C. 1997. Minorities and xenophilia. Paper read at the Christian Artists Symposium in Doorn, Netherlands.

Seymour, J. L., M. A. Crain, and J. V. Crockett. 1993. *Educating Christians: The intersection of meaning, learning, and vocation.* Nashville: Abingdon Press.

Shortt, J. G., and T. Cooling, eds. 1997. *Agenda for educational change.* Leicester: Apollos.

Shumway, N. 1995. Searching for Averroes: Reflections on why it is desirable and impossible to teach culture in foreign language courses. In *Redefining the boundaries of language study,* edited by C. Kramsch. Boston: Heinle & Heinle.

Simmel, G. 1950. *The sociology of Georg Simmel.* Glencoe, Ill.: Free Press.

Smith, D. 1995. Christian thinking in education reconsidered. *Spectrum* 27, no. 1, 9-24.

———. 1996a. Rediscovering a heritage: Lull, Bacon and the aims of language teaching. *Spectrum* 28, no. 1, 9-28.

———. 1996b. What hope after Babel? Diversity and community in Gen 11:1-9, Exod 1:1-14, Zeph 3:1-13 and Acts 2:1-13. *Horizons in Biblical Theology* 18, no. 2, 169-91.

———. 1997a. Communication and integrity: Moral development and modern languages. *Language Learning Journal* 15:31-38.

———. 1997b. Culture, conflict and communication: The troubled waters of modern language pedagogy. In *Reminding: Renewing the mind in learning,* edited by D. Blomberg and I. Lambert, 52-76. Sydney: Centre for the Study of Australian Christianity.

———. 1997c. In search of the whole person: Critical reflections on counseling-learning. *Journal of Research on Christian Education* 6, no. 2, 159-81.

———. 1997d. Power and mutuality in modern foreign language education: The possibility of a Christian orientation. M.Phil.F. thesis, Institute for Christian Studies, Toronto.

———. 1998. Knowing as wisdom in Blomberg and Comenius. *Journal of Education and Christian Belief* 2, no. 1, 27-37.

Smith, D., and S. Dobson. 1999. Modern languages. In *Spiritual, moral, social, and* cultural education: Exploring values in the curriculum, edited by S. Bigger and E. Brown, 98-108. London: David Fulton.

Soskice, J. M. 1985. *Metaphor and religious language.* Cambridge: Cambridge University Press.

Spina, F. A. 1983. Israelites as *Gērîm,* "sojourners," in social and historical context. In *The word of the Lord shall go forth,* edited by C. L. Meyers and M. O'Connor, 321-35. Winona Lake, Ind.: Eisenbrauns.

Standards for foreign language learning: Preparing for the twenty-first century. 1996. Yonkers, N.Y.: National Standards in Foreign Language Education Project.

Stevick, E. W. 1990. *Humanism in language teaching: A critical perspective.* Oxford: Oxford University Press.

Storti, C. 1994. *Cross-cultural dialogues: 74 brief encounters with cultural difference.* Yarmouth, Maine: Intercultural Press.

Stronks, G. G., and D. Blomberg, eds. 1993. *A vision with a task: Christian schooling for responsive discipleship.* Grand Rapids: Baker.

Swaffar, J. K., K. Arens, and M. Morgan. 1982. Teacher classroom practices: Redefining method as task hierarchy. *Modern Language Journal* 66, no. 1, 24-33.

Takalo, R. 1994. Cultural relativism, cultural tolerance and experiential knowledge. *Proceedings Journal of the North American Association of Christian Foreign Language and Literature Faculty* 4:237-48.

———. 1997. The role of culture and perception in determining Christian values. *Proceedings Journal of the North American Christian Foreign Language Association* 7:1-5.

Taylor, M. C. 1984. *Erring: A postmodern a/theology.* Chicago: University of Chicago Press.

Taylor, W., ed. 1984. *Metaphors of education.* London: Heinemann.

Tench, P. 1985. Teaching English as a foreign/second language. *Spectrum* 17, no. 2, 42-44.

Terrell, T., et al. 1996. *"Kontakte": A communicative approach.* New York: McGraw-Hill.

Terry, A. 1972. *A literary history of Spain: Catalan literature.* London: Ernest Benn.

Thornbury, S. 1991. Metaphors we work by: EFL and its metaphors. *ELT Journal* 45, no. 3, 193-200.

Todorov, T. 1983. *The conquest of America.* Translated by Richard Howard. New York: Harper & Row.

———. 1991. *Les Morales de l'Histoire.* Paris: Grasset.

———. 1993. *On human diversity: Nationalism, racism, and exoticism in French thought.* Cambridge: Harvard University Press.

Tucker, A. 1994. In search of home. *Journal of Applied Philosophy* 11, no. 2, 181-87.

Tucker, G. R. 1993. Language learning for the twenty-first century: Challenges of the North American Free Trade Agreement. *Canadian Modern Language Review* 50, no. 1, 165-72.

Uehlinger, C. 1990. *Weltreich und 'Eine Rede': Eine Neue Deutung der sogenannten Turmbauerzählung (Gen. 11:1-9).* Vol. 101. Freiburg: Universitätsverlag.

Vail, V. H., and K. Sparks. 1992. *Modern German.* 3rd ed. Orlando: Harcourt Brace College Publishers.

Van Brummelen, H. 1994a. Faith on the wane: A documentary analysis of shifting worldviews in Canadian textbooks. *Journal of Research on Christian Education* 3, no. 1, 51-77.

————. 1994b. *Stepping stones to curriculum: A biblical path.* Seattle: Alta Vista College Press.

Van der Toorn, K., and P. W. Van der Horst. 1990. Nimrod before and after the Bible. *Harvard Theological Review* 83, no. 1, 1-29.

Van Houten, C. de Groot. 1991. *The alien in Israelite law.* Journal for the Study of the Old Testament, Supplement Series 107. Sheffield: Sheffield Academic Press.

Vogel, L. 1991. *Teaching and learning in communities of faith.* San Francisco: Jossey-Bass.

Volf, M. 1995. A vision of embrace. *Ecumenical Review,* 195-205.

————. 1996. *Exclusion and embrace: A theological exploration of identity, otherness, and reconciliation.* Nashville: Abingdon Press.

Von Rad, G. 1960. *Genesis.* London: SCM.

Walsh, B. J. 1998. Homemaking in exile: Homelessness, postmodernity, and theological reflection. In *Reminding: Renewing the mind in learning,* edited by D. Blomberg and I. Lambert, 1-12. Sydney: Centre for the Study of Australian Christianity.

Ward-Wilson, R., and C. L. Blomberg. 1993. The image of God in humanity: A biblical-psychological perspective. *Themelios* 18, no. 3, 8-15.

Weideman, A. J. 1987. Applied linguistics as a discipline of design — a foundational study. Ph.D thesis, University of the Orange Free State, Bloemfontein.

Weinsheimer, J. C. 1985. *Gadamer's hermeneutics: A reading of truth and method.* New Haven: Yale University Press.

Wenham, G. J. 1987. *Genesis 1–15.* Waco, Tex.: Word.

Wierlacher, A. 1990. Mit fremden Augen oder: Fremdheit als Ferment. In *Hermeneutik der Fremde,* edited by D. Krusche and A. Wierlacher. Munich: Iudicium.

Wilkins, D. A. 1972. *Linguistics in language teaching.* London: Edward Arnold.

Yallop, C. 1993. Linguistic diversity. *Philosophia Reformata* 58, no. 2, 113-19.

Yoshikawa, M. 1982. Language teaching methodologies and the nature of the individual: A new definition. *Modern Language Journal* 66, no. 4, 391-95.

Index

aims, 55-124; academic, 29-30, 41, 114; affective, 113-15, 174, 177-78; economic, 31, 108-10, 113, 121; ethical, 31, 37, 41, 82, 85, 106, 110, 118, 122, 137, 140-41, 184n.42, 200. *See also* attitudes, virtue; missionary, 23-28, 44, 112; spiritual, 29, 30, 37, 41
alterity, 62, 88, 101
Anthony, Edward, 162, 163, 164, 167
applied linguistics, 156, 158, 159
approach, design, procedure, 162-69, 187-88
attitudes to others, 47, 64n.10, 67, 80-81, 82, 98, 101, 106, 114, 116, 123, 150. *See also* aims: ethical, virtue
Augustine, Saint, 22
autonomy, 9, 17, 117-18, 119, 173, 177, 184, 186; of learner, 49, 117, 138, 180, 182-83

Babel, 3-4, 7-8, 14, 15-16, 22, 209-16; and Pentecost, 14
Bacon, Roger, 20, 28-33, 34, 35
Baker, D., et al., 191-92
Bakhtin, Mikhail, 68-69, 71, 73
Bauman, Zygmunt, 90-91, 101, 117
belief, role of in pedagogy, 130-31, 153, 155, 163, 167-68, 187-89

Bible, 3-17, 30, 209-16
Bonhoeffer, Dietrich, 198, 200
Brueggemann, Walter, 9, 16, 213
Byram, Michael, 64n.10, 82n.9
Byrnes, Heidi, 188n.52

Calvin, John, 85, 207
Caputo, John, 91n.40
Cassiodorus, 23
celebration, 102, 142-43, 145
Charis Project, 191-205
Chastain, Kenneth, 70
classical culture and Christianity, 20-24, 40
Columbus, Christopher, 80-81
Comenius, John Amos, 20, 38-50, 51, 65; erudition, virtue, piety, 41-43, 46, 47-48; garden of delight, 50, 65; *Great Didactic,* 40, 41; *Orbis Pictus,* 39, 45-46, 48; playful learning, 49-50; vernacular languages, 44-45
communication, 22, 48, 60, 94, 150, 179, 183; breakdown of, 62-3, 66, 181; ethics of, 47, 150-52; possibility of, 60, 66, 120
communicative teaching, 150-51, 153, 180